Gender and population in the adjustment of African economies: Planning for change

Women, Work and Development, 19

Gender and population in the adjustment of African economies: Planning for change

Ingrid Palmer

Prepared with the financial support of the United Nations Fund for Population Activities (UNFPA)

International Labour Office Geneva

Palmer, I.
Gender and population in the adjustment of African economies: Planning for change
Geneva, International Labour Office, 1991. Women, Work and Development, 19
/Structural adjustment/, /Sexual division of labour/, /Woman worker/s, /Rural women/, /Demographic aspect/s, /Trend/s, /Africa south of Sahara/. 03.02.2
ISBN 92-2-107739-X ISSN 0253-2042

ILO Cataloguing in Publication Data

ILO publications can be obtained through major booksellers or ILO local offices in many countries, or direct from ILO Publications, International Labour Office, CH-1211 Geneva 22, Switzerland. A catalogue or list of new publications will be sent free of charge from the above address.

Preface

Structural adjustment issues, gender issues and demographic issues are all of great concern to policy-makers and scholars. To date, however, their intersection has not received sufficient attention.

These interrelationships take on added importance in sub-Saharan Africa where dashed hopes and falling real income levels have been part of the so-called lost development decade of the 1980s. Sub-Saharan Africa is also a region where women play a very important role in providing for family survival and, indeed, they often have primary responsibility for the production of food crops and trading activities; fertility rates remain extremely high, as does the reproductive burden falling on women; child labour continues to play a key role in the family survival strategy; and economic policies and incentives associated with structural adjustment programmes often unsuccessfully attempt to increase living standards by increasing economic efficiency.

This monograph by Ingrid Palmer addresses these issues by analysing how structural adjustment policies affect women's relative economic position, and in turn demographic trends. It also describes how gender and demographic considerations affect the economic efficiency, that is success, of structural adjustment policies.

The author's concern in this study is not in calling attention to social injustices and the need to rectify gender inequalities for its own sake (although she like almost everyone supports such a goal) but in seeing that gender considerations are systematically taken into account in economic policies. As the author successfully argues, structural adjustment policies and increased economic efficiency are unlikely to be achieved in sub-Saharan Africa, or indeed anywhere, unless gender differences in productive activities, resources, access to markets, family responsibilities, and so on, are taken into consideration. The author wants to achieve a dialogue with hard-headed policy-makers and economic planners who face difficult decisions about resource allocation and increasing economic efficiency. It is, to her, not just an issue of social equity but also an issue of economic efficiency.

What takes this book several steps forward in addressing structural adustment policies in sub-Saharan Africa is its development of a theoretical framework and perspective that takes into consideration gender dimensions that can be understood by economists. The author does not berate and browbeat policy-makers for being male chauvinists but shows them how policies can be made more effective by considering gender issues. Thus she makes an important contribution towards raising the dialogue to a higher plane. As a result she greatly increases the likelihood that society as a whole, as well as women themselves, will benefit from structural adjustment policies and, in turn, increases the chances that improvements in demographic trends will also be brought about.

Richard Anker,
Head, Target Group Policies Unit,
Employment Planning and
Population Branch,
International Labour Office

Executive summary

The study is intended to assist policy-makers to think systematically about gender issues in the contex of structural change in order to enhance sustainable development and population stability. It is not so much concerned with the impact of economic policies on women as with the impact of gender relations in factor and product markets on the effectiveness of policies.

The term "structural change" is used here to cover the economic strategies of demand adjustment (stabilisation), supply adjustment (market reforms) and transformation. Although these strategies overlap, and sometimes in effect combine, they are taken in successive order to make the analysis manageable. It is assumed that the final objective is the economically efficient use of resources and that planners are concerned with allocative efficiency in the long term as well as in the short to medium term. This study, then, is about gender constructs in markets and economic efficiency.

The gains from economic efficiency can be wiped out by uncontrolled population growth. Migratory shifts in population can work against the long-term economic interests of the country. Women's access to resources and income can greatly influence population variables. Planners should know, therefore, how their economic policies affect population variables via the economic, and consequent social, status of women.

Part I provides the theoretical framework for later analysis of the likely impact and effectiveness of the economic strategies and for identification of desirable modifications and interventions. Chapters 3 and 4 of this theoretical framework, which deal respectively with agricultural and non-agricultural market structures, use empirical information on the relative statuses of women and men in the markets for factors of production and products, as well as on the particular obstacles women face in these markets. The case literature is strongly suggestive of markets within the household as well as above the household level, particularly in the farming sector. Chapter 5 sets out in summarised form the main theories of change in population variables arising from economic and social factors.

Part II uses the theoretical framework to assess likely gender influences on the economic and demographic outcomes of economic reform policies. It begins by setting out the policy instruments of structural change based on improving allocative efficiency, and the way they are usually introduced and packaged. This is followed in Chapter 7 by commentary on the weaknesses of these instruments, as well as on new opportunities for reshaping strategies. The weaknesses depicted here are those generally understood to be the limitations of the reforms. Because this is a generic and speculative study, the available knowledge of the wide range of country experiences of the impact of these policies is reduced to essentials. Some gender implications are signposted. The opportunities arise from the lessons learned and the willingness to conceive alternative routes to reform and growth.

Chapter 8 provides a summary of how far and in what way gender has already entered the debate on policies of economic reform, which has mainly been on structural adjustment policies. It is easily concluded that the treatment of the subject of gender and structural adjustment so far has been from the viewpoint of the impact of structural adjustment on women rather than of the obstructions posed by gender factors to the effectiveness of market reform policies.

Chapters 9 and 10, the last two chapters of Part II, provide the argument for inclusion of a gender dimension in these policies of economic change by utilising the economic and demographic theoretical frameworks of Part I to analyse the likely outcome of the usual reform policies. The limitations of these policies arising from the absence of gender sensitivity are identified for the economy and for population variables, respectively.

Part III presents arguments and strategies for overcoming or mitigating these limitations. Chapter 11 deals with the implications of gender issues for policies directed at both static and dynamic market efficiency. Chapter 12 examines the possibility of adding a demographic dimension to the agenda of economic policies.

Chapter 11 indicates just how far structural adjustment programmes can go to eliminate gender-based market distortions in the short to medium term, and what other solutions are feasible within this time horizon by way of improved general policy packages and deliberate counterbalancing interventions. Inevitably there will be unresolved market distortions which must be carried over to the longer term and added to the agenda for economic transformation and the pursuit of new comparative advantages. At all times a sense of what is feasible or realistic is borne in mind. At the same time it is pointed out that there is an economic cost to the wider economy of not dealing with the huge labour overhead of women's reproduction work in the home. An approach to this uncharted territory for planners is outlined.

In Chapter 12 the absence of a relation between economic and demographic planning is commented on. This is followed by an exercise in modelling such a relationship and a description of a means to develop an agenda for a dialogue between economists and demographers.

The final chapter concludes that on the basis of the two theoretical frameworks the influence of gender on the economic and demographic outcomes of adjustment processes must be negative. The policies entailed in this do nothing to improve gender equity and reduce gender biases in markets, and may well make them worse. The most disturbing aspect is the likely effect on resource allocation within the farm household. But in the manufacturing and services sectors market liberalisation does little to eradicate or counter gender biases.

Policy instruments which could overcome gender obstacles to short- to medium-term efficiency include access to public sector facilities and counterbalancing meso policies. Eliminating gender biases in resource allocation during long-term transformation of the economy will require more serious action and will depend on planners' view of future social and economic relations between women and men.

If the gender bias, the weakest link in sub-Saharan economies, is not resolved, these economies may have an absolute advantage in no product and a comparative advantage only in lines of production based on the super-exploitation of women and a demand for children's assistance.

The new thinking on economic development that has emerged from the crisis in Africa and from the failure of early attempts to remedy it offers a unique opportunity to introduce gender issues into the planning process. What this study shows is that unless recognition is given to gender-based biases in markets, they could become worse through policies ostensibly designed to make markets more efficient.

Contents

Tables

Introduction 1

The purpose of this study is to help policy-makers to think systematically about how to take gender issues into account when drafting the agenda and planning the detail of programmes of structural change, in order to enhance their success. It should be stated at once that the focus of attention is not the impact of these programmes on women. It is rather how to identify and deal constructively with the effects of gender on the outcome of the programmes for the sustainable development of the economy and for population variables.

At a time when policy-makers are having to cope with so many different ideas on suitable packages of stabilisation and structural adjustment policies, it must appear almost perverse to impose one more frame through which to view adjustment strategies. It is accepted that there are significant non-gender issues involved in supply and investment responses to these policies and in reaching compatibility of goals of different time horizons. But it is contended that, without a gender frame in the analysis, certain significant costs of economic inefficiency and resource misallocation are likely to persist and that this will impair the chances of achieving sustainable growth.

The meaning of adjustment

The references given in this book refer constantly to "adjustment", although "structural change" is appearing more frequently now that corrective policies are merging with designs for fundamental transformation. For the sake of easy familiarity we use the term "adjustment", except in contexts when closer specification is called for. In these cases we refer to "stabilisation", "structural adjustment" or "transformation". It is worth noting at the outset what is implicit in all these terms.

Because of the institutional antecedent of the International Monetary Fund (IMF) often leading with a *stabilisation* programme and the World Bank following with a *structural adjustment* programme, adjustment has been seen as a first phase of demand-side adjustment plus a second phase of supply-side adjustment. (Where governments on their own have implemented adjustment strategies they have tended to follow this practice too.) More recently, to this has been added a further phase of long-term economic transformation as expounded, for instance, in the report of the

Economic Commission for Africa (ECA): *African alternative framework to structural adjustment programmes for socio-economic recovery and transformation* (ECA, 1989).

However, structural adjustment has been used to cover all three phases. For instance, a representative of the World Bank suggested that structural adjustment could be defined as: (i) stabilisation; (ii) adjusting prices to reflect supply and demand; and (iii) adaptation of policies, institutions, technology and management practices to promote efficiency and growth with equity (ILO, 1989a, p. 10). Speaking from notes at an Institute of Development seminar at Sussex University in August 1989, Tony Killick drew parallels when referring to the three perspectives of adjustment: (i) restoration of balance-of-payments viability (the IMF's view, and initially the Bank's view when its structural adjustment loans used to be seen as supply-side supports to the balance of payments); (ii) policy reform to raise efficiency of resource use and strengthen the institutional base (the present Bank view); and (iii) continuous adaptation to new opportunities for trade and comparative advantage in the process of economic transformation (the ECA view). Killick referred to (i) and (ii) as the economics of transition, or a medium-term adjustment preliminary to resumption of the development effort which entails transformation. Bank officials, on the other hand, have been heard to claim that the end purpose of structural adjustment was always (iii).

Nevertheless, experience has taught that policy reforms cannot be so easily partitioned. Stabilisation (demand adjustment) programmes have usually included reductions in government subsidies and the beginnings of reforms in the foreign trade regime which amount to first steps towards structural (supply) adjustment according to a narrow definition of structural adjustment as a correction of market distortions brought about by past government policies. Today demand and supply adjustment policies tend to run concurrently and are subject to continuous interaction. Also, acceptance of the fact that each country's economy needs a tailor-made strategy has brought about a proliferation of Fund and Bank loans and facilities that are interdigitated, and even sometimes seem to emanate from the wrong agency. It has finally been understood that dislocation in the economy during adjustment is not going to be as short-lived as the first estimates of the supply response indicated. Now there is multiple overlapping of stabilisation and efficiency reforms stretching over a long period. In addition, there is the growing interest in economic transformation. The word "adjustment" is used here to embrace all of this.

In order to make the following analysis manageable this study takes the policy packages in the order of the phases outlined above, before describing towards the end of Chapter 7 the scope allowed today for viewing all phases simultaneously.

The significance of gender in policy analysis

In no other region is making the distinction between women's and men's contributions to the family and national economies as important to successful policy formulation as in sub-Saharan Africa. Even in the event of rapid restructuring this region will be crucially dependent on processed or unprocessed primary products for foreign exchange for a long time to come. This dependency is tantamount to a dependency on women to find the resources and time to achieve more in the economic sphere. But women are also the main providers of everyday items of maintenance, which come from both self-provisioning and market-oriented production as well as wage employment. For a long time women in Africa have been placed under stress by the gap between their economic responsibilities and their access to resources. With increasingly small per capita resources in terms of quality as well as quantity, that stress is intensifying in ever-diminishing circles of resource rearrangements. Until it is relieved it must be seen as a constraint on the real options of policy-makers.

It is not easy to explain why economic planners interested in the rational use of resources have not, despite all the studies that have emerged since 1975, incorporated gender in their analyses. It may be that they have neither the time nor the disciplinary background to digest the mass of material with its strong sociological orientation. When "the role of women" is mentioned in five-year plans and in the papers of numerous governments and international agencies it is with regard to the fact that certain features of women's role can prevent a project or programme being successful. But it is rarely mentioned as a lead into the subjects of gender-based market distortions or what women's options and strategies are, relative to men's, in both resource and product markets. An analytic approach to these subjects could help to show how gender can influence the successful shift of resources to more efficient uses, a cardinal principle of supply-side adjustment policies. It can also help to define what would be a more efficient use of resources.

In sum, gender factors have a proper place on the agenda of strategic policy packages and investment priorities if allocative efficiency is really intended. But to do this we need to look at the effect that gender factors are likely to have at present on the outcome of adjustment. In particular, gender-based market distortions need to be identified and the efficacy of usual forms of market liberalisation in reducing them critically examined. This study, then, is about gender and economic efficiency, not gender equity as such, although it should not be supposed that gender equity must detract from market efficiency.

Adjustment and population variables

If the ultimate goal of adjustment is to raise per capita production and income and living standards, as it must be, then the policy instruments chosen for the strategy should encourage such resource deployment and contingent fertility decisions as would not dissipate economic gains in the long term. But there are grounds for believing that the typical package of policy instruments does not encourage this. To examine this more closely it is necessary to see how women and men are differentially affected by proposals for economic change, and in particular how women's survival strategies are influenced.

The report on *The state of world population 1989* (Sadik, 1989) points out that the deterioration of women's economic status, by leading to further uncertainty, locks women even more tightly into survival strategies which emphasise fertility and dependency.

Old sources of insecurity are aggravated. The hope of providing for old age with economic resources recedes further. As family resources become scarcer so discrimination against girls in nutrition, health and educational expenditure increases. More limited productive assets mean more intensive application of labour to maintain living standards. With diminishing chances of surplus economic accumulation and of ability to plan for a better future, women retreat into their traditional role of motherhood for securing labour assistance and their old age. But more children mean fewer resources to invest in their future.

Women's strategies for family survival in the face of this deteriorating situation have two direct effects on their contribution to the wider economy. They are less able to devote time to market-oriented activities, and the spectre is raised of population growth outstripping production increases. In turn this reduces the chances of acquiring a surplus to invest in higher productivity.

This was the generalised situation before stabilisation and structural adjustment policies were introduced. This study shows how, as they have been and may still be conceived, these policies could reinforce the circular deterioration that existed. It therefore becomes of crucial importance to develop ways of looking at alternative adjustment programmes to reverse rather than worsen the circular deterioration of women's economic status.

The state of world population 1989 points to "some of the costs of ignoring the needs of women: uncontrolled population growth, high infant and child mortality, a weakened economy, ineffective agriculture, a deteriorating environment, a generally divided society and a poorer quality of life for all" (Sadik, 1989, p. 1). It goes on to state that women should be a priority of economic planning. In any system of sustainable development in which human and natural resources are brought into a dynamic equilibrium, women play a central part. And investing in women means widening their choice of strategies and reducing their dependence on children for status and support.

Sub-Saharan African countries experience some of the highest rates of population growth in the world. Since the infant mortality rates are high and life expectancies low in comparison with most other parts of the Third World, this has to be due to exceptionally high fertility rates. Data bear this out. For instance, Kenya's total fertility rate of 7.8, and those of Zambia and the United Republic of Tanzania around the 7.0 mark, exceed those of 35 other world-wide developing countries recorded in a study (Potter, 1989, p. 191). Furthermore, while among African countries there is no obvious relationship between fertility and infant mortality rates, among the other developing countries there is a strong positive relationship. This suggests that there are factors other than the survival rate of children which have a major determining influence on fertility differentials within Africa.

However, African countries share with others a negative relationship between women's life expectancy and total fertility rates. It is highly plausible that aspects of women's status influence both these variables. How economic structures affect women's status should be a matter of concern to anyone interested in sustainable per capita economic growth. An appreciation of the case-study literature on women in Africa, the main population theories and the kinds of policy pursued under economic adjustment must cause apprehension about some possible demographic consequences of non-selective and hurried adjustment policies.

This amounts to a challenge to contemporary economic analysis. If adjustment means flushing out inefficiencies and waste, and developing new comparative advantages through investing in higher factor productivities, then a precondition must be recognition of the economic cost of gender-differentiated factor productivities and access to resources. With women's interlocking productive and reproductive roles, it is not tenable for adjustment strategies to ignore those roles that happen not to be commoditised. There are bound to be economic and demographic costs of inaction on women's status.

The approach of this study and related activities of international agencies

The approach in this study is to emphasise gender constructs of factor and product markets to indicate the kind of distortions and inefficiencies they give rise to. In this way it contrasts with much of the discussion on gender and adjustment, which is concerned with the impact on welfare, specifically a deleterious change in household consumption patterns. There are now international lobbies pointing out the greater vulnerability of women and children when household and government budgets are reduced as a consequence of these policies. The outcome has been an ongoing proliferation of household-level surveys, including those being undertaken by World Bank/United Nations Development Programme (UNDP) Social Dimensions of Adjustment programmes. In addition to information on consumption trends, a few of these surveys are expected to produce data on changes in men's and women's separate income sources and assets and, therefore, possibly describe the different strategies of survival that women and men have been able, or have been forced, to make. It is hoped that they will lead on to identifying policy prerequisites for more productive responses by the poor. But if the policy analysis of this mass of data proves difficult, there will be a temptation to revert to using these surveys mainly to record the damaging social and welfare aspects of adjustment policies.

There are current efforts to prevent this from happening. A new interest in empowering the poorest to contribute to national economic adjustment through a better understanding of their economic capabilities is gaining credibility, even in the most orthodox circles. It is not yet clear where all this will take gender issues, but it will probably come to rest largely with argument on the economic value of investment in human resources.

The ILO held a Tripartite Symposium on Structural Adjustment and Employment in Africa in October 1989. The meeting discussed the ILO's role and responsibilities in regard to adjustment. Within the Governing Body a consensus exists that the ILO has a legitimate and important role to play in monitoring the social consequences of adjustment and where necessary in voicing its concern (ILO, 1989a, p. 1). Therefore the ILO's role was seen as monitoring and evaluating macro- and micro-economic policies in addition to fulfilling its standing brief to follow labour market trends. The reports of the meeting did not mention women specifically, but if a concern with labour market trends is extended to all working conditions, market and private, the approach of this study rests within the ILO's broad responsibilities.

The study is not concerned with the social dimensions of adjustment in the sense in which that expression is commonly used, namely the welfare consequences. Gender is viewed here as an economic issue, not something to be relegated to the social sector agenda of government. The study is, however, concerned with certain social influences on the economic outcome of adjustment policies. Thus it focuses on women and men as producers, on how their respective incentives and capacities are likely to have been affected by adjustment policies, and, in order to correct their past invisibility to planners, on what are the prerequisites of women in particular being able to participate effectively in new economic opportunities. As a result it will include, inter alia, a concern about investment in human resources. However, the emphasis will be placed on women's relative access to factor and product markets and how this can be altered by adjustment programmes. The following chapters are therefore not concerned with recording gender-differentiated impoverishment resulting from adjustment programmes but rather with demonstrating how gender awareness in the packaging of adjustment policies can contribute to helping the poor escape that poverty through their own efforts.

It is not intended to debate the underlying principles of stabilisation and structural adjustment and transformation, but rather to assist in improving on packages of measures and programmes which often do not take into account potential adverse economic and demographic consequences—in this case those caused by gender factors.

Part I presents a theoretical framework for deducing the economic and demographic consequences of commonly applied adjustment policies. This includes the salient features of women's productive roles in African economies and of some widely held population theories. Part II begins by describing the range of adjustment policies that are usually applied, and continues with an examination of their weaknesses and the way these have created new opportunities for designing more sensitive policy packages. Chapter 8 provides a review of how gender has entered the adjustment debate, while Chapters 9 and 10 draw out the implications of adjustment policies for economic and demographic responses, respectively, as seen through the frame of gender issues. Part III develops issues of policy formulation from these implications.

Part I

A theoretical framework

Gender considerations common to all sectors 2

This chapter seeks to construct a means to identify the influence of gender on the operation of markets so that gender implications for the goals of adjustment and for appraising policy instruments and their packaging can be drawn out. The intention is to contribute relevant substance to the analysis and argument for a finer tuning of adjustment policies. It is assumed that what policy-makers are interested in knowing is the bearing that gender issues have on markets' allocative efficiency and their speed or impossibility of response to price signals and other policy measures.

There are four main gender considerations to keep in mind when looking at the functioning of markets.

The first is the element of *gender discrimination in access to resources or outlets for produce*. Discrimination is taken here to mean that resources are not going to those who can make best economic use of them. The reasons may be custom or social factors, or the implicit or explicit bias of government intervention. In nearly all cases gender discrimination in markets acts against women in favour of men. In the remainder the explanation is invariably an attempt by government to compensate women or to meet one of women's immediate practical needs. Compensation in the form of an allocated quota would mean a direct market intervention, but in the form of a transfer payment or an enabling support service it would initiate an indirect influence on markets in which women have a role. Both amount to counterbalancing distortions which should be distinguished from the cumulative distortions (social forces plus privileged access to economic services) that generally favour men.

But it is important to locate these compensations in the wider scheme of things. It is fair comment to say that the motivation behind them has been to make women more capable of delivering labour or produce for the achievement of planners' goals. It is a rare instance when intervention favouring women is designed to establish a sea change in women's control over resources or in their bargaining position in markets. Discrimination against women in markets continues to be rampant no matter how much of the social sector budget is spent on women or how many special women's projects are set up.

The second gender consideration is the *additional tasks women face in reproduction and family maintenance*. Regardless of which sector a woman is living and working in, she will experience the tax on her physical energies and time that biological reproduction demands. But gender constructs also oblige her to nurse sick family members, and to cook and clean for the household. In urban slums and in rural areas there will be the further tasks of collecting water and firewood. All this represents a labour "overhead", or tax, for women which they must pay before they can embark on income-gaining work or expenditure-displacing activities other than the elemental ones just described. It is true that this overhead is frequently traded at the margin against "economic" work. But this situation arises when women are so desperate for economic returns that they are obliged to forgo some degree of immediate welfare of the family. The point to bear in mind is that women face these fierce choices alone: their menfolk do not usually step into the breach and so rationalise the deployment of all adult family labour. Since men do not have to trade off their economic activities against their household responsibilities, this reproduction labour tax rests squarely on women and, like all taxes, it distorts resource allocation. An Organisation of Economic Co-operation and Development (OECD) report (1988) put the point in a pithy way. "If women did not perform these tasks, men would have to do so. We would then begin to speak of the important opportunity costs of male unpaid labour."

The effect is that this "tax" channels part of women's labour to where market forces would not direct it and presents a serious limitation of women's capability to engage in gainful work and entrepreneurship. It not only limits the time women can spend in economic activities but restricts them to activities that are compatible with their home schedule. From the viewpoint of economic analysis this amounts to gender discrimination and therefore a misallocation of women's total labour resources; and because one distortion sets up others, other resources are also misallocated.

The very fact that women's reproduction work leads to use values of goods and services means that it is productive to the household economy. At the least it displaces expenditure or saves cash income. Therefore it might be supposed that it is not strictly a labour tax from which women would gain nothing. But it is a tax in the sense that in this sector labour productivity is unnecessarily low because it has been so long and so thoroughly neglected. More importantly it is a tax in the sense that women thereby supply a resource, free of charge, to the wider community; namely, a replacement for the present labour force. When capital equipment has to be replaced, employers draw on their depreciation accounts which are clearly seen to lower profits and company tax. Biology and culture oblige mothers to bear the lion's share of the cost of a depreciation account for the labour force. Therefore when women return use values to their families with their domestic work it is because society has imposed upon them the responsibility for funding the labour depreciation account. There is no intention here to comment on societal values and the worth of family life. The purpose is solely to help policy-makers think systematically about the economic cost of these arrangements.

Thirdly, there is the question of *markets existing within household economies*. So far reference has been made only to markets above the level of the household economy. This would assume that the stock of all resources contained within the confines of all household activities faces the same set of market structures and incentives, and that those market structures and incentives are present, entirely and exclusively, above the level of the household.

This is patently not so. The case which is of crucial relevance to structural adjustment policies is when there are several lines of production below the household level and women and men hold separate accounting units among them. This occurs principally in agriculture but it can also occur in informal sector activities. And, of course, individual household members can have mixed portfolios straddling all economic sectors and including some wage employment.

There has been some debate about the appropriateness of a market analysis for what occurs within a household economy. This has been best exemplified by Sen (1984), who allows that households do not behave as corporately as has been supposed but criticises the notion of intra-household markets as an explanation on two grounds: *(a)* that the proponents of this explanation see market transactions taking place "in an imagined way at imagined prices and imagined wages (with demand and supply in balance as under a Walrasian tatonnement)"; and *(b)* that the inefficiency of this market rests on a particular distribution of benefits, or of "allocation of work and commodities", or on "who does what work and gets what goods and services" (Sen, 1984, pp. 373 and 375).

The first seems to imply that the hand of economics is not only invisible but imaginary too. However, there is nothing imagined in the way a woman assesses her chances of obtaining the going free market rate of interest from her husband when she lends him money, or that when she puts in a certain number of hours on his crop she expects a quantity of gifts or money to prevent her from doing something else with her time. The terms of trade, of course, are another matter. It is difficult to avoid the conclusion that in African agricultural households there are intra-household, albeit rigged, markets. An urban wage-earning household or one totally committed to a family-based enterprise is in a different situation. There are no claims for intra-household markets for inputs in these cases, except to say that when a wife shifts to an extra-household earning opportunity which returns to her greater personal disposable income she is operating in the labour market. Culture and personal family relations may determine the context of intra-household markets, but does not deny their presence. Monetised or barter-based exchanges of goods and services occur within the household.

Secondly, Sen, like so many others concerned with women's subordinate role in the household, concentrates on the distribution of returns to labour (benefits, commodities, goods and services); that is, the whole question of how far female family labour is unpaid and how "family income" is distributed or disposed of. This tells us nothing of the distribution of non-labour factors of production in the household: land, liquid assets available for working capital or credit, manure from livestock, and so on. Nor does it necessarily explain wholly, or even largely, why family labour is allocated as it is. It may well be the case in Latin America and Asia that these resources are utilised in some collective way. But the illustrations of the next chapter show that in the majority of African situations this is patently not so.

One does not need to deny the presence of affective bonds and co-operative forms of behaviour in the family, or pressures on women to forgo economic opportunities in order to hold the family together, in order to believe in the usefulness of looking at markets within the household. These things define the context in which economic forces play out their roles. Moreover, markets above the household are also shaped by social and cultural influences but they are still regarded as markets in their varied contexts. What is being pointed out here is that resources are misallocated because of these influences, and the best way of looking at this is through access to and exchange of resources. Sen's objection that intra-household markets are not monetised (although the ones under review here are subject to both monetary and barter transaction) implies that without this means of measurement the case for the markets is invalid. But problems of measurement should not stand in the way of agreeing that there is an allocation of resources based on different interests and bargaining and exchange, the basic attributes of a market.

A separate accounting unit of production is taken here to mean that the unit is *financially* autonomous. The rate of return is internalised over the unit but over no more. Returns to its activity must cover its costs and it must generate its own reinvestment. The unit is ostensibly neither subsidised by another accounting unit in the household nor itself subsidises another. Within the household women and men may be allowed to draw upon the stock of household-level fixed factors of production, according to customary practices of allocating use right to these resources, to form their own accounting units. But this does not entail combining costs and profits. To operate separate accounting units they must be responsible for mobilising other factors of production and for finding the wherewithal to pay for them (cash, produce or own labour). The corollary to this is the right to dispose of the produce or as much of it as is necessary to cover costs and give an adequate net incentive. It may be that more than one line of production is included in the accounting unit. In these circumstances the single manager of both has a reason for internalising the rate of return over the two activities and of deploying all resources efficiently between them but still *within* the one accounting unit.

However, the total of household-level resources need not be allocated efficiently *between* accounting units. In fact, there are likely to be highly imperfect factor markets within the whole household. The gender divisions of inheritance, marriage payments, savings, land and access to government support mechanisms join with the gender division of labour to ensure that there is a set of social and economic relations of exchange between accounting units. Some of these are no doubt what Sen had in mind when he referred to a "co-operative conflicts bargaining model". Both inputs and outputs can be offered in exchange between marital partners or with other members of the households. However, the terms of exchange between female and male household members need be neither equitable nor represent an efficient distribution of combined resources. The social aspects of gender impose their own definitions of correct exchange; in general they reflect bargaining power and status, and inevitably this means that the terms of trade are biased against women. This can be described as an asymmetry of obligations and responsibilities between women and men. This is a more accurate description of what happens than the expression "unpaid female family labour" because women rarely get nothing in return. It also sends an unmistakeable message to policy-makers who are concerned with the efficient allocation of resources at all levels.

The concern of this study is to gain recognition for these intra-household distortions in the appraisal of adjustment and transformation policies in order to see whether the policies counterbalance or strengthen these distortions.

The final disposition of incomes raises the fourth important gender issue of the distribution and absorption of resources within producing households through its effect on incentives and responses. This applies to both single and multiple accounting unit households. The intra-household control and distribution of income has been one of two major concerns of the debate on gender and adjustment so far (see Chapter 8). In the case where a whole household enterprise is in one line of production only, there is likely to be some gender division of labour. If women are additionally involved in non-economic work, a gender division could still be said to be rational should making domestic work women's concern be taken as given. However, rationality in the deployment of human resources in the household assumes a harmonious and corporate effort. Certain details are subsumed: that it is equally in the interests of women and men to operate at a certain output level so that net marginal utilities are felt in the same way; that the chosen technology fortuitously satisfies both sexes equally; and that there is nothing to bar a member of the household taking outside employment if that person finds a gratifyingly higher personal emolument there. Gender divisions in roles and codes of behaviour of women and men in the real world make nonsense of all these premises.

These four gender considerations of market operation will be referred to in what follows. Both factor and product markets are under examination here, but the labour market will receive particular attention because of women's multifaceted roles.

Gender in agricultural market structures 3

This chapter reviews the terms of access to resources that women enjoy relative to men and the way resources are exchanged within the household. This will provide the information base to later examination of the likely outcome of adjustment programmes in the agricultural sector.

Land rights

The relevance of studying land rights is not only that they determine individuals' access to land, but that this fixed capital base influences access to other factor markets. Commenting on the fact that women in sub-Saharan Africa generally only have usufructuary rights, an ILO report (ILO, 1988, p. 44) states: "Absence of land titles limits women's access to other productive resources such as credit, extension, training, technology and membership of peasant organisations which are generally directed at the male members of the household." This actually overstates the case. It is the insecurity of the terms on which women win usufructuary rights that is of importance. After all, secure lifelong tenancy rights ought to be tantamount to ownership, as they normally are on land settlement schemes. Although under traditional lineage systems individual men do not own land titles, they do have access to land in their own right.

In most of sub-Saharan Africa land is patrilineally inherited and where land has not been adjudicated it is distributed through the lineage. Matrilineal inheritance of land has characterised parts of Africa, notably within the Côte d'Ivoire, southern Ghana, Malawi and Zambia. Another major area of direct female acquisition of land is wherever Muslim law, which decrees that daughters should inherit half of what sons inherit, is still practised. This is mostly found in West Africa. As land becomes scarcer this may be modified to daughters inheriting movables or more liquid assets.

But Africa is predominantly patrilineal. This means that the majority situation is one of women obtaining usufructuary rights to land from their husbands' lineage group. The rationale of awarding women usufructuary rights to some land is that they should have the capability of fulfilling their socially prescribed economic obligations to the family. Except in instances of women's seclusion, this includes responsibility for supplying most or all of the family's food. The amount of land is usually in some proportion to their economic obligations. In theory, then, all members of a compound (a grouping of a few households bonded by close kinship or affinal ties), including wives, have a right to sufficient land to meet their food and financial obligations. In effect wives are allocated usufructuary rights as long as they are married to a lineage member. This is the first cause of women's insecurity of land use rights.

Although kin may live together in a compound (often a walled area) they are typically separated into different domestic groups. Agreement on land allocation may be reached through the compound head presiding over a meeting of adult males drawn from the related households in the compound. An example of this has been given for the Tiv people of central Nigeria (Burfisher and Horenstein, 1985). The practice is also in evidence in the Gambia (Dey, 1981). At this level allocation is simply between households, although the different household sizes are usually taken into account. The head of household, in turn, allocates the household portion of land between himself and his wife. In the case of polygamous households it is normally the case that each wife has her own cooking pot and therefore her own food fields.

With the size and demographic profile of households and compounds constantly changing there will be a need to alter allocatory decisions. This may be the reason for reports that women (and men) are sometimes allocated land on short-term arrangements. For instance, among the Hausa of the Niger plots are distributed to women on a yearly basis and a woman can find herself with different fields each year. A similar situation occurs in eastern Nigeria involving men as well as women. Here land is divided (at the start of every farming season) among adult male members of the patrilineage and widowed and separated women. Wives of male members have to await the subsequent allocation of land by their husbands. It is important to note that this source of women's insecurity of tenure over the same piece of land from year to year is exacerbated by increasing scarcity of land. Growing land shortage tends to exert a squeeze first and foremost on the quantity and quality of land assigned to women.

Agricultural modernisation as well as land scarcity has increased the profitability of land and weakened women's traditional rights to land for their own use. The introduction of export and industrial crops effectively alienated some land and family labour from food production. Irrigation schemes have done the same. In areas ecologically unsuitable for export or industrial crops more traditional forms of land use continue today.

Since women's land use rights are less secure than men's, women often lose access to part of their land with promotion of higher-productivity methods. Jackson (1985) reports that after implementation of the Kano River irrigation project in northern Nigeria pagan women were allocated smaller, inferior plots, often far from the compound, by their menfolk. Alternatively, they were given the use of a field in the wet (waterlogged) season but not in the dry (only irrigation) season. This is the third source of women's insecurity of land rights, which is associated with all measures to make agriculture more profitable and is therefore likely to be activated by adjustment programmes.

The traditional social organisation of land use cannot always contain competition over land between women and men when these changes arise. Dey (1981, p. 116) illustrates this with an example from another ethnic group in the Gambia:

> Although both men and women have a right to clear land which they then own, in practice men often try to prevent women from exercising this right . . . men time and time again denied that women owned rice land, insisting either that men owned the land themselves or that it belonged to the compound and was therefore under male control. Women, on the other hand, claimed that they owned much of the land they cultivated and had secure rights to use compound land.

Layers of customary laws, as well as residual traces of Muslim law, provide variation within what are generally patrilineal systems. In Burkina Faso a girl might be provided with a plot of land by her own family for her personal crops. Once married her husband's family would provide her with land. In western Nigeria a study showed that daughters were commonly given the right to use a piece of land within the patrilineal system but on the understanding that the property did not pass to their husband's lineage (Spiro, 1985). In the Gambia the *maruo* land a woman acquires for use on marriage is "inalienable while it is being put to the precise 'food for the pot' use for which it is assigned" (Phillott-Almeida, 1983, p. 19). But the retention of land within the lineage is jealously guarded.

The general pattern seems to be that daughters of the male members of a lineage could enjoy an allocation of land for their own use on condition that there was no chance of it being alienated from the lineage and that there was sufficient land to satisfy more important claims first.

In eastern and southern Africa women's contribution is more subsumed in the cultivation of "household fields" over which men have ultimate control. (This is far from being unknown in West Africa but it is more pronounced on the other side of the continent.) Likewise in eastern and southern Africa there are many cases of wives having personal land use rights. In Zambia the practice of granting wives use rights to some land appears to be clear in the case of polygamous households in which co-wives have separate houses, land and implements, and can dispose of surplus produce without their husband's permission (Haalubono, 1983). How definitive is women's separate use of a piece of land in monogamous smallholders' households is less certain. Monogamous households are likely to have smaller farms and therefore less potential for partition.

But the picture is not simply of farm households where men and women manage fields either separately or together. In one household there may be individual fields and joint household fields. For instance, under the *gandu* system of West Africa a group of related men and their wives farm together, but individual men and women might also have personal plots which they cultivate after labour commitments on the collective land are fulfilled (Jackson, 1985). A variation of this is practised in the Gambia

(Dey, 1981) and Burkina Faso (Fapohunda, 1987, p. 300). On the eastern side of the continent, despite women being less involved in own-account farming, there is evidence of jointly managed and individual fields (of both sexes) in the same household. Kumar (1985) has documented common and separate fields in different kinds of households in Zambia. She shows that there are many different combinations of jointly managed and separate fields.

Land adjudication and registration have been spreading for many years. The purpose of this policy is to confirm cultivators' rights to land improvements that they have put in. As such it has been seen, particularly by the World Bank, as an important pillar of agricultural adjustment. The change from a system of sharing, according to need, in the joint patrimony of conjugal dependants and progeny to a system of private ownership is expected to enhance farmers' incentives to invest in higher productivity. In the process land is overwhelmingly registered in the name of the head of household. "Legal systems have discriminated in land titling, by putting newly registered land in men's names (in their purported role as head of household), often overriding women's traditional rights to land use" (World Bank, 1989, p. 86). In Kenya a sample survey of 135 households affected by land adjudication included eight cases of the land being registered in a woman's name only, eight in a woman's and her sons' names, 34 in sons' names only, and more than 50 per cent in husbands' names only. The remainder were joint registration of husbands and sons (Pala-Okeyo, 1980). The category that is noticeably missing is joint husband-wife registration. That women should be on the register at all is due to recognition that they are guardians of their sons' land. When Okeyo asked land adjudication officers why more women were not registered owners, the answer was always: "Because it is customary: men own land and women do not own land." Even where there is legal provision for women to benefit directly from land reform, the practice can still be discriminatory. This was found to be the case in Burkina Faso and the United Republic of Tanzania, while a survey of Zimbabwean resettlement areas revealed that the legal and actual positions of women regarding land permits were different (ILO, 1989b, pp. 7 and 10).

The meaning of separate accounting units

The women in development (WID) literature on rural Africa adequately refutes the model of a homogeneous nuclear family acting as an integrated production unit and allocating resources rationally to obtain maximum possible total income from them.

The implications of a wife being allocated a piece of land must be that she has the managerial responsibility of mobilising the variable factors of production for its cultivation (through payment in cash, kind, labour or some exchange) and that she has the right to appropriate enough of the produce to cover outlays and satisfy the reason for that land allocation.

Otherwise "her land" has little meaning. Management does not have to entail ownership of the land; it is the usufructuary rights that are being managed. This gender division of management must be distinguished from the gender division of labour. When a husband helps a woman with land preparation he is not managing the land. "If a wife provides labour for her husband's agricultural activity, there is an exchange of agricultural by-products in kind or cash in recognition of this service. The terms of such intra-family exchanges reflect traditional practices and implicit spousal bargaining strength" (Fapohunda, 1987, p. 290). Through intra-household exchange of labour and other resources, the wife is funding the inputs of her husband's labour on her land.

The evidence of separate accounting units within households comes from illustrations of the rationale behind allocating land to individuals in the household, the way those same individuals acquire their resource base and the individuals' rights to appropriate and dispose of the produce as they see fit. Wife and husband may draw separate personal incomes from agriculture and associated activities to meet separate financial responsibilities. By tradition the great majority of women and men in African farming households have had their respective obligations to the family's maintenance demarcated. An ILO report (1988a, p. 43) put it this way: "In some cultures, particularly in Africa, conjugal couples have separate purses and consumption patterns." A World Bank report was more specific: "Women are guardians of their children's welfare and have explicit responsibility to provide for them materially" (World Bank, 1989, p. 86). To fulfil separate obligations women and men have had to find their own sources of goods or cash income.

But the picture is not always so clear-cut. In southern and eastern Africa women do not have as frequent or extensive own-accounting units as in West African countries. The result can be seen in the former regions in farming women's status, which is a combination of squatter on their husbands' (cash crop) land and their husbands' farming agent.

However, there is a common situation where women are significant, though partial, managers or decision-makers of the use of land but do not have ultimate control over inputs and outputs. These women are ostensibly operating farms on their own but with a husband making intermittent visits. Ironically, where governments and agencies have aimed to reach women farmers with services, it is these women rather than women farming on their own account (and therefore more autonomously) in male-headed farms that they have primarily in mind. The quite separate case of women clearly managing the farm household on their own is discussed later in this chapter.

Women's and men's crops

The idea that some crops are under the distinctive customary management of women is endorsed by the endeavours of governments and international agencies to reach women farmers with credit and extension services. In the WID literature there are numerous references to "women's crops" and "men's crops." But sometimes this separation is seen in no more subtle terms than "men's export/cash crops" and "women's subsistence food crops." This may be a useful shorthand for a summarised argument that is not expected to stand up to much scrutiny. However, an analytic framework needs more detailed reference points. It is useful to start by considering food and industrial/export crops separately.

Women receive the use of land on marriage in order to feed the family. For this reason the most common situation is that women tend to grow traditional foods while men grow food as a commercial staple. In areas suitable for their cultivation men would be seen growing industrial or export crops, perhaps in addition to the food staple. But this merely represents the two extremities of a spectrum of gender divisions of crops. Between them all combinations are seen. Nothing in this field should be seen as immutable.

In a world without money or market exchange men as well as women must be in self-provisioning food agriculture. However, monetisation and market development have happened. Today women may sell crops to buy in food, and the crops they sell may or may not also be food. Rural markets in Africa attest the surpluses of a wide range of foods produced and sold by women. Nor is it necessarily the staple foods that offer the greater "surpluses." It is a common characteristic of the poorest households that they are deficient in cereals because of limited land or particular production problems on extensive fields. In the time-honoured survival strategy of the poor, higher economic (and nutritional) value foods, such as pulses and legumes, are sold and lower-value cereals bought. Women cover one food deficit by selling other foods. This can mean that a higher proportion of secondary foods from household plots *(shambas)* is sold than the proportion of a staple cereal. If men grow the staple and women the secondary crops a situation can arise where women's food production is more market oriented than men's. At any rate, complete food self-provisioning might be hard to find among any class of household.

It is easily forgotten that men are often also involved in food farming. In countries as diverse as Kenya and Nigeria husband and wife might have their separate maize fields and/or cultivate maize jointly. The output of separate and joint fields can be directed to household granaries and the market in any combination. In Muslim West Africa husbands are sometimes responsible for providing part (the Gambia) or all (areas of western and northern Nigeria) of the family's staple foods so that they are heavily involved in non-marketed food agriculture. Women are able to sell considerable amounts of the output of their own food fields because their husbands' contribution to the family's food requirements can result in substantial marketable surpluses of female-managed production. This is a clear case of women farmers being the more market oriented due to cultural practices. Nevertheless, it has to be remembered that Nigerian women farm very much smaller acreages than men on an individual basis.

Elsewhere in West Africa husband and wife might both contribute to the family's food from their separate fields (see, for instance, Barres et al., 1976; Dey, 1981; and Spiro, 1985).

There are two principal, though not conclusive, determinants of whether a food crop is managed by women or men. The first is market access and the second is production technique.

When a staple such as maize is grown by men or jointly, surpluses are usually sold through official marketing channels, or were before these channels fell into a state of disrepair. The staple thereby becomes a tradable (import-replacing or export) crop. In as much as women's food surpluses do not reach large urban concentrations they cannot be considered as tradable crops. But to the extent that they can act as substitutes for staples they are "derivatives" of tradables. Through cross-substitution effects of income and price changes, they become surrogate tradables.

Gender division of crop management can also follow the introduction of new technologies. When the method of production is upgraded by the use of hybrids and chemical inputs, the staple can often become a man's crop. That is to say, when this new method is made available men are able to adopt it first, if necessary reducing the amount of land on which women cultivate it by traditional methods. In this way men have been able to emerge as producers of food tradables. One case in point is hybrid maize in Kenya. But an outstanding example of a gender hierarchy of yields for the same crop is that of rice in the Gambia (see later in this chapter under "The gender division of labour").

Two illustrations of the gender division of crop management in predominantly food-growing areas are given here. One is from Burkina Faso and the other from central Nigeria.

It is interesting to see that in Burkina Faso (table 1) men are mainly responsible for cereals, which constitute the bulk of self-provisioning foods, and women are strong in the higher-value foods which, given the number of fields involved, are likely to be more market oriented. Policy-makers in Burkina Faso do not, therefore, necessarily face a situation of "women's self-provisioning food agriculture and men's cash cropping". Men's majority role in cereals and cotton crop management means that they are more prominent in tradables while women's food crops are sold locally and nationally.

Table 2 shows how the Tiv women in central Nigeria predominate in the management of yams, maize, cassava and cowpeas, but also manage a considerable share of the benniseed crop and, to a much lesser extent, the water melon, millet and rice crops. Men predominate in the management of millet, rice, watermelons and, with the emergence of cassava as a cash crop, they are now growing cassava. Ranking all these foods according to their prominence as tradables does not obviously put female managers at one end and male managers at the other. But Nigeria is a good example of women's and men's crop portfolios and their relation to foreign trade regimes varying greatly within a country. In eastern Nigeria men manage "prestigious" crops such as yams, while women cultivate the "subsidiary"

Table 1. Fields planted to each major crop by sex of principal cultivator, Burkina Faso

Crops	Sex of principal cultivator (%)		No. of fields
	Men	Women	
Sole cropped:			
Millet	86	14	14
Red sorghum	100	–	11
White sorghum	69	31	10
Maize	100	–	29
Groundnuts	40	60	184
Bambara nuts	19	81	106
Cowpeas	84	16	6
Okra	2	98	96
Sorrel	2	98	44
Others	100	–	16
Inter-cropped:			
Millet/cowpeas	76	24	63
Millet/cowpeas/sorrel	68	32	37
Red sorghum/cowpeas	87	13	31
Red sorghum/cowpeas/sorrel	79	21	5
White sorghum/cowpeas	100	–	25
Others	58	42	44

Note: Pure stands of cowpeas are susceptible to severe insect attacks.

Source: ICRISAT, 1980.

crops of okra, cassava, cocoyams, maize and pumpkins. Among the Yoruba, it is the responsibility of husbands to produce staples such as maize, yams and cassava for the family—or to provide the money to buy them. In the north a wide range of food crops are grown by men. Millet and sorghum are the main staples (and are widely interplanted), and secondary food crops include groundnuts, beans, maize, rice, peppers, cowpeas and vegetables. Pagan women's main crop is sorghum, but they also manage a range of other crops, including millet, groundnuts and beans. Non-secluded Muslim women also grow a range of foods. Although women in the north manage much less land then men, there is considerable overlapping of women's and men's crops.

When it comes to main export or industrial crops the picture is also mixed but to a much lesser degree. In eastern and southern Africa these crops seem to be almost always men's crops apart from the case of women heads of household (Kumar, 1985). There are exceptions, however. Groundnuts, for instance, are also considered a woman's crop in Zambia (Safilios-Rothschild, 1985); cotton, tobacco and coffee provide other examples. But the great bulk of the literature on cases of women growing these kinds of crops on their own account come from West Africa. In the Bamileke region of Cameroon, while coffee is a main concern of men, some

Table 2. Female and male labour contributions to, and income from, staple crops: The Tiv people of central Nigeria (percentages)

Crop	Field preparation	Planting	Weeding	Harvesting	Income[1]
Yams	F: 50 M: 50	F: 80 M: 20	F	F	F: 80 M: 20
Millet	M	F: 20 M: 80	F	F: 50 M: 50	F: 20 M: 80
Sorghum	M	F: 20 M: 80	F	F: 50 M: 50	F
Cassava[2]	F: 25 M: 75	F: 75 M: 25	F	F: 75 M: 25	F: 75 M: 25
Maize	F: 25 M: 75	F: 90 M: 10	F	F: 90 M: 10	F
Rice	F: 10 M: 90	F	F	F: 50 M: 50	F: 20 M: 80
Benniseed	M	F: 50 M: 50	F	F: 50 M: 50	F: 40 M: 60
Watermelons	F: 25 M: 75	F: 25 M: 75	F	F: 25 M: 75	F: 25 M: 75
Cowpeas	F: 25 M: 75	F	F	F	F

F = Female; M = Male.

[1] Income refers to the value of the total crop, both the marketed and home-consumed proportions, valued at market prices projected by the project staff. [2] Women produce and control most of the cassava, but men are beginning to produce and sell some amounts.

Source: Burfisher and Horenstein, 1985.

women own coffee bushes on land they have bought (but never it seems on land on loan from husband or kin (Dieckermann and Joldersma, 1982)). Among the Hausa in the Niger a survey revealed that 60 per cent of the total value of output from women's fields came from groundnuts (Barres et al., 1976). In the Gambia women grow cotton and benniseed in the upper river areas. In southern Ghana a sample showed that one-third of (mostly older) women specialised in cocoa production on their fields (Okale and Mabey, 1975). A common pattern here is that women work for many years on their husbands' or relatives' export crop to be recompensed later with land or being able to buy land from their savings. In Burkina Faso cotton has been rapidly developed in the past decade or so. It is considered predominantly a man's crop, grown individually or by the compound group of men. But women also have experience of growing cotton. In a UNESCO project in the northern central area of the country among the majority ethnic group of the Mossi, women learned to grow cotton as a cash crop (McSweeney, 1979).

The WID literature suggests that women have a strong desire to produce export or industrial crops (but in their own right). This implies that, at least sometimes, they perceive the returns to be higher than for food production, however they impute the value of forgone food self-provisioning. The presumption that women hold fast to self-provisioning agricultural production, come what may, derives from observation of women's actions when they have no choice or when they fear that if they let go of self-provisioning output they will lose control of resources. It says nothing of alternative scenarios when their access to, and control over, resources are secured.

Although there are many instances of women growing industrial or export crops it would be wrong to assume that this production is on such a scale that women's and men's crop mixes bear comparison. They do not. And it is quite wrong to claim that the differences betweeen women's and men's crop portfolios are not significant or a thing of the past. In most cases of women growing industrial or export crops on their own account, the scale is of the order of a sideline. Nor do women and men usually enter production of these crops in the same circumstances. It is important to understand these differences when trying to assess the impact of adjustment programmes on women's own account agriculture relative to men's.

The gender division of labour

The division of labour is concerned with the typecasting of cultivation tasks. That this has been drawn up very much on gender lines is unquestionable, as witnessed by the WID literature. A summarised view might be that after land preparation (in which women are involved too) the bulk of the work is often done by women. The notion of a family labour force made up of "adult male equivalents" is useless except as a theoretical base with which to compare reality. But divisions are not rigid. Both sexes are sometimes involved in planting and often in harvesting. Or there might be a gender division of labour among the subtasks of planting and harvesting (including carrying produce from the field). The sharper the division of economic accounting units, the easier it is to see the quid pro quo for work done on the other's fields. In the Gambia, for instance, wives on an irrigated rice scheme agreed to work on their husbands' irrigated rice in exchange for the use of the land in the wet season when, although waterlogging reduced yields, those yields were still higher than the women's swamp rice yields. But in poorer households where women did not have swamp or dryland fields of their own to work (and therefore had no economic opportunity cost of working on their husbands' land to use as a bargaining chip), they were obliged to work their husbands' fields in the hope that from this the cooking pot at least would be supplied. Their control over the returns to their labour was much less than that of their better-endowed sisters. This is a good illustration of how women's own resource base influences the degree of asymmetry between women's and men's rights and obligations—and the true economic costing of female labour.

Some other examples from the WID literature fill in the picture of broad lines of labour specialisation with co-operation at the margin. Apart from the land situation the crop-mix of each person and male migration are also strong influences.

Historically, in Kenya, men cleared the land and looked after large livestock. Women undertook most or all of the rest: planting, weeding, harvesting and processing. There seems to be general agreement in the literature that the effect of male migration has been to add to women's tasks those of land preparation and looking after animals (Gathee, 1980; Monsted, 1977). Muriithi (1980) comments that when their husbands are away Kikuyu women take over all the work on cash crops, including digging, and still continue with their food farming. They also market the cash crops but do not control the cash income, which suggests that there is some other quid pro quo. Wills (1967) found in a study in Embu district that women spent half their agricultural time on men's coffee and maize crops. Where development of export crops is not so marked, the gender division of labour on food crops may be more traditional, except that male migration may be greatest from these less well-endowed areas.

Reports from Zambia suggest that the gender division of labour is less rigid than in Kenya, but that it can vary by crop. Hoe-tilling, in the absence of draft power or tractors, is performed by both sexes. But studies in several provinces have shown that women do most of the weeding, harvesting and post-harvest work on crops. They also share in planting. Men do more on land preparation and fertiliser application than women. A sample survey in Mpika (Northern province), Mazaluka (Southern province) and Mumbwa (Central province) indicated that women average 6.6 hours a day on agricultural work during the farming season compared with men's 5.7 hours (Due and Mudenda, 1984). An integrated rural development programme survey in Chinsali concluded that women undertook 44 per cent of all farm work (Allen, 1984). Thus in some areas women may not do most of the farm work. Another report from Zambia tends to confirm this, although there are variations in the gender division of labour among different tasks according to the amount of maize sold (Evans and Young, 1989). At either end of the scale of market orientation women do considerably more work than their husbands: when no maize is sold, women do about three times as much on-farm work and when large amounts are sold they put in 58 per cent more hours. Surprisingly, women and men do comparable amounts of weeding, while women are clearly more important for planting and harvesting. But the division of labour is also different by crop and by type of household.

Across the continent a similar pattern of division of land preparation is seen. In Burkina Faso, for instance, women's share of land preparation is likely to be greater when hand tools are used than when animal traction is available. Otherwise gender typing of field tasks in this country decrees that men clear the land and take a dominant role in land preparation, with women providing the majority of labour for sowing, planting, weeding and (depending on the crop) harvesting. Women can spend up to six hours a day in the fields (Lallemand, 1971).

No other country offers such widely diverse divisions of labour as Nigeria, with its very different cropping systems and cultural attitudes to gender relations. Information on the division of field tasks in eastern Nigeria is difficult to obtain. However, it is known that women perform some of the more intensive tasks of male-managed yam cultivation, as well as the much less labour-intensive tasks on their own cassava. Since yam and cassava are inter-cropped here on "men's land", this labour division might represent payment by women for land use.

A survey in the early 1970s among the Yoruba of western Nigeria found that 93 per cent of women helped on their husbands' yam, maize, tobacco and cassava crops, contrary to common assumptions that these women were not involved in field agriculture (Patel and Anthonio, 1974-75). More detailed research on the tobacco crop elicited the facts that fewer than 5 per cent of the women interviewed had anything to do with clearing the bush and preparing the land, while 77 per cent were involved in transplanting, 71 per cent in fertilising the plots, 87 per cent in topping and removing suckers and 94 per cent in harvesting. Surprisingly only 4 per cent weeded the tobacco crop. In this zone it is usually the older women who farm on their own account as well as trade, while younger women trade more and help on their husbands' farms. In the same region Spiro (1985) found from a survey that 25 per cent of women's time was spent in some farming activity. The only exclusively male tasks were clearing the land and burning the bush, and tractor ploughing. Women and men hoed, planted, applied fertilisers, weeded, harvested and transported crops.

Burfisher and Horenstein illustrated the division of labour over nine different crops among the Tiv people of central Nigeria (see table 2). Except for sorghum there is a close co-variation between who plants and who manages the crop (and income). Of all the field tasks, weeding, on all the crops, was found to be exclusively a female task. But harvesting is more of a shared task. One reason may be that sorghum follows yams in inter-cropping, and its planting date could coincide with the intensive weeding activity. In the north of the country the poorer and less secluded women are, the more field work they undertake. A survey of Zaria district concluded that "agriculture provides a limited amount of work for some women, who may assist in the cotton, groundnut, pepper and cowpea harvests if their husbands allow them to go out at these times" (Simmons, 1976). Jackson, drawing on the Kano River irrigation project, states that the gender division of labour is relatively inflexible, despite the seclusion of young Muslim village women. With the daily and seasonal commuting of farmstead women to the village this is possible. Jackson is more specific than Simmons: Muslim women in the project villages were responsible for most of the cotton, groundnut, bean and pepper picking, and helped with the millet and sorghum harvests. Planting used to be done partly by women, and still is in remoter settlements. Pagan women on the project performed different cultivation tasks, well beyond just harvesting—on *gandu* land, on their husbands' plots and on their own.

There is a pattern in all this. Women help their husbands in a more corporate manner if husbands have responsibility for finding the family's food. It is when women are allocated land to grow the family's food that divisions of labour (and quid pro quos) are more in evidence. That is to say, the more pronounced are separate accounting units the sharper the division of labour.

It is also a natural conclusion from the evidence of the Zambian case study mentioned above that the opportunity of earning cash income is a lure to husbands to work more in agriculture, while self-provisioning entails a more prominent role for women. This, together with the impact of male migration on women's work mentioned above, has implications for the results of adjustment programmes.

A final point is of relevance for policy formulation. Within Nigeria, at least, there is an inverse co-variation between women's involvement in field tasks and the extent of their processing and trading activities. It is plausible to suppose that this is the case elsewhere in Africa. But between the extremities of the range of this inverse relation there could be many different combinations of field tasks on the one hand, and processing and trading tasks, on the other. Some knowledge of the relations of production and exchange within the household would help to explain the rationale of what is observed.

Markets within the household

The separation of the divisions of management and labour indicate that women and men effectively exchange labour between their respective economic accounting units. This, together with the sexes' respective obligations to family maintenance, provides the framework for studying the circulation of produce, income and capital within the aggregate household economy.

The input of labour is mobilised through the division of tasks by gender. Women do not only work on their own crops, nor men only on theirs. The gender division of labour of field tasks encourages exchange labour between adults in a household. Basically it is not a case of one spouse helping the other through a labour bottleneck (although this can happen in addition). Men might do certain land preparation tasks on women's fields in exchange for women planting and weeding, and helping in harvesting on men's fields. Sometimes when the division of labour is not rigid, spouses appear to share certain tasks, usually planting and harvesting. But what is apparent from time allocation data is that the terms of labour trade between women and men are very unfavourable to women. Men can end up doing very little on women's fields. The labour disparity is sometimes, but rarely adequately, bridged by men making payments to their wives in cash or kind.

This unequal exchange is an illustration of the asymmetry of obligations and reciprocities between women and men. Nevertheless, within the limits imposed upon them, women make some fine calculations for the deployment of their resources. Their perception of what is a direct or opportunity cost to them is highly developed. If they produce the same crop as their husbands but experience lower yields this can be traced to unequal factors of production of the same quality (including land), emanating from causes within and outside the household.

It is in eastern and southern Africa that the image of women working as "unpaid family labour" is in greatest evidence. The crop that women work on in this way might be an export crop or a main food staple (which is often partly market oriented). For instance, in separate pieces of research in Kakamega in western Kenya, Moock (1973 and 1976) and Staudt (1985) chose to distinguish female-managed farms from male (or jointly managed) farms in reference to food-growing farms on which maize was the dominant crop. In the latter cases the maize accounting unit was jointly managed, although with unequal labour contributions and appropriations of net receipts. This indicates a more corporate, but still unequal, arrangement. Yet even in these farming households there will be women's sidelines of secondary foods directed to both self-provisioning and the market. An example of this is implicit in a contrasting view, also from Kenya. "The husband manages his own farm, producing cash crops . . . while his wife/wives work in their *shambas* with their children, and in addition work on the farm (husband's cash crop) as unpaid family labour" (Kongstad and Monsted, 1980). In Burkina Faso women work in their own condiment plots next to the compound, in compound fields and in the personal fields of themselves and their husbands. In exchange they receive help with land preparation (Lallemand, 1971).

In so far as some items of daily expenditure are purchased with the proceeds of these cash crops, the women are not, of course, entirely unpaid, since this displaces expenditure they would otherwise have to make. But the patrilineal basis to the allocation of the fixed factor of production, the bargaining power that this confirms on male heads of household and the fact that wives' labour is preferred to incurring a wages bill suggests something less than a free competitive labour market in the household. In fact, it is not unpaid family labour which is the lasting impression of WID sources on men's dominating economic accounting units, but the gross asymmetry of obligations and returns as well as the marginalisation of women's own accounting units. Women manage on their own account, but the gender terms of exchange of factors of production and of produce tend to be very unfavourable to them.

The clearest illustrations of intra-household factor and product markets come from West Africa, even though there may be additional fields cultivated jointly in this subregion. The structured asymmetry of these intra-household markets takes on many different forms not only between subregions and countries but within countries. Nigeria is a good illustration of this too.

Yoruba women's apparently unpaid labour is compensated by husbands' responsibility to provide the family's staple foods and by women's initial trading capital most frequently coming from their husbands in the form of a "gift". But it seems to be the case that Yoruba women are not directly remunerated for working on their husbands' farms. In contrast, there is considerable payment in kind within the Tiv household. However, payment is not made in the form of one balancing item. Several transfer payments can be made in either direction. "Women frequently receive millet from men to process and sell on their own account in return for their labour input on men's fields. Similarly, men usually receive some quantity of yams from women's fields in return for their participation in cleaning yam fields" (Burfisher and Horenstein, 1985). Moreover, foodstuffs may be sold within the Tiv household: a woman may buy millet or sorghum from her husband to make beer, or sell cassava on behalf of her husband and make a profit. Or a loan may be made between spouses, frequently with interest attached. The 20 per cent of yam output recorded as men's income in table 2 represents the amount women give their husbands for entertaining and ceremonies. Gender asymmetry of obligations and reciprocities there undoubtedly is, but within this restriction women are making their own calculations assessing direct and opportunity costs as well as returns.

In the Muslim north of Nigeria a dramatically different display of intra-household markets can be seen. Any tendency farther south of women being paid in kind for field tasks, thereby securing a raw material base for later processing and sale, is taken to an advanced state in the Muslim north. Unsecluded rural women may spend several days a week working on land from which their husbands will support them (Pittin, 1987). But husbands of secluded women have the responsibility of providing the family's food, as well as the water and firewood. Women will clothe and provide lunch for themselves and their children. They are also heavy contributors to daughters' dowries and sons' marriage expenses. The source of raw materials for their compound-based secondary and tertiary industries is remuneration for harvesting and, increasingly, threshing that part of their husbands' crop which is not sold directly. They may also process other farmers' crops for payment, glean the food fields or receive net produce from their own inherited farms. Husbands have no claim to their wives' earnings. The internal market of the household is highly developed and monetised. Women may lend their husband money or grain to provide the family food, charging interest for the loan. Some women may even buy grain from their husbands after the harvest and sell it back to them later at a higher price to provide the meals they share with their husbands (Jackson, 1985). Manure from compound livestock is sold to husbands for use on the food fields. These intra-household markets give rise to husbands' and wives' separate (current and capital) accounts. Secluded women can have equal economic status with their husbands and may even be richer.

It is very evident that the nature of these intra-household markets, compounded by the bias in farm support services towards male accounting units, has led to a misallocation of household-level resources, from the viewpoint both of factor deployment and of use of reinvestible surpluses. These markets are not static in character. Per capita resources alter as do opportunities above the household level. Changes intended by adjustment programmes can activate them in ways leading to unforeseen results, either improving or worsening the efficiency of resource use below the household level. To say that freeing prices will lead to the most efficient use of household resources is to ignore the terms on which intra-household markets operate.

Competition for women's labour and seasonal labour bottlenecks

Farming women may or may not spend longer hours in field agriculture than men. But when their other tasks (which include crop processing, water and firewood collection, child care and housework) are added, their working day becomes very long. A not unusual situation is that the domestic and economic sectors each appropriate about six hours of women's daily time. More commonly less time is spent in the domestic sector. Individual tasks intensifying at different times of the farming season and a shortage of labour at one time can be followed by an easing, or even some excess labour capacity, at other times. However, it is easy to make the mistake of assuming that absence of field work means women are having a much easier time. Jobs postponed are now caught up with; or some jobs have become more difficult. In the "off-season" women might spend a great deal of time stockpiling firewood; and they might have to walk up to 4 kilometres to collect water in this dry period.

It has been observed that women's workloads can be moderated in polygamous households: total workloads differ between single wife and co-wife status, as well as by age of woman. From a very small sample taken in Burkina Faso, McSweeney (1979) recorded a total daily workload of 11.3 hours for women without a co-wife against ten hours for co-wives. The gain of the latter came in household tasks. Kumar (1985) presents data from Zambia to indicate the same in a different way. In this sample women in polygamous households averaged 19 days of work per hectare, women in nuclear male-headed households 26 days, and women in female-headed households 40 days.

Competition for women's labour time is revealed by the use of children's labour. McSweeney shows that already at 7 years of age girls may be contributing several hours of work a day at pounding millet and spinning cotton, $4\frac{1}{2}$ hours at 9 years (including the additional tasks of fetching water and doing the laundry), $6\frac{1}{2}$ hours at 11 years (adding firewood portage) and $7\frac{1}{4}$ hours at 13 years. At 15 years of age a girl would spend $9\frac{3}{4}$ hours a day in productive tasks. Against this, boys of 7 years average $1\frac{1}{2}$ hours, and reach a peak of 6 hours at 13 years, to fall back to $4\frac{1}{2}$ hours at 15 years. The younger boys fetch straw for fuel and run errands for their mothers, assisting in hauling earth for construction and looking after the animals. At 13 years boys are active in market-gardening activities. Evans and Young (1989) give data to show that children under 13 years contribute significant fractions (around one-third) of their fathers' labour input, less of their mothers'.

Increased primary school attendance of children has been referred to in a number of countries as leaving women with a heavier burden. The absence of children during the day is a serious loss for women.

Two of women's field tasks typically present labour bottlenecks: planting and weeding. The latter in particular manifests itself as seasonal work stress for women. This is the rainy season when diarrhoeal illness peaks. It is also the "lean period" when food stocks are lowest. Pregnant women have been known to lose weight and seasonality of birth weights has been recorded. Breastfeeding is sometimes reduced or prematurely terminated at this time. Less water is collected and cooking might be reduced to once a day. Doubtless domestic work can be reduced under pressure by reorganisation and cutting corners. But if it is reduced too far there will be welfare costs, specifically maternal and infant ill-health in the short term and, if demographic theories are correct, demographic costs in the long term. How women trade off these costs at the margin for higher crop yields (so heavily dependent on their careful and multiple weedings) is a subject that has never been studied. The small amount of seasonal health data suggests that women do have to accept some trade-off because they cannot cover all tasks. That trade-off can be influenced by the new incentives intended by adjustment programmes.

Gender and farm support services

The comment is frequently heard that the problem of farm support services is that they are biased towards the large commercial farms and that they do not reach the entire smallholder sector. This was certainly true of the late 1970s and 1980s when these services declined following on general hard times for government. But it does not answer the question whether revived farm support services will address women farming on their own account or whether they will revert to the gender bias of the 1970s before the economic decline.

That that underlying bias existed is undisputed. The delivery mechanism, via farmers' co-operatives or parastatals, was directed to a male clientele. Male smallholders did receive heavily subsidised credit. There were small categories of women who were exceptions. For instance, in Burkina Faso, although credit is given in principle without distinction based on gender, it is granted through the intermediary of co-operatives, of which family heads are members. If a woman with two or three dependants can assure the co-operative of her ability to meet a repayment schedule, ordinarily there is no difficulty in admitting her to a co-operative in order that she can obtain a loan. But this is the case of a woman head of household. It does not mean that farming women's access to credit has become generalised. In Kenya, while some women have become shareholders in co-operatives on their own account, or jointly with their husbands, there has been nothing like a steady progression of female inclusion. Any future expansion of co-operative credit could be presented with an institutional framework that inadequately reaches women managing crops, even tradables or important horticultural crops, on their own account. There is nothing to suggest that institutional practices have altered. A recent World Bank report states that it is often more difficult for women than for men to gain access to information, technology and credit (World Bank, 1989, p. 86).

Co-operatives, of course, offer other services: supply of inputs, tractor services, technical information, livestock specimens and marketing facilities. But merely intensifying the activities of co-operatives does not overcome a bias against women farmers.

> In fact, disparities (in services received, *sic*) between female-managed farms and other types of farms widen as the value of the service increases, both in cost to the administration and in benefit to the farmer. Expensive strategies such as intensifying or saturating areas with services do little to alter these disparities. A bias against female managers exists, independent of other factors such as economic standing, land size and performance (Staudt, 1985, p. 56).

The male-staffed extension services overwhelmingly favour communication with male farmers (see Staudt, 1985). Special "women's projects" and a little agricultural knowledge in the home economics curriculum directed to women make no impact on the bias in the distribution of the most desirable public resources between female and male own-account farmers. In Kenya, after some effort to recruit more women, female extension workers are still a fraction of the total number. There is also the problem that they could offer a differentiated service. In theory, men and women in the service can train in *either* general agriculture and home economics, *or* general agriculture and agricultural engineering and soil conservation. In practice, the student extensionists divide the curriculum along gender lines with virtually all the female students opting for the first combination. Furthermore, once in the field they gravitate towards home economics focusing on welfare and nutritional issues. This factor, together with the high dropout rate of female extensionists, suggests there is no real substitute to directing the male-dominated mainstream agricultural extension service to women.

An alternative is to organise the demand for extension information in such a way that mainstream agricultural extension services are made easily available to women farmers. One way is to group farmers. This has antecedents in Kenya going back to colonial times, but it was neglected for most of the post-independence period. Now it has been revamped and claims are being made that a large majority of farmers reached by extension workers are women farmers. Extension workers have claimed that the farmers with whom they have the best contact are women.

Gender-differentiated yields

The absence of resource rationalisation can also be seen in differences in yields. When women and men grow the same crop in their own accounting units it has been noted that women's yields are generally lower than men's. The very fact of lower yields on land allocated to women is corroboration of the existence of their own-account farming. Of course, there are certain circumstances when a single manager might choose to concentrate yield-enhancing efforts only on part of his land. But these circumstances are never likely to be as frequent as the occurrence of lower yields on land on which "women's crops" are grown. One reason for the lower yields is that women are allocated inferior land. It may be less fertile, more fragmented or farthest away. Jackson indicated that this was so among pagan households in the area of the Kano River irrigation project in Nigeria. In the Gambia there is a hierarchy of rice yields with men getting the best land at the right time of year. Wherever there is a scarcity of good land, it can be expected that women will be found cultivating the marginal land more often than men.

But there is another reason for women's lower yields. That is that they do not have the same access as men to input supplies, information and credit. This bias might emanate from within the household through, for instance, women having to work compound and/or husbands' fields first, and therefore having limited remaining time for their own fields (see Jackson, 1985 and Spiro, 1985), or it may emanate from beyond the household, in farm support services.

Yet when women are able to incorporate new technical factors in their production functions the quality of their management, as evidenced by yields, is at least as high as men's. Moock (1973 and 1976) undertook a multivariate analysis of female and male farm managers in western Kenya which allowed for differences in factor use. The crop was maize. His conclusion was that "women managers of household farms are far better farm managers than men. A woman produces one-and-a-half more bags of maize with a given package of physical inputs. The regression coefficient is significant at less than 0.05 probability". He went on: "Not infrequently, government officials point to the preponderance of female managers by way of explanation for low agricultural yields in the area". But "women are generally more competent than men in Vihigia as farm managers, which is to say that women produce more output, on average, from a given package of maize inputs." The problem was that women faced obstacles in their access to these inputs. But there is also an implication here for the efficient use of public resources; the marginal return to these resources would be higher if some quantity of them were switched to women farmers.

Kumar (1985), in a survey in Zambia, analysed yields by three types of household: male headed (joint), female headed and polygamous. Yields were highest in male-headed households and lowest in polygamous households. Differences seemed to be closely related to labour input per acre. Probably because of their larger total acreage polygamous households used significantly less labour per unit of land than male-headed ones. Without animal or tractor ploughing and with much less fertiliser use than polygamous households, female-headed households maintained better yields by much harder work and a judicious mix of crops. But their individual crop yields were less than 60 per cent of those of male-headed households which utilised a great deal more family labour per acre.

Other gainful activities of farming women

The purpose of this section is to show that farming is not a "closed economy". It has to be traded at the margin with other opportunities and, given socio-economic stratification, there can be variations of income portfolios for both women and men.

In many parts of rural sub-Saharan Africa women are less inclined than men to be pure farmers. For men the alternatives to farming (migration or local government employment in the nearest town) tend to draw them away from farm activities. This means that when they farm it is usually their sole occupation. Women, on the other hand, undertake a wide range of work portfolios around their field agriculture. Declining productivity and profitability of farming has forced them to seek off-farm sources of income. Trading agricultural produce has long been another activity, with women often selling their husbands' cash crops for small commissions in cash or kind. Beer-brewing, making and selling snack foods, or processing produce for distribution farther afield are included in economic portfolios in all combinations. The growth of large commercial farms, and in particular the increased number of "emergent" farmers from the better-endowed end of the smallholder sector, has expanded the rural market for wage labour.

The picture is anything but uniform, and these extra incomes are not large. But they bear sufficient comparison with the value of women's own-account agricultural production, and returns to family welfare from women's work on husbands' crops, for women to adopt them even at the cost of working less on household land. Women are obliged to seek cash income because the amount that they and the children need is not assuredly forthcoming from men. The problem is less acute in parts of West Africa, where men are obliged by custom to provide a large part of the family's sustenance needs. But even here women can have a mixed and varying portfolio of farming and trading. For instance, trading is more important to women in western than in eastern Nigeria and, in general, the less farming women do the more extensive is their trading in processed and unprocessed foods. Cooking snacks and brewing beer for sale locally, especially to migrant workers, are frequent additions. But it is in the Muslim north of the country that trading in agricultural produce after value-adding processing is most marked. Snack foods may be made from beans, groundnuts, millet and soured milk. Some processed foods, such as groundnut cakes, are transported to Lagos and other southern cities (Pittin, 1987). Simmons (1976) reports from her three sampled villages in Zaria province that between 80 and 100 per cent of women were involved in trading. It would be wrong to assume that the scale of this activity represents pocket money for women or supplements to family income.

Simmons makes a comparison of gross farm income and men's off-farm income (from a 1966/67 farm management survey) with women's incomes (estimated from her own 1971/72 survey in the same villages). Average gross farm income for two villages were 199 naira and 215 naira per annum, respectively (9.60 naira equalled US$1 in March 1991). Men's off-farm income averaged 51.5 naira and 57.7 naira. Women's average incomes in the same two villages in 1971/72 were 55.0 naira and 163.2 naira.

In eastern and southern Africa women also have to take the acquisition of cash income very seriously. There is no doubt that men contribute to incidental maintenance expenses. But as one commentator on Kenya puts it, the "allocation of income from cash crops is a male domain" (Muriithi, 1980). Husbands do not perceive daily household expenses to be their obligation: "more than 40 per cent of them paid no cash or just occasionally purchase something" (Kongstad and Monsted, 1980). Thus women brew beer, weave mats, do a petty trade in snacks and undertake casual work on larger farms. Vegetables, pulses and root crops are traded. Large quantities of food are distributed in this way with little working capital. In many parts of Zambia farming women earn significant sums off farm. In Northern, Central and Southern provinces, fishing, field work on others' farms, and trading in food and clothing are sources of income. A study noted that more women than men earned off-farm income; in Southern province women earned almost three times as much as men (Due and Mudenda, 1984).

It is the agricultural wage labour market that holds some of the more interesting implications for strategies of agricultural development. The way women deploy their labour over a range of activities suggests an issue of opportunity costs of farming. It must be stressed that, given intra-household economic relations, opportunity costs are felt at the individual level as well as the household level. Sometimes the former is predominant. It is reasonable to ask why, if women are so interested in off-farm work, they should bother with their own food farming at all? Or, if it is to be regarded as a good thing that they should concentrate on technical improvements in their food farming in future, what will they implicitly be asked to forgo? What calculations do women make at the margin?

If women do not hire casual labour to free themselves for farm work elsewhere it has to be assumed that the returns to other activities are less than for their own farming. The reason that they do not expand own-account farming is invariably because their access to land is limited. Therefore other activities provide accretions to the (imputed or real) returns to own-account food farming. These are not necessarily accretions to self-provisioning production. Considerable amounts of their own-account food production might be destined for the market. But they are accretions in the sense that more cash income must be found after the production possibilities, at current technical levels, of available land have been fully exploited; and there remains some labour time for additional activities, usually in the slack season. The year-round presence of women wage workers who also do some farming indicates that not all categories of farming women are fully stretched by household-level farming, probably because of lack of agricultural resources.

The female agricultural wage labour market is furnished by the unequal distribution of cash crop acreage. Three categories of farmers might be presumed: rich, middle and poor. Kongstad and Monsted (1980), writing on western Kenya, depicted their different labour deployments thus: rich farmers hire in supplementary labour; middle farmers mainly rely on family labour, but may both hire in and hire out labour; poor farmers rely on family labour but because they have such small farms family labour is also hired out. The bulk of the labour that is hired in and out is most often female.

But farm size is not the only determinant of the labour market. On the demand side the influences are ecological conditions and cropping patterns. Where ecological (and climatic) conditions allow highly diversified cash cropping, such as in Kisii district in western Kenya, while total labour requirements are large, the seasonal profile is relatively flat and family labour might be relied on by greater numbers of middle farmers. For instance, pyrethrum and tea can be continually harvested throughout the year. At low altitude the cash crops might be sugar cane and cotton which give rise to seasonal peak labour demands that cannot be met so easily by family labour. If two crops of maïze a year are possible, as in Kakamega and Kisumu, there will also be a seasonal labour market.

There is, therefore, a matrix of locality-specific demand and supply factors of a rural wage labour market that is highly stratified by gender. Women and men have their respective economic opportunity costs that they experience individually. It is not feasible to plan structural changes in smallholder agriculture on the basis of a presumed homogenised household labour force.

The consequences of ignoring gender-differentiated labour deployment issues is dramatised most strongly in the case of female-headed farms.

Female-headed farm households

Given the high percentage of female-headed smallholdings in Africa it is difficult to talk of a sustained internal dynamic to the small-scale farming sector without addressing their particular needs.

Staudt reported that 36 per cent of farms were headed by women and Moock 33 per cent in the same province of western Kenya. Muriithi points out that the prevalence of these households in Kenya is greater in areas of lower agricultural potential. Quoting figures for around 1974 she claims that in Eastern and Coast provinces the figure is 27 per cent, compared with 19, 22 and 23 per cent in Western, Rift Valley and Nyanza provinces, respectively. But Gathee, writing five years later, gives a figure of 95 per cent for Kisii, a high potential area. Kershaw (1975-76) noted in a study of Kikuyu families that men who migrated to town to find work mostly came from households with less than 2 hectares. Small farm size may therefore be another determinant of the frequency of female-managed farms.

Figures for the proportion of farm households headed by women in Zambia vary widely, both between and within provinces. But they are also very different between the 1980 census and the 1982-83 Farm Survey, despite both defining a household in terms of common residence—cooking and eating under the same roof. This means that co-wives (as well as widows and divorcees) head their own households. This definition is of use to economic planners only if the unit of consumption is the same as the unit of production. Co-wives are certainly undertaking own-account farming, so that in their case the primary units of consumption and production would be the same. But unless proved otherwise, it has to be assumed that the great majority of women in monogamous households do *some* own-account farming too. Identifying recorded female heads of household for receipt of credit and extension would therefore exclude a sizeable proportion of women's agriculture. Even so the official data on these households in Zambia are worthy of note. On a district basis the range recorded by the census is 35-50 per cent, with the highest percentages tending to be in Northern and Luapula provinces. The Farm Survey range is from under 10 per cent to 43 per cent.

Southern Africa is reputed to have the highest percentages of female-headed households: 40-60 per cent in Lesotho and 35 per cent in Swaziland (Palmer, 1985). In Botswana studies during the 1970s reported levels of 20-43 per cent (Fortmann, 1984, p. 454).

The figures are probably lower for West Africa. But Bukh (1979), writing in the late 1970s when many male Ghanaians had migrated to oil-rich Nigeria, gives a figure of 42 per cent for the Ewe in south-eastern Ghana.

A major problem of assessing the frequency of these farms is that of definition. This is not just a statistical matter. It raises issues for the tailoring and targeting of farm support services. For instance, who takes which decisions? At one end of the spectrum husbands may be resident but commuting to daily formal sector employment. At the other end they may live and work far away, returning once a year or even less frequently. Even in the latter case major decisions, such as which cash crops to plant and over what acreage, may be taken by husbands. The day-to-day or month-to-month management decisions of mobilising a labour force or deciding how carefully intra-cultivation field tasks are to be done would be left to women. But if they do not also pay for the inputs and appropriate the returns, this kind of decision-making does not amount to own-account farming. Therefore another crucial subject of targeting is identifying the individual who is the "financial manager." For simplicity's sake it has to be assumed that the individual who is responsible for raising the working capital (credit and cash inputs) is the same individual who controls the financial returns. The WID literature is replete with references to men finding the cash requirements for cash cropping and controlling the returns, even when wives are left to manage during the growing period and actually undertake the selling of the crop.

However, some women have been able to raise credit through their own co-operative membership and would appear to sell the produce on their own account. These women are most likely to have husbands who appear least frequently or never. If widows are added to this category there is then a percentage of farms which are managed by women in the fullest sense. The studies by Moock and Staudt imply this kind of complete management when they refer to female-managed farms. Gathee's very high percentages probably include women managing within a production scheme laid down by their husbands.

Characteristics of female-headed farms include gross undercapitalisation (sometimes lacking simple field tools), below average farm size, acreage left uncultivated, fewer cash crops grown, very low adoption of improved varieties of food crops, and hiring out of labour to other farms. The women heads also tend to be significantly older on average than other farming women.

The critical factor that leads to this deterioration in own account farming is the depletion of the family labour force by the absence of the adult male. Fortmann (1984, p. 457) illustrates this with figures for differences in average family size between male- and female-headed farm households in Botswana. But it is not simply a reduction in the total "adult male labour equivalents"; family labour for ploughing is specifically absent. Draft animals are frequently absent too. The result is that some combination of oxen, tractors and male labour has to be hired. The information network on the supply of these inputs is not always easily penetrated by women on their own. The result is seen in lower ploughing rates for female-headed farms (ibid.). When the services are hired, women often find themselves at the end of the queue for them so that planting dates might not be optimal. Sometimes the promised hired male labour does not turn up at all or does not do the job properly because of women's limited ability to supervise authoritatively. The final cost is a factor in estimating net monetised returns. For instance, a Rural Income Distribution Survey in Botswana found no difference in yields of sorghum of male- and female-managed farms, but female-headed households averaged net profits of 7.91 rands per acre compared with 11.57 rands per acre (1.83 rands equalled US$1 in March 1991) for male-headed households (Palmer, 1985).

Lower net returns affect the profitability of using credit. A study in Malawi noted a close relationship between defaulting on repayments and the mean labour units available to the households (Chipande, 1987, p. 320). Labour-deficient households were unable to manage these particular labour-intensive crop packages that were linked to the credit facilities.

The outcome of the problem of labour deficiency is that female-headed farms frequently leave part of their acreage uncultivated and seek more work off farm. There is some evidence from southern Africa that women farming on their own spend less time working on household land than women in male-headed households (Palmer, 1985). Smock (1981) mentions the different patterns of earnings of male- and female-headed farm households in Kenya. She quotes an Integrated Rural Survey to conclude that female-headed households earned more from regular wage employment than other farm households and that as a consequence male-headed households consumed a greater proportion of their total food output. This should dispel the idea that male migration necessarily leads to the "feminisation of farming" and a retreat into self-provisioning agriculture.

But it should not be supposed that being on their own and suffering a labour deficiency prevents women from cultivating export crops. Kumar (1985) analysed cropping patterns on jointly managed and individual fields for male- and female-headed households, respectively, in plateau and valley villages in Eastern province in Zambia. She found it impossible to generalise about crop specialisation by sex, but did conclude that women's crops differed by type of household:

> Thus in joint households, maize (local) is most likely to be managed by men alone or jointly with women, while groundnut is most likely to be grown independently by women. However, in female-headed households, 83 per cent grow local maize independently. What is striking is that in joint households, while women are involved in the joint production of major cash crops, such as hybrid maize, cotton, and sunflower, they do not undertake such production on their own. This is not the case for female-headed households, nearly a third of whom are found to grow cotton or sunflower.

Nevertheless, the household labour supply, rather than returns to labour, can determine which cash crops are grown. In the Malawi study quoted above female-headed households concentrated on groundnuts rather than maize or tobacco, despite groundnuts being more labour-intensive (total number of hours worked per hectare) than maize and providing smaller returns to labour than both maize and tobacco. The reason was that the labour requirements for groundnuts could be spread more evenly throughout the year whereas maize involved sharp seasonal peaks of labour input (Chipande, 1987, p. 323).

There is clearly a need to design crop packages and support services to farmers bearing in mind gender and type of household.

This long chapter has illustrated the many ways that gender influences the organisation of production in farming households. The division of labour is well known. But planners need to take into account the gender divisions of land management and type of crop managed when designing packages of incentives and supports. To the extent that efficiency of household resource use is the objective of agricultural adjustment policy it is necessary to understand that in households where women and men have separate accounting units resources, such as labour and working capital, move to their most efficient use when women enjoy equal access with men in land and other factor markets and in product markets. Unequal access means unequal barter or bargaining capabilities and suboptimal resource allocations. Without this reckoning some of the simplistic formulations of adjustment packages could lead to greater economic inefficiency in agriculture.

Gender in non-agricultural market structures 4

Already some indication has been given that those whose main occupation is farming can also earn income through wage employment, processing activities or vending. Non-agricultural market structures therefore extend beyond main urban areas, through rural towns to rural areas. Although the primary concern here is with urban gainful activities, one study is included to illustrate that there is already a rural base on which to build servicing and value-adding activities, not only to complement agriculture but to supply farmers with a range of consumer light manufactures and services.

The literature on adjustment frequently refers to different responses of the formal and informal sectors. It must be supposed that the explanation lies in what are regarded as their distinguishing characteristics. These have changed over the years.

An early distinction that was made was between organised (formal) and unorganised (informal) economic activity. Then the informal sector came to embody illegal activities just tolerated by the authorities; allegedly because they pass unenumerated and unrecognised, even though the sector might acquire its inputs from the formal sector or sell its output there. Stewart (1981) points out that some activities, such as beer-brewing, are more obviously illegal than others. The degree of illegality has often rested on the degree of competition with the formal sector. Certainly the informal sector produces similar kinds of goods. But it is frequently pointed out that it mainly provides goods and services for low-income groups. Its substantial trading and value-adding activities (especially of food) supply essentials at lower cost, even if also of an inferior differentiated variety. Demand substitution between the sectors can therefore be expected when prices and incomes change. The informal sector is also characterised by indigenously (and, consequently, endogenously) devised production methods, an unorganised and unprotected labour force and extraneous sources of working capital. Indeed one definition of the informal sector is that it cannot obtain official credit. Small amounts of capital, a degree of factor substitution between capital and labour (if only in being able to put on another shift at short notice), ease of entry of new participants and minimal skills required are much-vaunted supply-side features which suggest flexibility of response to a new set of production incentives.

But there are gradations of informality. Enterprises do not have all or none of the above characteristics. They range from smaller versions of formal sector enterprises, which adjust to inequitable competition in factor markets by adopting somewhat different production functions, to the casual on-and-off petty trading or value adding.

It is useful to depict three categories of non-agricultural production: the larger modern formal sector, a small-scale intermediate sector which links into official credit sources and may even be able to obtain imports, and the most informal sector (which can fulfil a need very quickly but is limited in what it can do). The available data show that women and men, respectively, participate to different extents in each of the three categories.

The modern formal sector

Women's participation in the formal sector has always been slight. A number of reasons have been put forward. On the supply side, it is said that formal sector employment requires a level of literacy and education which has given men the edge (see, for instance, Date-Bah, 1977, for Ghana, and Smock, 1981, for Kenya). Or it is claimed that women have been unwilling to submit to the regularity of shifts and have preferred the flexible hours of the informal sector.

On the demand side, employers may favour male employees because of their past experience with them and because of the supposition that the jobs are "men's". But employers may also be sensitive to female employees being less reliable through absenteeism and more expensive through maternity leave and crèche requirements (Smock, 1981). Anker and Hein (1985), concerned to redress the emphasis on supply-side reasons for the poor showing of women in formal sector employment, elaborate on the influences of recruitment policies. Employers surveyed in Ghana and Nigeria were variously apprehensive about the costs of absenteeism, maternity leave and lower productivity during pregnancy. It is these factors, and the way they give rise to employers' "statistical discrimination", that—according to one theory—explains much of the lower recruitment of women after such things as gender differences in experience and qualifications have been allowed for. Statistical discrimination means that average differences between categories of candidates are used to discriminate against all members of the category averaging a poorer score. In effect, "some women have spoilt it for all women". "If an employer believes that women are *on average* more likely than men to be unstable, less qualified, etc., then he will tend to discriminate against women even if he knows he may be wrong in certain individual cases" (Anker and Hein, 1985, p. 76). Moreover, employers are reluctant to hire women for jobs that have hitherto been almost exclusively held by men.

It has been a characteristic of sub-Saharan Africa that when urban industry was embryonic, men were there first. Men took the first employment in the formal "producing" sector, with the result that employers became accustomed to male workers. Lagos in the 1960s captures this well with 41 per cent of employed males in "crafts, production processing and labouring" against 7 per cent of employed females. Outside the small category of professional or technical workers, "men are mostly employed in the 'modern' sector while women are in the 'informal' sector" (Fapohunda, 1977). Across the continent the supply of male workers was still abundant and already in the urban economy when African countries embarked on their post-independence drive for import-replacing secondary industry. Expansion of the formal sector was not maintained into the 1980s so that women were not given much of a chance of joining men in it. Within the formal sector women have generally benefited from two growth occupations: secretarial work and teaching. But these two occupations are for the better educated. For other women there has been almost nowhere to go apart from the urban informal sector.

Despite an understanding of how women's low relative participation in the formal sector occurred, it comes as a shock to see how low this participation is in Africa, and relative to Asian and Latin American participation rates.

In only a very few African countries are official employment figures broken down by sex. Unfortunately, the nearest one can get to formal sector employment is through the official data on waged employment, which includes, for instance, a primary producing sector that cannot be assumed to be waged employment only on formal large-scale farms and estates. However, a very large proportion of it has to be regarded as indicative of employment in organised enterprises well integrated into formal institutional structures. While there is some representation of the informal sector in these tables, it is not likely to influence significantly the overall picture here. Therefore we can describe these as formal sector figures. The self-employed are excluded here. The data come from the ILO *Year Book of Labour Statistics,* which draws on labour force sample surveys, general household sample surveys and surveys of establishments of a certain importance (which in effect means a minimal size).

Table 3 shows the disposal of women's and men's waged employment by subsector in three African economies. Total female employment as a proportion of total male employment ranges from 12.9 per cent in Malawi to 21.3 per cent in Kenya. Women's participation in waged employment is still only a fraction of men's. It is in the manufacturing section that women's participation is least, and lower than in other world regions. Except in the case of the United Republic of Tanzania these ratios are higher in the primary producing sector. Women do best overall in the service sector (trade, restaurants, hotels, finance, insurance, etc.). They are particularly strong in Kenya and the United Republic of Tanzania in community, social and personal services, which includes the government sector. Many African governments have tried to give a lead on gender equality of employment to the private sector by following an affirmative action policy on employing women. But the share of women in public sector employment cannot necessarily be seen as a precursor of general female participation rates in the formal sector (Anker and Hein (eds.), 1986). The past also says nothing about how this affirmative action

Table 3. Waged employment by subsector in Kenya, Malawi and the United Republic of Tanzania, 1980 and 1986 (thousands)[1]

	Kenya		Malawi		Tanzania, United Rep. of	
	Males	Females	Males	Females	Males	Females
1980						
Subsector						
Agriculture, hunting, forestry, fishing	186.4	44.9	157.1	25.1	72.3	5.9
Mining	2.2	0.1	0.6	–	4.3	0.4
Manufacturing	128.2	13.1	38.0	2.0	70.3	9.6
Electricity, gas, water	9.6	0.5	3.8	0.3	12.6	1.2
Construction	60.7	2.4	32.6	0.2	23.0	0.9
Trade, restaurants, hotels	63.2	7.3	23.9	3.2	27.7	4.0
Transport, storage, communications	48.9	6.3	16.5	0.9	49.4	2.8
Finance, insurance, etc.	33.4	6.3	11.2	1.0	10.1	3.0
Community, social and personal services	296.3	95.8	44.5	9.5	128.7	46.2
Total	829.0	176.8	328.2	42.2	398.3	73.9

1986

Subsector						
Agriculture, hunting, forestry, fishing	199.6	48.8	158.4	29.0	67.6	6.8
Mining	5.4	0.1	0.3	–	3.7	0.5
Manufacturing	147.9	16.9	51.8	16.5	82.0	9.1
Electricity, gas, water	16.7	1.5	4.3	0.4	18.6	1.8
Construction	52.6	3.1	28.6	0.3	19.7	1.4
Trade, restaurants, hotels	78.9	15.6	36.3	2.9	35.4	2.6
Transport, storage, communications	50.4	7.1	25.0	1.5	52.6	2.8
Finance, insurance, etc.	44.8	11.2	11.8	1.3	11.3	4.7
Community, social and personal services	375.0	144.2	52.3	11.5	157.7	56.5
Total	972.0	248.5	368.8	63.5	448.7	86.2

[1] Totals may not add up exactly, owing to rounding.

Source: ILO: *Year Book of Labour Statistics 1988.*

holds up when government payrolls are reduced and manpower rationalised.

Table 4 provides information on different manufacturing industries. Separate data for men and women are not available in the case of the United Republic of Tanzania. The data for Kenya show that women do best in food and quite well in textiles and garments. This could be seen as an extension of their traditional skills. More surprisingly, they do compar-

Table 4. Male and female employment in selected manufacturing industries and total manufacturing, Kenya and Malawi, 1980 and 1986 (thousands)

	Kenya		Malawi	
	Males	Females	Males	Females
1980				
Subsector				
Food	28.8	5.4	11.9	0.04
Beverages	{ 4.7	0.4 }	1.4	0.02
Tobacco			6.5	0.80
Textiles	17.7	1.9	5.3	0.10
Garments	4.3	1.0	1.9	0.10
Leather and products	1.4	0.1	0.07	–
Wood products	8.5	0.6	1.4	0.04
Paper and products	7.1	0.8	1.3	0.03
Chemicals	11.0	1.2	2.2	0.11
Non-metallic minerals	5.8	0.2	2.4	0.13
Fabricated metal products, etc., of which:				
Fabricated metal products	(10.4)	(0.3)	(1.7)	(0.02)
Transport equipment	(17.8)	(0.3)	(0.2)	(0.01)
Total manufacturing	128.2	13.1	38.03	1.90
1986				
Subsector				
Food	37.8	7.2	19.6	2.35
Beverages	{ 6.2	0.4 }	2.1	0.05
Tobacco			5.4	1.30
Textiles	29.4	1.7	6.7	0.40
Garments	5.8	2.3	3.0	0.20
Leather and products	0.8	0.1	0.1	–
Wood products	7.6	0.4	3.8	0.09
Paper and products	9.9	1.1	2.0	0.20
Chemicals	12.7	1.4	2.3	0.25
Non-metallic minerals	5.2	0.2	1.5	0.11
Fabricated metal products, etc., of which:				
Fabricated metal products	(9.6)	(0.5)	(2.8)	(0.06)
Transport equipment	(15.7)	(0.2)	(0.1)	(0.01)
Total manufacturing	147.9	16.9	53.3	5.31

Source: As for table 3.

atively well in the categories of wood and paper products. Women in Malawi do not have a similar foothold in these industries. They do better in the tobacco industry. Women generally do very badly in the heaviest industry, metal products.

There is no reason to believe that in other African countries women hold a significantly higher share of formal sector jobs than in Kenya and Tanzania, or that they have a lower participation rate than Malawian women. Across the continent there are relatively few women in formal sector employment; and participation is least in manufacturing.

The intermediate sector

In between the modern formal sector and the very flexible informal sector there is what has been called the intermediate sector, composed of modern small-scale enterprises (SSEs), employing ten to 50 workers. These are reputed to be included in official statistics (World Bank, 1979). Clothing (garment) manufacture is believed to be substantially more important as a source of employment in this intermediate sector than in the full formal sector. Carpentry and furniture making is the second largest intermediate industry and competes closely with the formal sector. These enterprises often have higher capital requirements and more employees on average than garment-making. A very small percentage of intermediate sector employment is found in food manufacturing enterprises. On balance, because of the product mix the sector includes a higher proportion of women in its labout force than do industries in the large-scale formal sector.

There are also differences by location. The major industries of the intermediate sector are found in urban "sites", although these may not be in large towns. It is probably true of most sub-Saharan African countries that women's participation in non-agricultural activities rises fairly steadily, moving from urban areas to small rural towns to rural areas, and from formal to intermediate to micro-enterprises.

There is evidence of substantial scope for capital-labour substitution in the small-scale sector (World Bank, 1979). The evidence for this seems to be that capital-output and capital-labour ratios within a single industry have been observed not to change consistently in the same direction with size of enterprise. It is not known what situations have been aggregated to produce such information. But the point is taken that the smaller the enterprise the more easily work can be reorganised to change these input ratios. To the extent that women are more prominent in these enterprises than in large formal enterprises, flexibility of production functions has a gender dimension.

These enterprises, like the more formal ones, have suffered from idle capacity during the years of economic decline. The difference is that they could well increase employment and output significantly without much additional investment. On the other hand, low entry barriers may inhibit greater utilisation rates by those already in the field. Initial capital investment comes from personal savings, loans or gifts from relatives and friends. Funds for expansion tend to come from retained profits. But very little capital comes from the formal lending institutions. This means that male entrepreneurs do not enjoy much privileged access to cheap credit. But relying on personalised sources of funds may mean that men are able to find initial and working capital more easily, because women tend to spend their earnings on consumer essentials.

A case study in Zambia confirms much of this generalised sub-Saharan African picture. This study of SSEs covered smaller towns and rural areas. A sample of 68,000 households was undertaken. All enterprises consisted of fewer than 50 employees, but 98 per cent were found to employ fewer than six people. The survey found that a great many more people were employed in this way than formerly thought. The ILO has estimated that the total Zambian informal sector employed 200-300,000 (1988a). The survey indicates that the true figure might be in the order of 575,000 (Milimo and Fisseha, 1986). This is to be compared with the official total of national wage employment of 360,000, with manufacturing accounting for 48,860 in 1986.

The SSEs supplied large shares of the surrounding market: beer-brewing, 94 per cent, knitting of garments, 78 per cent, food and grocery shops, 43 per cent, petty food trade, more than 80 per cent. There were several other characteristics of SSEs deduced from this survey which are relevant to adjustment programmes and which have gender dimensions.

First, the enterprises became increasingly dominated by manufacturing as they moved into rural areas, and the reverse for services and trade. But manufacturing became more important at the small-town level when charcoal-making and beer-brewing are excluded.

Second, the smaller the enterprise the less likely it was to have a secondary line of production. Ninety per cent of proprietors with fewer than five employees (including themselves) had no secondary enterprise, whereas 53 per cent of those with more than ten workers did. Overall only 10 per cent of SSE proprietors had a secondary enterprise.

Third, relatively bigger enterprises were found in catering, other services, trade and foods. Services tended to operate with more than two employees. Nearly 85 per cent of catering and a little less than 50 per cent of trade SSEs employed two persons. When manufacturing activity was included, about two-thirds of all SSEs comprised one-person units and another 18 per cent two-person units.

Fourth, data on percentage shares of women's ownership and employment within each SSE group showed that the share of female ownership was greater than the share of female employment in both manufacturing (62.7 per cent against 56.6 per cent) and services (60.3 per cent against 53.8 per cent), and in all three types of location. While vending became steadily more "feminised" as the enterprise moved to more rural locations, manufacturing in the SSEs saw maximum participation of women in rural towns. Female ownership of garment, food, beer-making and vending enterprises were in nearly all categories over 80 per cent, with female employment not far behind.

The informal sector

The discussion above was on small-scale enterprises. The smaller ones could be said to merge into the informal sector. Moving into rural areas, small-scale industries tend to be more of the traditional crafts of weaving, blacksmithing and pottery, and to be single-worker enterprises. Where appropriate, agricultural processing can add much to this small-scale sector. The great majority of these micro-enterprises consist of the self-employed owner, alone or with one assistant. Apprentices and wage labourers become gradually more important as population density rises. There is, then, a gradation of enterprises which responds to market outlets and labour supply. Micro-enterprises satisfy demand that comes from small rural towns and rural areas, and have proliferated since independence.

However, truly informal activity undertaken in large urban areas should also be mentioned. It is impossible to conceive some of these activities as "intermediate". They have been well described in a study of married women in a peri-urban township of Lusaka. Hansen (1975) sought to explain the small number of women employed. With husbands more directly exposed to urban industrial organisation the women found themselves more restricted to the townships. Thirteen per cent of the sample did miscellaneous work permanently in the township, while another 11 per cent worked from time to time locally. The women's activities were mostly in trading products of personal use, such as food, beer, charcoal, clothes and handwork, which were often produced intermittently to meet a periodic need or a particular shortage. Hansen gives the example of shortages of cooking oil, bread and onions to illustrate the adaptability and responsiveness of these women in petty trade. Initial capital came mostly from relatives or friends which in fact bound the women to their surroundings and incurred obligations from which some of them disengaged with difficulty. But it was not just the occasional opportunity that caused the intermittent nature of these activities. They had to fit in with women's family responsibilities which were not always regular by month or year. Also, a display of enterprise was sometimes in response to immediate need for income. The spontaneity of much of this activity means that the women do not go through the formal bureaucracy for a licence to operate.

Given the need for additional income, the small numbers of women involved have to be explained. The illegality surrounding many production or trading lines, and the periodic police raids, signal interruptions in the flow of business. With the trouble involved in avoiding the authorities there must be clear need and opportunity to start up. This leads Hansen to talk of female entrepreneurship operating as a social form in a niche. Exploitation of the niche is illegal and therefore periodically entails costs. Perhaps more importantly, there are social costs arising from competition for the limited market opportunities. The women try to avoid this by trading in differentiated products (for example, different kinds of beer). But hostility could develop and customers were not always secure. One important limiting factor was lack of urban work experience. To operate in the niches or risky interstices of the economy required knowledge of the urban habitat. Hansen concludes that the main asset behind female entrepreneurship is urban experience, which was limited in the case of these outer-suburban women.

The informal sector can be distinguished from the intermediate sector by its legal uncertainty, its very weak and erratic resource base, and the volatility of competition in the market. It is a last resort for those seeking new coping strategies. Financial losses happen easily to the inexperienced. Much of the new activity arising from people seeking second and third sources of income does not have these characteristics, but consists of small enterprises employing a few people.

The formal, intermediate and informal subsectors of non-agricultural activity are not compartmentalised. Each faces costs and returns influenced by demand and supply conditions in factor and product markets which are derived from conditions in others. An alteration in prices and profits in one subsector cannot be contained there. Incentives targeted on one will inevitably affect incentives in the other two. Factors of production can move between them. The conditions under which this might happen are discussed in Chapter 7, under "Industry's supply response".

Population variables in socio-economic change 5

This chapter does not claim to offer an exhaustive coverage of theories of movements in population variables during socio-economic change. Instead the main theories are summarised and their relevance to the African context commented on.

The demographic transition

The idea that there is a demographic transition emerged from the observation that pre-industrialised societies exhibit high fertility and high mortality, while industrialised societies exhibit low fertility and low mortality. In between something happens—either reactively and endogenously through felt socio-economic changes and perceived life assurances, or exogenously through the introduction of ideas and practices from outside.

Whatever the explanation, and in nearly all cases it will be some mixture of both propositions, a concomitant observation is that during the transition population initially increases rapidly because the mortality rate declines well ahead of the fertility rate. Thereafter the fertility rate begins to fall, though often following an interim period of even higher rates. The theory of the demographic transition rests on aggregations. In this simplistic notational form it says nothing about socio-economic groups let alone personal circumstances, but without this information changes in determinants cannot be charted. Moreover, it has become apparent that this demographic transition is taking an unconscionable time in some areas of the world where the more ostensible signals for a decline in fertility are positive. This is particularly true of African countries in the decades after independence, when health and education advanced and the modern economy reached many people.

Caldwell (1982) has offered the explanation that net flows of wealth from children to parents have to be reversed before a fertility decline is rationally based, and that such a reversal will not occur until the emotional ties and economic obligations between biological parents and their children become stronger than attachments to a wider group, whether consanguineous or affinal. In sum, the nuclearisation of the family has to arrive first. Caldwell considered that families in Europe passed through this cultural change even before mortality started to decline. In contrast to this, commentators on African demography stress the continued strength of kinship and affinal attachments, particularly in the case of rural Africa where in many situations the advantages of nuclearising the family or reducing family size are not apparent, to women at least. Oppong and Bleek (1982) mention the conclusion Fortes came to after studying the Ashanti of Ghana that reproductive behaviour would not change much until the corporate lineage organisation lost its influence. It is not easy to see, particularly in West Africa, how nuclearisation would develop endogenously where it has not developed already.

Caldwell also claimed that an idea, exogenously introduced, could change attitudes to the family in the Third World. This is to ascribe influence to an exogenous variable independent of the basis of livelihoods or net flows of wealth. In practice it is difficult to isolate the influence of an exogenous idea on reproductive behaviour because it can affect that behaviour through its influence on intermediate determinants.

But what are the supposed determinants of mortality and fertility rates which allow these rates to move towards or away from the demographic transition in response to socio-economic change?

Theories of mortality

The relevance of mortality rates is that they affect people's estimates of the number of children that will have to be replaced by further births. There are different reasons for wanting a certain number of surviving children. But here it is enough to believe that reduced mortality rates eventually lead to a decline in fertility. However, mortality rates at the micro household level are subject to much more uncertainty than aggregate statistical results. Thus couples may hedge against unknown risks by having more children than statistical averages warrant. An analysis of Kenyan fertility determinants concluded that mortality and fertility were strongly positively related (Anker and Knowles, 1982, p. 178).

It is widely assumed that mortality rates are reduced by the improved nutrition and general welfare that come with higher income. But there is only so much that private income can do. Some health-enhancing basic needs can only be satisfied communally, at a level above the family. The advent of preventive public health measures has had a significant impact on mortality rates. But there is nothing preordained about the order in which determinants of mortality decline take effect. The substantial decline in mortality rates in the United Kingdom is reputed to have occurred while there was still poor nutrition but when vaccination campaigns against endemic diseases, sewerage and safe water supplies became an accepted item on the public health agenda.

The efficacy of some supposed determinants of mortality change which focus on the family as a whole has been questioned on the grounds that their effects are subject to the pattern of family welfare activities. The criticism is best exemplified by the case of child mortality. While increased income does bring better health to children, this is assuredly so only when the parent responsible for maintaining and caring for the child has free access to the income necessary to bring about improvements. Otherwise the theory incorporating income has little meaning. Infant survival also depends on the health of the mother and her ability to breastfeed at some length and practise adequate infant care. A harassed, undernourished woman is less likely to have healthy offspring, regardless of "family" income. Therefore the way higher incomes are deployed—and usually this depends on how they are obtained—is crucial to the net mortality effect.

While mortality rates undoubtedly affect fertility, this does not rule out the possibility that fertility rates influence mortality rates. High fertility places physical stress on mothers and jeopardises the nutrition and care of growing infants. Frequent reproduction brings risks to both mother and child. Very young mothers who are still growing themselves are particularly affected by the nutritional drain of pregnancy, and sometimes by their bodies not being large enough to have unobstructed childbirth. Physically inadequate mothers are part of a cycle of malnutrition that raises mortality rates and that is difficult to break. Very young or malnourished mothers give birth to low-weight babies for whom common diseases are more lethal than for healthy babies, or weak babies suffer from stunting and chronic disabilities, leaving them open to above-average mortality rates throughout their lives. It has to be expected then that the health and reproductive status of mothers is one determinant of mortality rates.

Theories of fertility

The economic theory of fertility

The economic theory of fertility (ETF) provides a consumer durable demand-oriented explanation of fertility. It assumes that households set out to maximise their total satisfaction by pursuing (consumption) preferences among commodities subject only to the constraints of costs and available resources. Children are viewed as one of these commodities that must compete for resources. Therefore the demand for children rests on their relative utility, their relative cost and total income. A change in any utility or cost, or in income, can alter what is considered an optimal package of commodities to be acquired by the household.

The absence of a supply-side explanation is an obvious omission which is taken up later. Here we look more closely at two main aspects of regarding children as commodities.

First, in its simplest form the theory assumes that children are viewed as commodities for consumption or some final gratification. Implicitly this means that households are already in the era of net transfers of wealth from parents to children. But children in developing countries, particularly in Africa, have an additional utility based on their contribution to household economic activities, whether income gaining or expenditure displacing, or displacing the labour of other family members. As such, children cannot be seen as merely competing for household disposable income with other consumer goods; they help to generate that very income. Theoretically, this productive value could be an additional utility enhancing the preference for children (while altering total disposable income or reducing the cost of children at the same time). But this interpretation is no longer the usual micro-economic consumer demand analysis assumed by the ETF. Nor, in the African context, can this value of children be treated as an addendum to the ETF because it is a subject of its own. That is to say, in sub-Saharan African countries reproductive behaviour may still be mainly governed by a net flow of resources from children to parents.

Second, there is the question of at what level costs and benefits of children are felt. The ETF has sometimes been called "the new household economics theory of fertility" to emphasise that decisions about fertility are assumed to be taken at the household level. In this case, for analytical purposes, the household is taken as the smallest unit of reproduction. The couple feels and acts as one perfectly homogenised unit even though, still as a unitary being, it sometimes takes account of the opinion of close relatives. Because demand is aggregated at the family level individuals' felt utilities and costs are passed over. But the importance of emphasising women's felt costs and benefits of children (as consumption goods) has won increasing recognition.

Disaggregation of the household unit is also relevant to assessing the impact of children as economic producers.

While the ETF concentrates on economic determinants it does not necessarily preclude non-economic influences. The theory's causal relationships "operate in a particular cultural, economic, institutional and historical setting, which conditions behavioural responses" (Mueller, 1988). Many untoward empirical relations between fertility and economic determinants have been explained under the rubric of accompanying lifestyles and expectations. But the characteristics of the non-economic environment are assumed to remain constant; only the economic determinants change. The ETF is therefore of limited use in explaining or predicting fertility when there is dynamic change on a broad front. But it is a very broad front. There is always the possibility that new ideas will trigger a fertility decline, or emerge more influential than shifts in the balance between costs and benefits of children. Certainly in South-East Asia, the fast and substantial fertility reductions cannot be explained by consumer demand theories. African fertility is often said to be determined by women's status being bound up with membership of a wider network. The obvious conclusion is that modes of production must alter first through structural change. That may well be, but it does not preclude some fertility transition if African governments demonstrate the commitment of South-East Asian governments.

Socio-economic determinants of fertility

The principal socio-economic determinants of fertility as described in the demographic literature are reviewed in this section. To the extent that they can be translated into economic costs and returns all but the last two (demand for children's assistance and support to parents in old age), which do not comply with children as consumer goods, could be incorporated in the ETF.

If *income* increases then an immediate consequence is a rise in demand for children because more children can be afforded. This is a straight income effect. Anker and Knowles (1982, p. 177) found in their Kenyan analysis of fertility determinants that income had a positive effect. Indeed, the positive relationship between the level of economic well-being and fertility was one of the strongest and most consistent findings of the study.

Were demand for children actually to fall as an immediate consequence of an increase in income, children would be regarded as an "inferior good". In fact, empirically children do sometimes prove to be an "inferior good" but this is over the longer term when other things have had time to change with income. For instance, some sources of new income bring with them new lifestyles or a change in the non-economic environment. Expectations may rise such that parents strive to endow children with capabilities which require investment of resources. When this happens, the cost (and "quality") of children rises with income. At the same time the utility, as distinct from the "consumption value", of children may be diminished through the parents' new ability to invest in labour-saving technology or to hire labour, and perhaps because parents' concern to have surviving children for old age weakens. The result is that at a higher income marginal utility and cost are equated at a smaller number of children. Couples in this position and facing decisions on the creation of a family choose to have fewer children than they would otherwise.

It can be seen that the immediate income effect and the later discovery of new horizons in life with higher income can present divergent conclusions on the impact of income. Frequently, in the case of the latter, income is viewed by analysts as a proxy for socio-economic modernisation which causes fertility and income to be inversely related.

The evidence for these assumptions through the establishment of positive or negative relationships between fertility and income is inconclusive. But developing countries exhibit a positive relationship between income and fertility more frequently than industrialised countries (Farooq and DeGraff, 1988). There is also evidence to suggest that fertility rises with initial income increments, thereafter to decline.

However, the acquisition of higher income, as well as its use, is widely recognised as influencing fertility decisions. It is argued that since gainful employment must be given up to look after children there are opportunity costs of having children. Because child care is considered overwhelmingly a woman's task, the argument devolves on the way women's role conflicts give rise to a trade-off between children and women's income. The more remunerative is women's employment the greater the opportunity costs. Therefore, fertility is assumed to be negatively related to *female labour force participation* (more strictly, paid employment). Should employment opportunities for women increase, these costs of forgone income will be felt by greater numbers of women. Should employment opportunities for women decline following contraction of the economy, these costs will not be felt so widely. They are, in fact, new indirect costs of having children. On the other hand, there should be a positive income effect on fertility resulting from increased income from women's employment.

This assumed inverse relationship between female labour force participation and fertility has caused a great deal of contention. Are researchers observing the fact that women with high fertility choose not to seek employment, or that women who actively participate in the labour force choose not to have many children? And do either or both of these apply only to formal sector employment? Are there some categories of women who have to work, willy nilly, for the reason that a large family has to be fed and clothed, whereas those with few children are not under such pressure to work? Are these working women found mostly in the informal sector where they can combine child care and gainful employment to a degree? And in what employment circumstances is it valid to argue that women, hard pressed by all their tasks, need children to take over some of them? It is in the areas of what kind of labour force participation and employment is being assumed, and of the scope for delegating child-care and domestic tasks to a range of co-opted assistants (including children), that the ETF has met some of its sharpest critics. There is therefore a pressing need to disaggregate the female labour market.

The evidence of a negative relationship between female labour force participation and fertility has been stronger in industrialised countries than in developing countries, and stronger in other regions of the Third World than in Africa. Kenya, for instance, offers quite inconclusive evidence. Anker and Knowles (1982, p. 179) offer the explanation that where alternative sources of child care are either inexpensive or readily available within the family, no major conflict arises when the wife attempts to combine work with raising a family. It is a persistent finding that women's employment in agricultural activities and in work at or near the house has a neutral if not a positive effect on fertility (Youssef, 1988). This is consistent with what is known of cultural practices of child care in Africa, and is discussed below.

Research findings for urban areas can produce a similar picture. Data from urban Nigeria indicate that female labour force participation has little effect on fertility except in the case of formal sector employment (Farooq, 1985). One Nigerian study (Okpala, 1989) put urban women in three categories: the civil service, the self-employed and housewives. Fertility was lowest among women in the civil service, but there was not much difference in fertility between the self-employed and housewives. One important finding was that part-time workers had fewer children than full-time workers. This could imply that those with more children have to work full time for economic reasons, or it could simply mean that part-time workers enjoy higher levels of education or the economic freedom to choose how they work and how many children they have.

Because opportunity costs of a woman's time are frequently estimated, by researchers on the basis of her educational level, *education* is also seen as negatively related to fertility. The assumption is that the higher the education level the greater the income forgone by staying at home. As with more remunerative employment opportunities, further education for women cause children to "become" more expensive without actually incurring any new direct cost. Or education could encourage parents to alter their consumption preferences away from traditional family lifestyles with large numbers of children. A possible positive effect of women's education on fertility could be that educated women know how to improve their health, and this makes reproduction easier. Of course this knowledge also extends to matters of family planning methods and to the health value of child spacing. This was, in fact, the case in an ILO/University of Nairobi survey which found that better-educated women were more likely to visit, and return to, a family planning clinic (Anker and Knowles, 1982, p. 176).

The same study found that at the micro level the more education advanced beyond functional literacy the lower fertility was, while below this level the inverse relationship was weak. However, with relatively few women educated to this level, at the macro (aggregate) level there was found to be a positive relationship between women's education and fertility—in urban as well as rural areas. Were women's education beyond functional literacy to stand proxy for formal employment, then this kind of employment participation could be inversely related to fertility. But there is a confounding influence. The general prosperity of these better-educated households, which in the Kenyan case (at least) encouraged fertility, might also be due to the (educated) husband's earning power. The inverse relation between women's education and fertility was stronger and more consistent in rural areas. This is surprising because rural areas are more strongly characterised by compatibility of work and child care through support networks. Education in rural areas might then have the power of a new idea; or the confounding influence of educated husbands' greater income contribution might be less in rural areas because there men tend not to put so much of their income into the family budget; or it might be simply due to the fact that average rural fertility is very high indeed and modern influences can only lower it.

Globally, research indicates a consistent inverse relationship between women's education and fertility. In a review of World Fertility Survey countries the negative relationship held, in 40 per cent of cases, after controlling for duration of marriage, urban/rural residence, wife's occupation and husband's education (Farooq and DeGraff, 1988). But what has also been noted is that the intensity and shape of the relationship between these two indicators varies. For instance, fertility may not decline continuously with additional years of women's education, but may sometimes rise. Perhaps of greater long-term significance is the finding of the World Fertility Survey analysis that the relationship between desired family size and education was consistently monotonically negative, and between contraceptive use and education similarly positive.

Fees and other expenses of *children's education* constitute a direct cost or, in contrast to the income effect, a price effect. There may also be an indirect cost if the children forgo some gainful or contributory work to undertake education. Giving rise to costs for parents, children's education must be seen as negatively related to fertility. A negative relationship between education of children and fertility decrees that, with a given disposable income, a rise in the average cost of a parental commitment to education will have a depressive effect on fertility. An increase in family income would, of course, allow more to be spent on children's education (directly or indirectly). But how this income effect is distributed between more children (to educate) and more expensive education for children already born depends on a number of things.

Anker and Knowles concluded from their Kenyan study that the intense desire for children's education did not have a negative effect on fertility (1982, p. 175), implying that education was viewed as an essential and not an expenditure which competes with other consumer durables. Here then is a clear positive relationship between children's education and fertility at the micro level, but a statistically significant negative relationship at the macro level. It is possible that at the macro level the concentration of schools in urban areas means that the aggregation of all situations in the macro analysis was unable to isolate the influence of urbanisation on fertility.

For poor parents, children's assistance is frequently a direct benefit. In the literature on the economic basis of fertility the *demand for children's assistance* is mentioned in the context of the need to augment parents' labour. This determinant raises the utility of having children, although not, as already pointed out, as a consumption good.

One other direct utility of children is their *support to parents in old age*. This arises when parents take the view that they will not have secured sufficient resources to maintain themselves when their working lives are over. State pensions for the aged are not feasible in developing countries. The alternative of assuring old people that they will be looked after by the community, which has allegedly halved China's birth rate in less than ten years, cannot readily be transplanted for other reasons (Sadik, 1989). This source of demand for children, which amounts to guaranteeing sufficient numbers of long-surviving ones, is affected by levels of income and expectations of an accumulated surplus at the critical time. An increase in income should have the effect of reducing this component of the utility of children.

Gender factors in socio-economic determinants of fertility

The importance of identifying socio-economic determinants in relation to women's roles has been mentioned in the case of employment and education. The opportunity costs discussed were caused by women's additional maternal and domestic tasks. But nothing was said to suggest that the effect of this opportunity cost was not felt by the whole household in a uniform way.

Since the ETF is formulated as a theory of how the household or family decides on fertility, it uses a level of aggregation which does not give due weight to individuals' utilities and costs of children. It implicitly assumes that these utilities and costs are felt equally by mothers and fathers. In an African context this is refuted by separate financial responsibilities to the family, with women usually bearing day-to-day maintenance costs, and men the larger intermittent items. But there is much variation within as well as between communities. In a Kwahu community of south Ghana, for instance, the amount contributed by fathers varies enormously. Some contribute nothing at all, while others give more than required by custom. Mostly contributions are below the norm. What is highly relevant to this discussion is that "wives can never be certain how much of the parental costs husbands are going to share" (Oppong and Bleek, 1982, p. 28). It is therefore important to ask the questions: Whose direct costs of children are we talking about? Are those who contribute little to the cost of children interested in family planning issues? Furthermore, income forgone by having to care for children and the home can be seen as an opportunity cost that falls on a woman since the income would have eased her financial responsibility to the family. This is not a case of a wife passing up the opportunity to augment her husband's income. It rather concerns matching financial responsibility with financial ability at the individual level.

Utilities of children, particularly the value of their labour assistance, are likewise experienced differently by mothers and fathers. Because of the crucial importance of women's special maternal and domestic tasks, and therefore the far more acute role conflict for women, demand for the assistance of children is usually couched in terms of the need to augment women's labour in *(a)* domestic tasks and/or *(b)* farm or informal sector work. It is often claimed that if a woman's "productive work" lies in household farming or the informal sector, children can be useful in these activities as well as in domestic tasks.

But if children represent a utility to women in their work, what becomes of the opportunity cost (forgone income) of having children? The answer lies in the many different class and occupational situations women find themselves in. For some the opportunity cost is positive, for others it is effectively negative. The degree of formality of the employment is one influence. Access to child-care support at the early stages of the family life cycle is another. An individual woman could combine her own initial infant care with some informal or agricultural work, but proceed to better-remunerated formal sector employment when older children are able to assume child care and domestic responsibilities. As mentioned above, the demand for children's assistance could help to explain observations of a positive relation between women's labour force participation and fertility.

Mueller (1988) points out that the ETF pays little attention to women's non-market time. She suggests three classifications of activities: *(a)* market work (including self-provisioning); *(b)* housework (including child care), and *(c)* leisure. The theory sees the trade-off (role conflict) between *(a)* and *(b)*. But, says Mueller, it could be between *(b)* and *(c)*, or within *(b)*. Oppong (1983) puts it more bluntly when she says the assumed trade-off has been that between occupation and parenting, whereas other housework and leisure also have their trade-offs.

Because the impact of *old age security* is influenced by asset and marital status, concern about it can be experienced in quite different ways by women and men. Kenya provides some interesting findings on women's attitudes to old-age support (Anker and Knowles, 1982). Significantly more urban than rural women do not expect support from children when they are old. There was also a strong negative relationship between expectations of support and the women's educational levels. Further, there was no relationship between these expectations and amount of land owned. Very few women own land, and if women's insecurity over divorce, widowhood or land sale after adjudication exists, it makes little difference how much land the husband owns. A "rich" farming wife in this situation will still want surviving sons.

This leads to another gender aspect of old-age security. Despite the greater importance of girls' than boys' labour to women, women may state preference for sons more than do men, in that boys stay within the family to inherit and preserve family property. Son preference is, therefore, a form of planned old-age security that is particular to women because of their tenuous hold on "family assets". Rwabushaija (1988) also refers to the value of sons to women, especially in the event of divorce or widowhood. One could hypothesise that the more insecure women feel about their access to land and their economic future, the stronger will this son preference be. Other commentators (such as Oppong, 1988b, and Youssef, 1988) have generalised this by pointing to the importance of high fertility as compensation for women's low status. High fertility helps to confirm the rights that women do have and contributes to their economic survival as well as social prestige.

Cultural factors

The socio-economic determinist view of the influence of women's employment participation and education on fertility has been criticised because of its neglect of the cultural context, especially the way costs and benefits of children are shared by kin or affinal groups. It is not simply a case of the cultural factors modifying theories based on socio-economic determinism. Some situations in Africa would indicate that culture overwhelmingly determines reproductive behaviour.

The literature on population variables deals with the impact of "modern" and "traditional" culture. The influence of modern culture, which is allegedly anti-natalist, is found in new settings. For instance, participation in some of the more formal kinds of employment can bring women into contact with new role examples, knowledge of women with smaller families and of the means to family planning. Thus female participation in a formal labour force can also be a proxy for women gaining access to new ideas, regardless of the extra sum that is earned. Employment might be supposed to build on the foundations laid by education to allow a woman to become an independent and self-sufficient member of society. In the event, however, too much of this modern cultural influence was expected from women's entry into modern employment, and the model of transformation has not always been backed up by data. This cultural change has mainly been seen among urban middle-class women.

Women's education is also believed to introduce a cultural effect which depresses fertility because of the greater access of educated women to knowledge of better nutrition and child-care practices. "The families of educated mothers are likely to be healthier as well as smaller. Mothers' education may be even more important to her children's health than flush toilets or piped water or even food intake" (Sadik, 1989). Educated women also tend to marry at a later age. On the face of it this represents a change in the cultural environment, rather than an alteration in costs and utilities of having children.

The thesis on the traditional cultural influence on reproductive behaviour can be summed up as follows: women obtain support from a network wider than the nuclear family to reduce role conflicts, but there is a price to pay in terms of high fertility for maintaining this network of support.

The notion of African family systems as being basically bounded conjugal units has little support in the African anthropological literature. Realisation is spreading that in Africa the conjugal pair may not be multifunctional. It may not be co-residential, it may not eat from the same pot or to the exclusion of others, it may not bear all the costs of child maintenance, least of all "jointly", and it may not be the locus of decision-making. Units of consumption and of production are not the same as each other, and the unit of biological reproduction is something else. Different groups of people co-operate in food production, distribution and consumption (Oppong, 1987). Anker and Knowles (1982) draw attention to the fact that production and consumption relations are governed by social norms and affinal expectations. Husband's lineage and the extended family are the source of land and flows of money and assistance. In this situation status is acquired through having many children. For women especially the lineage may provide a court of appeal against perceived unfair treatment over crop disposal (Locoh, 1988, p. 57). Kinship ties provide a wide network in which people share problems and successes in life. Affiliation can help with job opportunities, and migrants to cities can live with a relative or friend until they find a job. These considerations of support from and loyalty to the wider group do not rule out the possibility of couples making conscious decisions about fertility, but they could be incorporated in costs and benefits.

This bonding has to be confirmed and renewed through a multiplicity of exchanges by assuring the next generation of the group. Women in particular must be careful to fulfil the expectations and meet the norms of the patrilineal group that they have married into and to demonstrate their loyalty to it. There is hardly a better way of doing this than by producing sons for the lineage. Another way of achieving this is to share the parental responsibility for other children. In the process "children learn the art of maintaining multiple links with several family units in the kinship group" (Locoh, 1988, p. 55). Locoh also argues that the trend in rural Africa is from large extended compounds (a segment of the lineage) to nuclear families enlarged by more distant relatives. Group child-care practices are more restricted, but child care can still be shared beyond the parents.

What all this means is that while conflicts between women's employment and child-rearing may not be as great as implied in formal theories, and therefore the negative relationship between fertility and employment is to be questioned, the basis to these work-sharing arrangements actually exercises a pro-natal pressure. As long as women receive assistance from this network and not from a source which does not require numbers of children, fertility will remain high no matter that the socio-economic signals indicate that matters should be otherwise. To this extent Caldwell (1982) was correct in basing the demographic transition on the nuclearisation of families. However, in as much as women's autonomy is increased by it, employment participation may allow women some independence from consanguineous and affinal ties without clear nuclearisation of the family, and this could encourage a decline in fertility.

While demographers and anthropologists rightly point out the cultural influence on fertility behaviour, it would be wrong to have this discussion hanging on the assumption that nuclearisation will always encourage fertility reduction. Much depends on modes of production and, in farming communities, land tenure systems. Nuclearisation of the rural African family means a small-scale production enterprise dependent on its own family labour as much as possible before utilising exchange or wage labour. Anything which encourages this, such as land registration or incentives to increase production, will buttress the forces inducing high levels of self-exploitation. The nuclear family can therefore be seen to gain from enlarging its own labour force.

Of course, the cultural environment varies between situations and can be altered by level and form of socio-economic development. It is difficult to calculate the costs and benefits of children when resource use and the sharing of parental responsibilities are continually changing. But it remains possible for the cultural environment to prevent any inverse relationship between women's education and employment, on the one hand, and fertility, on the other. Socio-economic variables may have to alter very substantially to subdue cultural factors. And for many women in developing countries they doubtless have not altered sufficiently.

It has been claimed that the most carefully executed studies show a lower fertility in polygynous marriages, although the difference is small (Pebley and Mbugua, 1989, p. 339). However, studies in Cameroon, Ghana, Lesotho and Senegal, after excluding childless women and allowing for wife's age and marital duration, indicate no statistical difference in fertility. Discussion of the effect of polygyny on fertility usually concentrates on the supply side. One supply-side aspect is the difference in the reproductive lives of first and later wives. For instance, whereas in the case of a study in Kenya both senior and junior co-wives shared lower fertility, a study in Côte d'Ivoire showed only junior wives having lower fertility than women in monogamous unions. In some instances polygyny would have been the outcome of the barrenness or subfecundity of the first wife. The standard explanation has been sexual abstinence usually covering a long breast-feeding period. Also several wives may mean less frequent intercourse with any one.

A study in Senegal supports this explanation but suggests the operating mechanism is the age difference of spouses (with some wives a good deal younger than their husbands) and the greater likelihood of temporary separate residence (Garenne and van de Walle, 1989). In addition, data on birth intervals could be interpreted as lower fecundity of old men rather than less frequent intercourse. Nor are hallowed sexual practices among polygynous couples always respected today. A study of Kenyan agro-pastoralists concluded that fertility was not influenced by marital status and that the vaunted longer post-partum sexual abstinence taboos of polygynous couples have not been supported by empirical evidence (Mulder, 1989). In East Africa post-partum taboos have been much eroded.

Another reason for lower fertility in polygynous households may be less work stress among women in them. Where co-wives co-operate to rationalise child care and other tasks, women in polygamous families have less need of children's assistance, or of kin or affinal support networks. Thus it might be supposed that women in monogamous marriages have a greater need to confirm kin and affinal ties through reproduction. However, Mulder comments that among the agro-pastoralists she studied co-wives' co-operation is of no particular advantage because there are informal co-operative networks among women and because co-wives might be settled at a distance from each other. This suggests that marital status does not influence dependency on these networks beyond the family.

It is widely assumed that a strong cultural influence on reproductive behaviour operates through rural-urban migration and that fertility and migration are inversely related. Certainly where migration entails separation of the couple, rates of conception must be affected. But more importantly, migrants are said to be a selective and motivated group, mentally already on their way to urban lifestyles. Health and family planning services, which are more readily accessible in urban areas, provide both publicity and means for reproductive control. Results of (worldwide) analyses show that the "coverage of public care in the community was closely associated with an individual respondent's practice of a modern contraceptive method" (Potter, 1989, p. 203).

But if migrants are rooted in rural life, attitudes may be slow to change. Locoh makes the point that urbanisation does not necessarily lead to nuclearisation. Networks of kin, polygyny and child fostering provide complex living arrangements. A migrant can only join a settled urban household if he is already in some relation to it. Nor can it be assumed that both the husband and wife migrate. In Africa especially, migration might be for the husband only, leaving the wife on the farm. There is nothing certain about migrant husbands transmitting their own urban cultural attainments to their wives remaining in rural areas. This return to the village should agriculture become more profitable may even increase rural fertility rates through a greater male presence.

One conclusion that Anker and Knowles drew from their Kenyan study was that in urban areas, which are in a state of flux, traditional values do seem to be breaking down and children are no longer valued so highly as economic resources (1982, p. 180). Such a state of flux is suggestive of rising expectations. But a state of flux can also follow economic policies which make livelihoods increasingly parlous or at best speculative. It is very difficult to decide from the literature whether the outcome would be greater fertility (hedging bets and securing supportive networks) or lower fertility (abandonment by the wider group in a desperate economic situation).

Theories of rural-urban migration

Rural-urban migration is a feature of demography with major implications for policies. It has consequences for both the sending and receiving areas. As new economic strategies are being put forward by governments, the subject of a more appropriate distribution of population becomes more important.

Rural outmigration affects the supply of farm labour by raising wages and can either lead to smaller farms being only partially cultivated or cause large farmers to adopt labour-saving machinery, or both. The experience of African countries suggests that outmigration has contributed to declines in per capita crop output, if not in aggregate crop output. Worsening poverty ensues with its usual effect on mortality rates and health indicators. In urban areas the labour market becomes more crowded, there being weak price-responsive adoption of appropriate technology in the formal sector at least. Municipalities have their resources stretched coping with spontaneous settlements and health hazards.

The sex and age profile of local populations is affected by migration, and this in turn can influence crude birth and death rates. Spouses are physically separated or marriages might be delayed, affecting fertility rates. The urban experience should change expectations associated with having children. Oberai (1987) summarises the issues for fertility when he questions whether migrants have lower fertility than their rural cohorts because of initial selectivity (they wanted and were able to have a share of modernity), subsequent adaptation (influenced by fertility behaviour in urban areas) or disruption (physical separation of spouses).

Theories of migration have emerged from observations that people move as a result of both push (poverty forcing departure) and pull (attractive options elsewhere) factors. A natural outcome of this was to see migration as an equilibrating factor, with people moving from labour surplus to labour deficit areas. This has often been based on the notion of a dual economy of a subsistence farming sector (with the marginal product of labour close to zero) and a modern industrial sector of full employment (Oberai, 1987). The problem with this is that the equilibrating mechanism is far from perfect, the marginal product of labour in farming is clearly not in the environs of zero, and unemployment abounds everywhere although some places are preferable to others if one is underemployed or unemployed.

A theory, put forward by Todaro, is that a migrant holds a favourable view of a combination of expected urban incomes and the probability of winning them. A later refinement of this theory implies that there is an equilibrium level of urban unemployment or underemployment (that is, a level tolerated by migrants) determined by the difference between formal sector wages and income forgone in agriculture. But both the original and the refinement are based on the relativity of rural and urban incomes.

However, the theory based on differential earnings has lost some credibility with the continued migration to African towns and cities despite worsening unemployment and living conditions in them. The neglect of rural areas no doubt contributed to maintaining the relative attraction of urban areas. Diversifying the family income portfolio to minimise risk has been put forward as an explanation. This is also seen as influencing the decision as to which member of the family should migrate. But in Africa, where women are usually responsible for day-to-day maintenance of the children from their own income, risks have to be identified at the individual as well as the family level. It is obvious that mothers are more indispensable than fathers. For the young unmarried it is a different matter. Girls as well as boys may move to urban areas not because of any risk spreading but because they do not wish to have a lifetime of the village environment. This is linked to the alternative view that education has been the main mechanism of rural to urban migration through its effect of alienating school leavers from agricultural activities. For these young aspirants the move to urban areas was social mobility itself (Adeokun, 1989, p. 272).

An important feature of rural outmigration is that it is often done by steps—moving from village to rural town to provincial town to city. Some research findings support the suggestion that this reflects a reluctance to move far from home. Evidence from Kenya suggests that male migrants prefer rural to urban life, that their migration is temporary, that the majority own land or expect to inherit some and that a relatively high proportion of income is remitted home (Anker and Knowles, 1977). This is supported by a survey of migrants from Lesotho working in South African mines, showing that migrants would be prepared to return to farming if it produced about 60 per cent of their mining wages. There was great variation around this figure. What the survey failed to make clear was whether this was just cash income, or included the imputed value of other farm output. Since most of the imputed value would be produced by the wife left behind, presumably the 60 per cent refers to the cash component only. In addition, the remaining 40 per cent could be accounted for by the additional cost of living away from home. Even so, these two examples indicate that the attraction of urban lifestyles may be more to do with income differentials than "being where the action is". If true it hints at a potential reversal of migration, without including reverse step-migration, if policies make agriculture more attractive.

A general weakness of migration theories is that they do not explain what has changed for the women left behind. Studies from southern Africa show that they alter their economic portfolio, taking on more wage employment (Palmer, 1985). This is far from the image, depicted in theories of migration, of women left on the farm but receiving remittances to supplement the poor returns of smallholder agriculture, which is assumed not to have changed much since the male migrant took "surplus labour" with him. A potentially very important consequence of male migration for population can be seen in the set of studies drawn on by Palmer: there is evidence that kinship and affinal bonds weaken when the husband/male relative is absent. The wife does not get the ploughing assistance from her husband's male kin or she gets it too late, and so on. If the support a woman receives from bonding is weakening under the impact of male migration, then the need to confirm such bonding through high fertility ought also to weaken. Correspondingly, these women will acquire more economic autonomy, though at a personal price, and may start taking decisions in their lives not hitherto contemplated. This will not be true of matrilineal areas, such as found in southern Ghana and Côte d'Ivoire, where male migration leaves kinship and affinal ties intact.

If these theories of causal relationships in demographic change have validity, then population variables could be significantly altered by policies of economic adjustment and transformation. Given that, the issue becomes: "What alteration in population variables is desirable and how far can economic policies be tailored to bring them about?"

Part II

Adjustment programmes and the influence of gender on economic and demographic outcomes

Adjustment programmes are designed to arrest the economic decline of the period following the mid-1970s and to unravel the effects of government intervention in markets, preparatory to a resumption of real economic growth. Here a thumbnail sketch is given of the cause and nature of sectoral decline as an introduction to the adjustment measures taken.

From dates of independence to the first rise in oil prices in 1973 real per capita growth rates were positive in sub-Saharan Africa. Almost all countries embarked on some industrialisation, mostly import replacing, and selected technology from a narrow range of options on offer. During the period export markets were buoyant enough and capital inflows generous enough to support this kind of industrial growth as well as the burgeoning state sector without extracting a crushing "surplus" from agriculture.

The increase in the price of oil imposed a new burden on the balance of payments of all countries except those exporting oil or petroleum products. There followed world inflation, rising interest rates and growing debt repayments. Some African economies enjoyed temporary respite with price increases for their exports. But overall rates of increase of gross domestic product fell precipitously and to well below population growth rates. This situation continued into the 1980s when the problems of declining international terms of trade and a cutback in inflows of capital investment and credit were added.

The earlier growth of industrialisation tapered off. Overvalued currencies meant that exports and import replacements were less profitable and imports more profitable than formerly. The response of rising levels of protective tariffs and tighter quantitative restrictions contributed further to the ensuing inefficient distribution of resources, while at the same time failing to prevent increasing underutilisation of existing capacity. The reduction in real consumer purchasing power led governments to increase subsidies on essential goods, particularly on food staples. The resulting worsening of the fiscal deficit added to domestic inflation and currency overvaluation. Producers of exports faced weaker incentives through both lower real prices and lack of consumer goods to buy. This gave a further twist to the gap between exports and imports and rising foreign debt. The reactive relationship between government budgets and balances of payments was leading to contractionary spirals of ever-diminishing output.

This summary of the economic crisis in sub-Saharan Africa overlooks the many different individual country circumstances. But there is no intention here of embarking on a comprehensive overview of the continent or even to take individual countries as representational cases for analysis and for offering policy prescriptions, although illustrative references may occasionally be made. Instead Part II is a deliberate continuation of the provocative thesis put forward in Part I.

Part II begins with an explanation of the nature of adjustment policies in Chapter 6. Chapter 7 then identifies what have been considered main weaknesses of adjustment packages in Africa and discusses the opportunities for improvement that have developed as a result. Pointers to relevant gender issues are indicated briefly. Chapter 8 reviews how gender has been dealt with so far in the known literature on adjustment. Finally, Chapters 9 and 10 draw out the gender implications of Part I for the economic and population outcomes of adjustment polices.

The range of policies commonly applied 6

In Chapter 1 different views of the meaning of adjustment were presented. It was pointed out that the meaning had changed over time as policy priorities and mixes altered with experience. Here adjustment is taken to include demand management, restructuring of markets and long-term transformation. It makes for simpler analytic presentation to separate these three as much as possible, noting only how they interact.

This chapter provides a summary review of what these three packages of adjustment policies comprise and how they are supposed to work. But first we define their purposes.

The objectives of adjustment policies

No two African economies have the same set of characteristics, nor do they face the same diagnosis of their problems. In theory, then, adjustment packages ought to differ by country, and in fact have done so. However, the policy instruments used and the kind of packaging and sequencing of them bear many similarities between countries. The main reason is that, given the present tight international capital market, the International Monetary Fund (IMF) and the World Bank are the main sources of much-needed additional resources, and these two agencies have, until recently, run orthodox programmes. A few African countries have devised their own adjustment packages without resorting to these agencies, but their packages usually at least include a common range of policy instruments.

The initial phase of demand management is to bring about a decline in domestic demand in order to reduce fiscal deficits (and therefore inflationary pressure) and to release resources for exports (and therefore redress the external deficit). Following some gratifying degree of stabilisation of national accounts over a very short period, a programme of structural adjustment will progressively remove the obstacles to resources and products finding their most efficient use and true economic prices. Subsidies, fixed prices and restrictions will be phased out. Competition will be encouraged. Free pricing and liberalisation of market structures will eliminate biases, discrimination and other sources of distortions. Beyond this saving of resources for their most effective use to further development and, perhaps, an augmentation of resources through liberated entrepreneurship, there is the goal of deliberately investing to realign the economy towards new productivities and new comparative advantages. This will be growth from directing national surpluses and external funds, not just from eliminating waste of the current stock of resources.

Whereas the IMF has been associated with stabilisation programmes of short-term (one to two years) duration, the Bank has been concerned more with lending for structural adjustment over a three- to five-year period. The relation between these two lending programmes rests on two aspects. The stabilisation policies will, of course, have an impact on variables after the short term and will not have a neutral effect on the progress of structural adjustment. But there is a more deliberate relationship between the two sets of loans. Lending by either agency has been conditional on agreeing a diagnosis and accepting the remedial policies. During the 1970s IMF conditionalities were "low" but they became increasingly "high" in the 1980s, although since 1986 things have become easier. The Bank has its own conditions for structural adjustment loans which it started offering in the late 1970s. But increasingly during the 1980s the Bank offered loans only if an IMF stabilisation programme had been agreed. This is known as cross-conditionality. The Bank provides loans for both aggregate goals and sectoral goals.

Because of both these aspects of the relationship between stabilisation and structural adjustment, it is important that the agenda of issues for structural adjustment is borne in mind at the stage of designing the earlier stabilisation package.

Both kinds of adjustment are directed to remedying two problems: *(a)* the external and internal imbalances, and *(b)* the price distortions and allocative inefficiencies which impede growth. The two problems are not mutually exclusive. For instance, while producer and consumer subsidies are the major cause of internal (budgetary) imbalance they also distort markets by favouring the use of certain factors of production or the consumption of certain final products. Because of this, resources are not used in a combination and to a set of purposes which reflect the true conditions of their demand and supply. Some resources (or owners of resources) are being under-remunerated while others are being over-remunerated. This situation might represent an urban bias, a particular sectoral bias or a gender bias. The market distortions and the allocative inefficiencies that have been built up are far from being slight. The removal of typical subsidies and protection measures of the past two decades would cause major market alterations in sub-Saharan Africa.

Subsidiary to this main objective are some immediate objectives. The strictures of the economies of sub-Saharan Africa require new growth to emanate mainly from agriculture. It could be said that governments in general have increasingly talked of agriculture as a priority because of the very slow progress in deregulating agricultural markets and improving farm support services, and because it has become apparent that nothing much was going to change until agriculture had shown signs of movement. The objectives of agricultural adjustment include self-sufficiency in food staples, increased import substitution of both products and inputs, expansion of exports, improvements in the livelihoods of the farming population and rationalisation of the sector's budgets.

The immediate objectives for manufacturing seem to be more uniform across all countries. The need is to restore utilisation of efficient industrial capacity and create new viable industries. The objectives are to raise the international competitiveness of industry and to move to new comparative advantages in import substitution and exports. It is also frequently hoped that industries will look to local supplies of raw and intermediate inputs.

Another objective has come to the fore with years of experience of adjustment. Initially, fiscal concern concentrated on reducing the overall deficit. Later, when persistent large deficits and declining quality of crucial services demanded a detailed agenda for correction, budget rationalisation and targeting were given priorty.

Stabilisation

Stabilisation programmes act initially on the side of demand through fiscal and monetary restraint. On the fiscal side government expenditure is cut, thus reducing public sector demand for resources. This policy package tends initially to consist of an approximate "across-the-board" percentage cut in expenditure, although there are always some items of expenditure held sacrosanct. Inter alia, the government wage bill is reduced and subsidies are scaled down.

Monetary restraint is exercised by reducing the effective supply of credit. This is done by raising the price of credit or by cutting allocations of cheap official credit, or by a combination of both. Credit is therefore taken up and used only when it is profitable to do so in the scheme of stabilisation. Otherwise enterprises have to adapt in some other way.

Formal sector wages are affected directly by cuts in government emoluments and indirectly by reductions in subsidies and increases in the price of credit to productive enterprises. Domestic demand for consumer goods and, consequently, production inputs contracts because the real aggregate purchasing power of pay packets has fallen. But producers' demand for inputs declines because of this and also because, with a rise in interest rates, both capital investment and working capital are more expensive. Thus, even before policies to deliberately alter prices of inputs and outputs are introduced, demand for factors of production must diminish.

With reduced consumer and producer demands "absorption" (of resources) is moderated. With this there is less demand for imports and for those goods that could be exported instead. Some of the latter are now happily liberated from domestic consumption to earn foreign exchange. Reducing aggregate demand, therefore, benefits both sides of the foreign trade balance: imports decrease and exports increase. These hopes rest on the domestic demand for imports and exports being sufficiently responsive to the measures of fiscal and monetary restraint.

Accompanying this enforced reduction in domestic demand for resources there are often some initial steps to rationalise the foreign trade sector. The situation is likely to be that there has existed a tangle of quotas and tariffs to ration foreign exchange among competing groups. Rationalisation will aim to simplify the regime and prioritise some imports (and all possible exports). Eliminating quotas and altering the tariff schedule sometimes constitutes the entire policy change in the foreign trade sector during the stabilisation period. It is usually designed to eliminate privileged access to foreign exchange and to improve the competitive basis for its deployment. In other cases devaluation is added to increase the price of foreign exchange more directly. Either way the intention is to increase prices paid for imports and received for exports in order to switch expenditures from imports to domestic production, and from production of goods not exported to production of exports. This switching of capital, labour and other resources, once the new price signals are received, ought, according to the earlier orthodox scheme of things, to be achieved in a very short time.

That the IMF's performance criteria have to be met in this manner means that elasticities of demand must be activated quickly and new demand signals speedily transmitted to domestic producers, importers and exporters, who in turn have to expand or alter their portfolios in a brief time period. This period has in the past customarily been set down to last a couple of years. In practice, however, because of the experience of delays in demand and supply responses, it has been extended into the mid-term era of structural adjustment; that is, it is active concurrently with steps towards market liberalisation. In addition, the magnitude of budget deficits, and the rigidities and vested interests that have to be overcome in eliminating them, are such that the process of budgetary contraction might have to be progressively managed at least throughout what is called the medium term of three to five years. Controlling the fiscal balance might now have to be seen as a problem extending into the longer term, although its nature will change radically from the first brutal cuts. The mechanistic moves to monetary stabilisation of the late 1970s and early 1980s are giving way to using government capital and current budgets more discriminatingly to effect specific sectoral interventions while the budgets are contained in the aggregate. The interest of the international lending agencies in this new schematic agenda opens up possibilities of intercession on behalf of neglected economic issues and ignored potential agents of change.

The instruments of fiscal and monetary restraint will impinge directly on those in goverment employment and on the most formal of production and trading enterprises which have enjoyed subsidies and allocations in the past. For those workers and entrepreneurs who have never been embraced by development policies in this way there should be no direct impact. The indirect impact, of contraction in consumer demand and formal competitive suppliers in difficulties, will be mixed.

Structural adjustment

This concerns adjustments in factor and product markets to lead to a pattern of production in which resources are paid their true economic (approximately alternative use) cost. The policies include some aspects of stabilisation strategies, such as reducing subsidies and devaluing the currency, but this time with the purpose not of reducing aggregate demand but of eliminating price distortions. It is for this reason that the World Bank, the lender for structural adjustment, favours devaluation (freeing of the foreign exchange market) more than the IMF, which will settle for other means of reducing imports and increasing exports that may maintain distortions.

The policy instruments of structural adjustment include phasing out the subsidies to, and the monopoly rights of, public enterprises and trading parastatals, raising interest rates towards free market rates and phasing out credit quotas, as well as devaluation. This time these measures have the primary purpose of improving competition for resources so that they are used in the most efficient way to respond to final market demand. Again these workers and producers who have not been shown favour in the past will improve their competitive edge. Prices of all resources will gravitate towards their natural absolute and relative levels according to the real forces of supply and demand. In the process resources will leave unprofitable ventures and switch to profitable ones. If this involves greater demand for a certain resource, then its price will rise relative to other prices and this will call forth a greater supply. The markets are working efficiently, and goods are being produced at least cost and in the proportions consumers are demanding, given their incomes and purchasing patterns.

There is no doubt that certain categories of producers who have not been favoured in the past by official import or cheap credit quotas can "come into their own" in the new scheme of things. The process of altering competitive edges amongst suppliers, begun indirectly under stabilisation, continues in a more deliberate way. But caution must be exercised over seeing market forces sweeping away all barriers to true competition at all levels of production of goods and services. Stabilisation and structural adjustment deal with market irregularities brought about by government intervention. Other sources of market imperfections require longer-term treatment, often dealing with the social fabric and distributional issues, and amounting to structural transformation.

Under structural adjustment switching resources is taken much further than under stabilisation. Because one of the reforms is devaluation, imports will be discouraged and exports encouraged more directly than under demand contraction. Factors of production will be used more in accordance with their newly available proportions. Some long-neglected factors will experience a rise in demand. It is understood that, during this phase, switching and mobilising resources will take time and that there will be dislocation and unemployment because old production will disappear before new production can come on stream. This is why even the early structural adjustment loans from the Bank were over the medium term.

The implicit assumptions of this strategy are that the new price signals are the right ones and are sufficient to achieve significant liberalisation of markets, and that resources can be switched in response—all over a three- to five-year period. In particular, it is implicitly taken for granted that there are no major obstacles to the eradication of imperfections in markets that freeing prices cannot overcome. With this belief there is no need to fear that decontrolling prices will set up new market distortions, or that continued distortions in some markets will pervert the use to which efficiency gains in others are to be put. Across the broad phalanx of markets, then, imperfections will be progressively and continuously on the retreat if only prices are freed.

Longer-term adjustment

There will be unfinished business from what are bound to be protracted efforts on fiscal and monetary restraint. There will also be continued reverberations from the actions taken during the medium-term structural adjustment programme. Changes earmarked for action on the medium-term agenda, but unexpectedly found to be problematical, will have to be moved to a long-term agenda or a "phase two" medium-term agenda. This is already happening.

But there is another adjustment agenda, which used to be thought of as the stage following structural adjustment, on which quite new economic directions as well as population problems would be tackled. That is to say, after rectifying internal and external imbalances, and eliminating inefficiencies, questions about new comparative advantages and specialisations generating an internal dynamic to the economy and promoting regional trade could be dealt with. These questions take the debate into the area of investment in new factor productivities and of stretching the purpose of institutional reforms to channelling resources deliberately into certain uses or to certain target groups. The end product is an economy which is competitive, efficient and sustainable, but one which has developed resources, not merely reallocated the existing stock more efficiently. Now there is a body of opinion which claims that these subjects are not postponable. It is said that stabilisation and structural adjustment programmes will not work, or will be easily blown off course by shocks, because the economy itself is inappropriately structured. Moreover, the preconditions for population control ought to be embedded in economic policies immediately, otherwise those policies could contribute to the looming crisis in factor proportions. This agenda is longer term in the sense that it will occupy decades; but the argument is that it should commence now.

The agenda laid out in the ECA's *African alternative framework . . .* is in fact an example of such an amalgamation of structural adjustment and long-term transformation. But it notably argues a role for the human dimension of this great effort. The ECA publication (1989, p. 25) states that:

> . . . the conventional SAPs [structural adjustment programmes] are inadequate in addressing the real causes of economic, financial and social problems facing African countries which are of a structural nature. There is therefore an urgent need for an alternative to the current stabilisation and adjustment programmes in Africa. Such an alternative will have to take into consideration, among other things, the structure of production and consumption and the people who are the main actors in the development process.

While it is fairly well understood what the purposes of transformation should be, the range of policy instruments to be used, let alone their packaging with other adjustment programmes, is still weakly developed. So far it has been accepted that under "adjustment with transformation" there will be moderations in budgetary reductions (especially in social services and subsidies on essentials), the credit squeeze and interest rate increases, price incentives offered to tradables, total import liberalisation and market liberalisation. There must also be a deliberate attempt to influence the allocation of fixed and recurrent resources to strengthen and diversify production capacity, improve the level of income and the pattern of its distribution, pattern expenditure for the satisfaction of needs and strengthen institutional supports. The ECA publication centralises human conditions. In doing so it shows similarities with the Social Dimensions of Adjustment (SDA) programmes of the World Bank and the United Nations Development Programme (see Chapter 7). The difference is that the ECA paper foresees an immediate incorporation of these long-term developmental policies into current planning practice, while the SDA programmes are more experimental in intent.

This chapter has described briefly the purposes and means of the different forms of adjustment programmes. It has also indicated that experience with the first, more orthodox, policy packages has opened the way to new perspectives on purposes and means. These are taken up in more detail in the next chapter.

Weaknesses and opportunities of adjustment packages

7

The weaknesses of demand and supply adjustment policies have received a great deal of attention, and there is little fundamental disagreement about them. Basically they stem from the unreality of the assumptions of the policies described in the previous chapter. But experience has led to the identification of improvements in macro-level strategies and the development of micro- and meso-level policy detail; as well as to the quest for policy instruments of more fundamental structural change. In these can be found the first tentative signs of official recognition of the relevance of gender issues for the success of adjustment. But much more than this, they open the door to extensive dialogue on the impact of gender on the outcome of adjustment.

Weaknesses

General

An overriding comment in the case of sub-Saharan Africa is that the structure of its economies renders the customary stabilisation policies even less effective, and in certain instances (such as when there is inadequate external support) actually counter-effective. The policy instrument of devaluation, when it is used, is singled out for special criticism. It does not work as it should in these economies because world demand for Africa's export is inelastic and much of the formal sector of African economies has, in the short term at least, an inelastic demand for (dependency on) imported inputs. Unless it is possible to develop new exports and input substitutes quickly, this weakness will remain and the objective of external balance will have to be spread over a longer time.

A widespread comment on stabilisation policies has been that they were formulated by identifying macro-level targets expressed in money terms without any clear links to real variables. This arose because it was too readily assumed that macro policies would elicit real responses at the micro level via the market forces that existed or that were newly brought into play. Therefore a major criticism of adjustment strategies has been that they greatly overestimate elasticities of supply through not giving realistic consideration to likely reactions of producers. At issue is the speed and efficiency with which factors of production can be switched to new uses or incorporated in new methods of production. The shorter-term stabilisation strategy emphasises tradable goods (more frequently concentrating on the export side of foreign trade). It is implicitly assumed that either resources move from non-tradables to tradables or unemployed factor capacity is "absorbed". The instrument chosen to produce this effect is changes in relative factor and product prices, principally through devaluation.

It is now admitted that the first stabilisation programmes greatly overestimated the capability of markets to respond in terms of efficiency and greater production to less government intervention. "Actions to reduce demand within inflexible production patterns reduce imports only by cutting real output and consumption, and may do next to nothing for exports" (Colclough and Green, 1988, p. 2). The consequences of this are profound. Because of weak (expansionary) supply responses of even inherently competitive industries there is a real danger that (contractionary) demand effects of stabilisation programmes will dominate the impact of exchange rate adjustment. In this case it is not easy to justify the inflation which inevitably follows devaluation. Consequently, a short-term stabilisation programme may not be an appropriate path to restoring external balance. More time and resource may be required to rectify the causes of the external imbalance through measures acting on the real economy. And the real economy includes a gender dimension.

An unsustainable programme to remedy balance-of-payments and budget deficits makes the success of structural adjustment measures more problematical because too many immediate objectives, not all compatible with each other, are being pursued at the same time. These measures, in any case, face structured rigidities in markets which laissez-faire or price liberalisation policies at the macro level cannot always weaken. Green (1986) remarks that the IMF prescription offers an export strategy that goes no further than "generalised higher price prescriptions". However, there is now apparent unanimity among critics, including the Fund itself, that constraints on the free operation of markets do not disappear when prices are changed. It has almost become conventional wisdom to assume that price changes are necessary conditions, but rarely sufficient conditions. Thus it is accepted that biases in the exploitation of resources persist. Streeten (1987) makes the valuable point that while price signals are suitable to do the bidding of planners in slow, gradual change, they are inadequate or plain wrong for large and sudden changes. The implication of this is that even if the diagnosis of the economic malaise is perfectly correct there is no unique, inimitable path to a resolution. There emerge options on the means to overcome market biases, some of which are gender based.

Behind this overview of criticisms several specific planning problems recur in the literature.

The threat of inflation

Internal balance was one of the two objectives of adjustment programmes. But achievement of this objective has often proved unexpectedly difficult and presented a serious planning problem. In this study the threat of inflation is seen in relation to entrepreneurial confidence and capability. It should be noted at the outset that the desirable alteration in absolute and relative prices which were formerly artificially suppressed is conceptually different from generalised inflation. The problem is that the first often leads to the second.

Generalised inflation creates uncertainty and a costing nightmare for producers. It is particularly damaging to any policy goal of switching resources to new technologies or uses (that is, structural adjustment). Producers will not gamble on otherwise promising new production while absolute and relative prices are in turmoil. It is difficult to overestimate the damage that inflation inflicts on the adjustment process. Any means to limit it merits consideration.

Under adjustment programmes demand contraction is deliberately intended to cause deflation in the sense of reduced uptake of resources (domestic "absorption"). This it certainly does. But the policy instruments of fiscal and monetary restraint used to achieve this have a highly inflationary content in terms of price increases. Domestic inputs become more expensive because of higher interest rates and reduced subsidies. Both inputs and consumer goods which are imported also become more expensive because of higher interest rates and devaluation. If, as a consequence of higher priced inputs, enterprises close down, this will add to inflation by reducing supply. The assumption is, of course, that new input costs and output prices of producers will bring forth a new pattern and level of production which at least moderates the ensuing generalised inflation.

Monetary and fiscal restraint can reduce supply more than demand in the short term not only because of a slow supply response but because those in need, the newly unemployed or impoverished, will use money balances or sell personal assets to finance their demand for essentials. As near and distant relatives help each other out, those still in steady employment no longer save from their current income.

Thus one of the most potent criticisms of past stabilisation programmes is that they did not achieve their own goal of price stabilisation; and, with that, the political difficulty of reducing subsidies and nominal wages in the public sector grew. The stabilisation process was stymied.

When structural adjustment policies are added, with the hope that economic contraction is reversed, inflation can become much worse. Devaluation is now undertaken in earnest while fiscal restraint continues and interest rates approach free market rates. So certain input costs are still rising.

Much depends on supply response for price stabilisation. It is assumed that inflation will abate as producers increasingly develop more profitable lines of production and technologies in response to relative price changes. But the uncertainty created by the very presence of inflation inhibits entrepreneurial capability. Moreover, rigidities/immobilities in domestic factor markets mean that labour, management, fixed capital and credit lines do not move easily to other productive uses or to recombine in more economically efficient technologies. If factors of production are not mobile between uses and technologies, then the hoped-for supply increase to combat inflation will not be forthcoming. The immobility of factors, or the stickiness of markets, could cause a rise in real prices in some factor and product markets without any real hope of the desired production changes.

There are two reasons why incorporating a gender perspective could help in the fight against inflation.

First, if it can be supposed that the more flexible the technology used and the more open factor markets are to new influences the greater will be mobility of factors of production, then the technologies used by women and men, respectively, and women's and men's differentiated statuses in factor markets, have a bearing on any attempt to moderate inflation.

Second, enterprises which have never enjoyed input cost favours in the form of subsidised credit or privileged foreign exchange rates should be better able to weather price adjustment. The call of "unfair competition from imports" tends to be heard mostly from enterprises of notable formal structure formerly protected by tariffs and import quotas. The relative importance of women and men as entrepreneurs and workers is different in the privileged and unprivileged sectors, with women relatively more significant in the latter. If governments wish to target micro-level policies on the formerly unprivileged sector they may have to overcome obstructions that women particularly face in factor and product markets.

If it is found that a great deal of women's activities are marked by flexibility and adaptability but that they have been especially neglected by services designed to improve production, then "betting on women"could become a deliberate counter-inflationary policy instrument. Conversely, ignoring this gender dimension could make inflation a more problematic consequence of stabilisation and structural adjustment measures.

The elusive trade balance

The theory of adjustment assumes that devaluation improves the trade balance by encouraging exports and inhibiting imports. In this way external balance is achieved. The success of this strategy depends, on the demand side, on the price elasticity of *(a)* world demand for exports and *(b)* domestic demand for exports and imports. Because of the nature of the price elasticities of these demands, devaluation tends to prove a weak instrument for resolving the external deficit. Conversely, to make any impression on the external deficit devaluation (and therefore inflation) would have to be massive. On the supply side there have often proved to be rigidities limiting the expansion of exports and producers' capacity to absorb higher-priced imported inputs.

For the great majority of sub-Saharan Africa's current exports, world demand is fairly inelastic. This means that if exporters do increase their supply in response to an initial rise in price in domestic currency terms, they will only succeed in driving down the international price or adding to unsold stocks. Krueger (1984) has pointed out that countries that have followed an outward-looking policy of export promotion have been able to adapt more easily to adjustment policies than countries following an inward-looking policy of import replacement. There seem to be two reasons for this. First, the outward-looking policy has encouraged the development of new post-colonial and diversified exports, principally processed primary produce, whose world demand is more elastic. Second, import-substituting and export manufactures bear different technological features. Krueger (1983) argues that export orientation of tradables responds better to structural adjustment programmes because its chosen technologies are based on the factor proportions of the countries' endowment, regardless of the foreign trade regimes, whereas import-substituting manufactures use much higher capital-to-labour ratios. Labour legislation, privileged access to credit and import licences give rise to high capital-to-output costs, and these have been the principal characteristics of import-substituting manufacturing. To the extent that jobs in import-substituting manufacturing have been overwhelmingly filled by men while women tend to have a relative prominence in the new export manufactures, there should be something of a gender division of labour between the less and more responsive parts of secondary industry. Any encouragement of the latter may need to deal with the particular conditions of the supply of female labour.

Domestic demand for export goods is supposed to be reduced by the effect of fiscal and monetary restraint—or by income elasticity of demand. However, apart from staple foods, exports which are also consumed *en masse* in the country are not usually the most essential of goods. For instance, African countries are not known to be great exporters of textiles. Therefore a significant reduction of domestic demand for goods which are also exported will come about when the purchasing power of those who tend to buy non-essentials is curtailed. Nevertheless, it should be pointed out that the domestic market does not compete very greatly for exported goods. In the case of imports, there will be a number of goods now regarded as essentials. Their price elasticities of demand will be relatively low. To the extent that they involve raw materials not often produced in African countries there is little chance of higher prices acting as an incentive to import replacement. Gender would have a potential relevance if purchasing patterns of women and men were different, as between essentials and non-essentials, and their personal disposable incomes were affected differently by adjustment programmes.

The aggregate demand factor

In the above discussion on inflation, mention was made of supply falling faster than demand because producers faced contracting domestic demand in addition to a cost squeeze.

The theory of stabilisation implies that supply can stabilise because *(a)* there will be a greater demand for exports, and *(b)* consumer demand will switch from newly expensive imports to newly created import replacements. It has just been argued that the first is not always feasible, at least within a few years, because external demand cannot be depended on. The second assumption depends partly on how total demand and its composition are affected by cross-substitution price and income effects.

A persistent downward trend in mass purchasing power (after money balances are exhausted) raises the possibility of a downward spiral in economic activities. Less total mass purchasing power leads to lower effective demand, with consequent less output and employment. The cycle is repeated; a multiplier is at work. Demand falls but so does supply. One means of halting the downward spiral is to try to shape the pattern of consumer—and producer—demand in favour of goods produced from domestic materials by flexible production functions.

Mass income, or purchasing power, will have been eroded and the public sector wage bill reduced. Some formal sector employees will have been made redundant in the first cost squeeze during stabilisation. Monetary restraint and some devaluation will have set off a price rise which reduces the value of remaining incomes. Money balances do not last for ever; income elasticities of demand have to come into play. The informal sector does not escape these effects. Colclough (1988) mentions that in Zambia the contraction of urban consumer demand threatened incomes in the informal sector because it was dependent on incomes of formal sector workers. It is difficult to gauge how far a shift to cheaper, inferior goods produced by the informal sector might have a mitigating effect. It is very plausible that one part of the informal sector loses while another part gains. The pattern would depend on income and price effects, together with their cross-substitution influences. There are very likely to be gender-differentiated losses and gains.

Income elasticity analysis assumes that all close substitutes are directly affected by changes in income and that a new set of preferences emerges from a new income. Non-essentials (of all qualities) will be forgone or reduced. Expensive forms of essentials will be eschewed for cheaper inferior versions. The income elasticity effect operates in a similar way to the cross-substitution price effect; new consumer choices have to be made. But it is different from the price effect in one respect at least. The pattern of revealed consumer preferences is influenced by how the reduction in purchasing power is distributed between women and men, as well as between income classes. This may be brought about by the gender division of employment and income, by how much of "household" income a woman budgeting for family needs has available to her, or even by expenditure on the social sector budget.

Income and cross-substitution effects could cause markedly different demand patterns in product markets. If there is some gender specialisation amongst substitutable goods then female and male producers will probably experience different changes in demand for their products.

Industry's supply response

The result of stabilisation and structural adjustment policies for industry was expected to be varied. Although some industry would not be viable after devaluation and freeing of input and output markets, it was always assumed that these reforms would give a new lease of life to other industries previously discriminated against by government interventions. Freed prices would force a more efficient deployment of resources which would in itself generate expansion of output.

However, the practice of reforming industry has proved a protracted affair. Import licensing remains an important policy instrument in many African countries because dismantling protection has been more difficult than expected. One reason may be the vested interests of state-owned industry, but another is certainly the problem of redeploying resources.

Despite this there is still much optimism about inefficient manufacturing going out and efficient, competitive manufacturing coming in. The optimism extends to a felicitous counterbalancing of departures and arrivals. It is true that data show some countries experiencing a decline of old industries alongside the development of specialisations and rises in value added per worker (UNIDO, 1989), but this is far from universal. For some countries the new lean competitive manufacturing sector has been elusive.

In predicting secondary industry's response it is helpful to consider two aspects: *(a)* the changes in relative prices of tradables and non-tradables, or product price signals, and *(b)* movement in factor markets in response; that is, expenditure switching and/or higher factor absorption rates.

Prices of tradables will rise relative to those of non-tradables. The incentive is to boost production of tradables. Factories producing import-replacing final consumer goods are already working at well below capacity. They also tend to use imported inputs which will now be more expensive. It would not take much to shut them down if credit lines became more expensive and subsidies were reduced, even supposing the cost of labour per unit of output could be made to fall substantially. The finished product might still be cheaper to import. As for a factory producing exports, if it is not also using imported inputs it will be heavily dependent on increased supplies of primary produce, which places the responsibility for produce response on the farming sector involving very significant gender issues.

The second aspect, factor market movement or expenditure switching, is determined by elasticities of demand and supply of all inputs. The elasticity of demand is, in turn, determined by the range of potential production functions. If, in the short term, technology cannot be changed, and there is no possible factor substitution within the technology used, then an unavoidable increase in the price of one factor will lower prices for all complementary factors; or, if there is downward rigidity in these prices, output is cut back. The transitional factor price increases and loss of production would be less if the method of production allowed for some factor substitution or if some technological variant were available.

Substitution of one factor for another, or flexibility of technology, is associated more with the informal sector than the formal sector. Moreover, the formal sector is customarily more dependent on imported equipment, spares and even raw materials which will now be priced more highly.

Alternative domestic supplies of these inputs are usually not readily available, or available in the quantities required, for years. Formal sector nominal wages cannot easily be reduced to accommodate other cost increases. Real wages could be induced to fall despite union bargaining, but this waits for inflation to do its work, and therefore postpones the orthodox correcting mechanism of the markets. Reducing the wage bill through redundancies, with non-substitutability of other factors for labour, must lead to a corresponding fall in output. In the meantime manufacturers face cost rises almost in proportion to the much-vaunted product price increases. Frequently the result is closure or further underutilisation of capacity because the goal of switching factor use, or altering the production technology within formal sector enterprises, is beset with problems.

Another problem of conceptualising factor switching is that the market for each factor is not "homogeneous" over both the formal and informal sectors: exit and entry of a unit of a factor of production involved in the informal sector can be governed by other than marginal price changes. Certainly the informal sector manufacturers' credit market (if there is such a thing) is different from the formal sector's credit market. Labour too has different supply conditions in informal and formal sector markets, particularly in the case of the self-employed or family business. It is far from clear how higher wages in the formal sector actually bid labour away from the informal sector. There is bound to be a gender dimension to the non-homogeneity of these credit and labour factor markets.

One source has gone so far as to say that the informal sector "consist of activities in sectors without formal factor markets and therefore characterised by no *market* separation between the returns to labour and the returns to assets" (Addison and Demery, 1985, p. 29). The self-employed, the co-operative and the small intimate firm combine returns over all factors of production and do not apportion returns to each to justify the production function. A degree of this is probably the case because small enterprises have maximising goals other than pure monetary profit. But neoclassical micro-economics must be some kind of reference point if relative prices change dramatically.

Even if a factor of production has homogeneous characteristics in all sectoral markets, the markets themselves may experience features which lead to different prices operating. If we can assume total mobility of factors between all sectors and uses, then the factor of production which is used more intensively in (the now supposedly more profitable) tradables production than in non-tradables production will enjoy a disproportionate increase in price, unless it has a highly elastic short-term supply, which is unlikely even in the case of labour. There is, however, some doubt whether this favourable income position is shared by units of this same factor in other parts of industry: the new price signal is not transmitted to the entire market of that factor. There may be geographical, institutional or social obstacles to much relocation of the input. Moreover, production of tradables might utilise factor A intensively in the formal sector but might utilise another, factor B, intensively in the informal sector. That factor

A probably equals capital and factor B labour comes readily to mind. But factor A might also be labour, although of a certain kind (for instance, male) with its different supply conditions from factor B (for instance, female labour).

For several reasons, then, national factor markets are not operating according to the book, and the usual price signals cannot be relied upon to alter this. Policies to promote allocative efficiency have to be more discerning.

If gender influences these characteristics of factor markets and flexibility of production functions then any strategy arrived at to improve market efficiencies ought to take gender factors into account.

Supply functions for agricultural products

With so much uncertainty about demand for urban output emanating from export and urban consumer requirements, much dependence for lifting aggregate purchasing power is bound to rest on increases in agricultural incomes.

An increase in the price of a good elicits a greater volume of output if *(a)* producers have the capacity to produce more, and *(b)* they have the incentive to seize an opportunity to earn more income. On both these grounds there has been much concern expressed that the producer price increases of stabilisation and structural adjustment could cause a contraction of agricultural production—either of tradables or of non-tradables, or both.

When analysing the possible course of supply response it is helpful to bear in mind several things:

- farming households produce tradables, surrogate tradables and non-tradables from their partially fixed stock of production resources;
- farming households produce for both own consumption and sale;
- farmers are supposed to show a response by the end of a stabilisation period (one to two years) since agricultural exports are to help to improve the balance of payments;
- there is what has been called a "behavioural black hole" relating to farmers' objectives and strategies which neoclassical micro-economics cannot illuminate.

An implicit assumption made about the beneficial impact of producer price increases is that small farmers' supply is price elastic. There is now much debate about the period required by farmers to mobilise for greater output to demonstrate this elasticity.

However, at the outset it has to be recognised that higher producer prices may not get through to farmers. Inefficient parastatal marketing, unpreparedness of private traders to enter a newly deregulated trading sector, and inadequate transport and storage facilities can all impair the price signals en route. A measure of liberalisation of agricultural input and output markets has taken place in all countries which implemented adjustment policies. In many cases it would be more accurate to say that the free markets that were operating despite official input supplies and parastatal marketing monopolies merely spread further. Nevertheless, despite the presence of free markets, mainly in the field of food crops, one of the biggest obstacles to effective structural adjustment in agriculture has been the inability of quasi-governmental institutions, which for one reason or another still have an important role to play, to pass on the full benefits of higher producer prices because of their extremely high cost management. There is no doubt that weak management of the main parastatals and their inability to reform themselves have affected government ability to continue with price deregulation (and fiscal control). Frequently attempts to co-opt the private or co-operative sectors to augment infrastructural resources have exposed their capabilities as limited. The private sector has worked well where it crept into a profitable vacuum. But it has been laggardly in expanding into new roles on request.

The delay in achieving intended reforms of market institutions has therefore limited the effect of price deregulation on production of tradables. This offers the chance of incorporating other institutional reforms which would weaken gender-based distortions in agricultural factor and product markets.

Another cause of a slow transmission of greater incentive to produce tradables lies in the rise in unit cash costs of tradable output which emanates from adjustment policies. Profitability is immediately weakened.

It can also be the case that some non-tradable crops are substitutes for tradables in the domestic market, such that when the price of the latter rises consumers switch to the less preferred, but cheaper, non-tradable. The outstanding case of this is a rise in domestic demand, and therefore price, of millet and sorghum, in response to a consumer switch from the now hugely expensive maize. But the same could be said of a new interest in fresh vegetables and fruit if tinned produce becomes much more expensive. The fact that some crops are both foreign traded and domestically consumed while others are only domestically consumed means that price substitution effects can weaken the intended incentive of adjustment-induced price increases.

This has led some commentators to conclude that all crops are tradables and that it is not useful to pursue the distinction between tradables and non-tradables. Before sight is lost of the original purpose of this distinction it should be remembered that cross-substitution effects are reactions to an initial impulse and that other crops become substitutes under different time horizons. There are also, of course, limits to substitution. What is of particular note for this study is that the crops receiving the initial incentive signal may be grown by one sex, and the reactive substitutes by the other.

More than this, however, some (tradable and non-tradable) crops are also consumed by the farming household. Social and familial structures, resting on tradition as well as a rational guard against uncertainty, usually lead a farming household to underwrite its maintenance by first setting aside some produce for own consumption. Differences in post-harvest glut prices and later scarcity prices may be seen by some economists as a neo-classical micro-economic explanation for own consumption. But even if there were very little difference between these prices households might still earmark some output, and select a crop mix, to meet a large part of the family's food needs. There might be limited switching of resources from self-provisioning production which provides immediate use value to the household.

Price changes will nevertheless have a net favourable effect on tradables, potential import-replacing crops as well as exports. The capability of farmers to respond with a supply increase depends on their crop mix and the availability of extra resources, within short- to long-term time horizons. Excess capacity cannot be assumed. Land may or may not be fixed in the short to medium term but acreage expansion requires great labour application. Seeds will be in fixed supply, in the very short term at least. Chemicals are likely to have experienced a price jump because of their import content. It is quite possible that the price of chemical fertiliser rises faster than the price of the tradable good.

Agriculture is labour-intensive. Unlike in the case of manufacturing, labour can substitute partially for capital and land by being applied more carefully and intensively to the different tasks. But the supply of labour for the tasks that would require labour intensification to produce higher land yields is not very elastic. These tasks come at seasonal labour demand peaks. The stock of household labour is usually already fully stretched, and labour is hired at a premium. There is not much evidence of excess labour capacity at the crucial times of the year.

A switch of resources from non-tradable crops to tradable crops would be problematical. Price changes alone will not necessarily trigger the switch. Land under non-tradables (usually traditional foods) may not be suitable for growing tradables. Also tree crop exports require a gestation period after planting. There may never have been any working capital or credit lines for non-tradables, so that there are no units of this factor to switch. Labour is the only factor that could be switched.

There are many very important gender issues involved which are elaborated in Chapter 9. But it can be pointed out here that they make the switching of factors of production more difficult.

Capacity can be increased through government intercession. But reductions in the government's agricultural current budget are likely to mean the erosion of farmer support services such as credit and extension, while cuts in the capital budget will probably threaten research into higher productivity and infrastructural supports. Smallholders who might spearhead a boost in output, because their land yields could be lifted substantially through a more flexible and less capital-intensive technology, are unable to enjoy efficiently operating markets. But government action to remove these market inefficiencies is a longer-term matter.

Mention needs to be made of another weakness in supply response of agricultural output. This comes not from diminished net price incentives but, ironically, from the possibility of a successful rise in net income. The weak response of farmers to higher prices has sometimes been put down to the lack of goods to spend the income on, and the unwillingness of farmers to hold money balances during inflation. One instrument of stabilisation and structural adjustment is to limit imports, including imports of consumer goods. Domestic production of consumer goods may also be affected deleteriously. Rural communities are last in the queue to receive supplies of consumer goods. The little that is imported will be taken by urban consumers, and that little will be highly priced. Thus farming households may not be able to find consumer goods to buy in exchange for their money income, and even if they can do so, the terms of trade between agricultural produce and manufactures may be as low as previously. The true incentive, to have purchasing power to buy goods, will not exist. There is no point in producing more if higher producer prices mean that the previous net income can be obtained by producing less. Beyond that money balances would have to be kept, but perhaps for a long time during which inflation will eat into them. The higher the crop price, the less has to be produced to obtain the previous situation. Supply on the market is inversely related to price.

The clearest example of this was in the United Republic of Tanzania during years of particular shortage of consumer goods. The situation has been described thus:

> Our major thesis is that peasant supply response changes radically and becomes perverse once the consumer goods market is heavily controlled . . . Whereas consumer goods were readily available in rural areas in Kenya, in Tanzania they were subject to severe shortages whether purchased at official prices or on the repressed and highly fragmented rural black market . . . The peasant will, therefore, choose to do only enough work on coffee to pay for the goods which he expects to be available, since further coffee production would be wasted effort, yielding no additional consumption. In this situation, an increase in the barter price of coffee will reduce coffee production, unless it coincides with a changed expectation of availability of consumer goods . . . An increase in the price of coffee will then induce an equal proportionate reduction in supply (Bevan et al., 1987).

It has been suggested that in the very short term there would be a positive response to price increases—before stocks of consumer goods disappear altogether. Then output falls, possibly dramatically. At some future date, when short-term production obstacles are overcome and structural adjustment is able to deliver consumer goods, output will keep rising. In this scheme of things there is no monotonic increase in supply of agricultural produce.

Given all these considerations the agricultural supply response might be muted or delayed. However, a strongly positive response can be achieved if favourable price relatives attract household resources away from other deployments. In particular, if male labour returned to family farming, bringing with it cheaper ploughing services and some assistance in other agricultural tasks, a new willingness to invest resources in correct and annual ploughing could lead to any combination of acreage expansion, higher yields and a shift to crops for which ploughing is crucial.

Opportunities

The opportunities that have arisen for reshaping adjustment strategies on the basis of experience stem from a greater appreciation of what is possible in the short to long term, and involve a return to the idea of using resources discriminatingly. The desired end result remains sustainable growth through the efficient deployment of, and investment in, resources.

New attitudes to adjustment

There is a different climate of opinion today from ten years ago. The World Bank, concerned with the viability of its longer-term loans, has an interest in urging the IMF to offer more realistic conditions. The Fund, in turn, instituted Structural Adjustment Facilities (SAF) in 1986 and Enhanced Structural Adjustment Facilities (ESAF) in 1988 to cover three-year programmes of stabilisation with concessional finance. These facilities are arranged in conjunction with Bank loans. The Bank shares the widely accepted view that expenditure-switching policies do not work in the very short term of stabilisation programmes, and without extra resources would operate with difficulty in the medium term. For its part the Bank has moved towards Sectoral Structural Adjustment Loans (SECAL) which earmark funds for the restructuring of certain sectors, including the social sector, and which are accompanied by more detailed planning and targeting. They cover a period of up to five years. This prolongation of the adjustment process and the greater specificity of loans offer new opportunities for detailed corrective action and closer targeting of policy instruments. Gender-based biases in factor and product markets can now be more easily addressed.

The goals of a more competitive industrial base could be partly achieved through micro-economic policies in the foreign trade and monetary sectors. But as with agriculture there comes a point when this signalling through prices loses impact, and deliberate action on factor productivity is needed. Some governments have already acted on this. Kenya has gone some way with an Industrial Sector Adjustment Programme whose immediate objectives are to encourage investment and to increase efficiency and flexibility of the financial system, as well as to reform incentives. Most recently, in 1989, the Government set out to improve credit availability to the informal sector and to establish new tendering procedures that favour informal sector firms in bidding for government contracts. Nigeria has an industrial policy which emphasises small- and medium-scale enterprises as a source of employment creation and industrial development. In so far as it reaches the small entrepreneur and the aspiring self-employed this policy should improve the efficiency of public resource allocation which has been biased towards large entrepreneurs in the past. If women as well as men are reached, the gender bias in resource allocation should also be weakened.

There has also been discussion of alternative paths to agricultural rehabilitation and development because of institutional weaknesses of agricultural markets. Some crops, such as staple substitutes or secondary crops, may benefit more from new price relatives or cross-substitution price effects because they can find domestic markets not dependent on parastatal networks. The policy environment is favourable to recognising the case for investing some part of the input and extension supplies in them, as well as in export crops or the purported import-replacing food crops. If a new agenda for structural adjustment policies in agriculture is in the offing, then there will be many gender aspects to take into consideration.

Alternative routes to stabilisation and restructuring are also being debated. The 1989 ECA contribution to discussion on, essentially, "which way African economies and how?" puts forward a more realistic view of the real task ahead by rejecting the assumptions of orthodox adjustment programmes.

The way policy objectives have evolved can be seen as implicitly drawing out gender issues more starkly than previously. The growing concern with agricultural supply responses obliged planners to look closely at whom they need to influence, and how. Also, the more recent government statements of intent on small-scale manufacturing and the informal sector herald less reliance on the adaptability of the old formal sector enterprises.

Budget rationalisation and credit reform

Increasing attention is being given to using government capital and current budgets to channel resources in ways that encourage a more strategic shaping of the adjustment process. This new direction—using government budgets as an instrument of intervention in improving factor productivities and supply responses—opens the door to possibilities of drawing women's unremunerated output of goods and services into arguments about the efficient allocation of resources.

Attempting a reduction in the aggregate budget deficit is usually the first measure of a stabilisation programme. But however drastic these cuts, they seem never to have been enough to obtain internal balance. At the end of the 1980s African governments are still struggling to bring down their deficits as a percentage of GDP. There are, therefore, two pertinent aspects to the experience of expenditure cuts to consider: first, they are often introduced years before the other stabilisation interventions and therefore early enough to affect the outcome of other macro-economic policies at the micro level; and, second, they continue beyond the medium term into the long term. It is often wrongly supposed that budget reform is taken hurriedly in a situation of crisis management.

In fact there is frequently a long run-up to fiscal retrenchment during which there are plenty of signs of the inevitable to come, and time to plan sectoral reductions. For instance, the Zambian Government was making major reductions in expenditure six years before the first agreement with the IMF and the beginning of the depreciation of the kwacha in 1983. Kenya also was cutting per capita public expenditure on health, education and the social budget in the 1970s as part of a broad policy response to external and internal imbalances. In Nigeria the large fiscal deficit was tackled by an across-the-board cut in expenditure (which excluded the subsidies to parastatals and agriculture) in 1983, at the same time as the first steps to rationalising and liberalising the foreign trade regime were taken but a full three years before the foreign exchange auction (a "second-tier" foreign exchange market whereby commercial banks were permitted to let market forces dictate the rate of exchange) and anything like an adjustment programme was adopted. The United Republic of Tanzania made major reductions in investment projects, froze civil service wages and salaries, and shifted resources to productive sectors in its 1982 programme, just a year before major devaluation.

This long process means that fiscal and financial retrenchments are not to be seen as simply slamming the brakes on aggregate demand as a curtain raiser to structural adjustment strategies. There has been time to use them to change direction and to influence the targeting of macro-economic policies from the start. Policy instruments, in so far as they emanated from budget allocations, did not have to wait upon aggregate macro-level policies somehow "clearing the ground" for them, as strongly suggested by the early literature on adjustment. We can see, then, that there has usually been time to draw up an agenda of selective budget cuts to reap maximum positive effect of the macro-economic policies. Utilisation of the budget to promote greater supply response could have been started at the earliest phase of demand management.

This selective use of budgetary resources is a subject taken up by Stewart (1987). Stewart uses the term "meso" for policy action which improves the impact of a given macro variable through the allocation of resources and/or the deliberate distribution of income. Meso policies can also be used for a deliberate distribution of improvements in factor productivity. For instance, they can be used to empower the poor to contribute better to economic growth, an important element of programmes promoted under the rubric of "social dimensions of adjustment". (Meso policies are discussed further under "Adjustment, growth and equity", below.

Today budget rationalisation is widely seen as an important policy instrument for raising factor productivities (in both the government and private sectors) to elicit a better response to any market incentive. This finer tuning of public resource allocation is an objective that is growing in importance and constitutes the bridge between structural adjustment (managing the economic legacy efficiently) and real transformation. As such it presents many opportunities to raise the question of the influence of gender on the efficacy of budgets. That cuts in social sector budgets preceded reductions in producer subsidies means that the early experience of fiscal retrenchment included a gender bias in the outcome for production because the former expenditure is much more supportive of women's economic activities and the latter more supportive of men's.

Raising interest rates has been difficult because of the strong vested interests of past beneficiaries of cheap credit. The first moves have frequently been towards requiring banks to award quotas of credit to priority sectors, sometimes accompanied by the raising of interest rates. In Nigeria, for instance, the progressive raising of real interest rates from 1986 to the final abolition of ceilings in August 1987 was accompanied by sector-specific credit allocations imposed on banks, with at least 50 per cent for high-priority sectors.

But even sectoral allocations are at too macro a level to reach into the workings of credit markets among producers. Without accompanying reform of credit institutions and delivery systems, sectoral allocations merely mean that those who are normally first in the queue will gain if they are in priority sectors. Some amelioration of this credit bias could come from budget allocations to make producer support services more effective, so raising the demand for credit from formerly neglected target groups. However, given the inability of governments so far to go below the level of sectoral allocations and to reform the structure of access to credit, monetary policy has not been able to direct credit to less visible, but potentially highly profitable, producers within priority sectors.

Some countries are beginning to rectify this. Institutional reforms of credit markets may be moving up the agenda and may be imminent in some countries. The IMF is alive to the issue. Despite the United Republic of Tanzania achieving positive interest rates in early 1987, the Fund concluded in 1989 that problems of credit demand and use are structural in nature and therefore cannot be resolved meaningfully by monetary measures. That would have to be done through an adjustment programme which tackled structural constraints and discrimination. But the detailed planning of this requires an answer to the question: "Improving access to credit for whom and removing whose structural constraints?" Governments do not always seem clear about what kind of producer they want to encourage this year, next year and sometime. It is far too soon to make any comment on whether opportunities to counter gender biases in credit markets have been developed in plans to restructure these markets.

Adjustment, growth and equity

Enough has been posited to indicate that there are theoretical weaknesses in orthodox adjustment programmes. While it would be difficult to find any agency or development economist supporting former orthodoxies, it is useful to mention two issues that invite a fundamental reorientation of strategy in order to indicate how open the field is for new ideas on what adjustment ought to be about.

First, there have even been questions on whether the analysis of the economic malaise to be corrected is appropriate. Green (1986) claims that there has been no diagnostic flexibility in respect of varying economic structures, diverse economic situations and causal patterns of imbalance. Killick (1989) has questioned the strategy in a similar way. Colclough and Green (1988, p. 2) point to the fact that lags between the use and effect of a policy instrument are almost always underestimated in these programmes. Moreover, "initial measures are typically adopted without adequate attention to identifying either optimal sequences or sequential interactions". So we have issues of phasing, lags and sequencing in determining the policy package given the diagnosed malaise and the stock of internal and external resources with which to meet it.

Second, the major practical weakness is that markets cannot be made to perform as policies intend. Certain inefficiencies require treatment other than laissez-faire macro-economic instruments, and for more than five or even ten years. Until this is done there is no guarantee that the weakening of some inefficiencies or biases will not provide room for others to expand into.

But beyond the diagnosis and the practicalities there loom questions about the ultimate objectives of adjustment. Streeten (1987) asks: "Adjustment to what? For what? Of what? By whom? And how?". The response from the orthodox side would be that adjustment policies are value free and objective. They aim to use mechanical policy instruments to rectify the national accounts. The development strategy of a government and the distribution of the burden of adjustment is not the province of immediate corrective adjustment policies. But this narrow interpretation does not answer Streeten's questions. Moreover, the value-free approach assumes that there can be only one policy-mix option for correction once the goal is defined, whereas in fact there are many. Each option incorporates, implicitly or explicitly, a set of value-weighted objectives and in the real world can bring about its own end result. Nor does the value-free approach ensure that economic efficiency is enhanced in all people's lives. As Streeten notes, the assumption that if only efficiency policies are pursued everyone will be better off in the long term, with occasional losses on the way, is false. Some can be consistent losers. People may be losers not only on the consumption and welfare side but also in terms of productive assets and skills. It is the economic effectiveness of people that this study is concerned with.

These comments introduce the links between adjustment programmes, on the one hand, and growth and equity, on the other. In what follows, the scope for viewing all phases of adjustment and growth simultaneously can be seen.

Countries whose primary resource sectors had been especially blighted by the common policy of an overvalued currency and protected capital-intensive industry are no longer only concerned with flushing out inefficiencies. In Nigeria, for instance, present macro-economic policies are intended to link manufacturing more solidly with primary production. This vertical linkage should supply an internal dynamic and develop new comparative advantages. Thus policies of economic transformation are beginning to accompany stabilisation and structural adjustment programmes.

Basically what is emerging in the new commentary on the long term is that there are alternative routes, and routes which have a better chance than the minimalist orthodox approach, to achieving lasting improvements in the external and internal balances on which to build a more viable economic order. At the macro level present lending conditionalities are too high and repayment periods too short. Relaxing them would permit attenuation of the adjustment process at the micro level, thereby giving producers room to move factors of production to new growth poles.

Governments' concern about where new growth or a new impetus for development is to come from has led to forms of intervention which amount to modification of stabilisation and structural adjustment strategies in order to include long-term transformation at the outset. As already mentioned, Kenya and Nigeria are now selecting adjustment policies which give greater prominence to small-scale manufacturing partly as a result of the sluggish response of large-scale, more capital-intensive industry.

But these sectoral shifts of attention do not comprise in themselves a strategy of growth and of developing new comparative advantages. For that there has to be a policy on promoting investments in factor productivities. It is difficult to see how this can be formulated without due regard to the special features of the factor of labour.

Alongside the reassessment of the strictly economic objectives of adjustment packages there has been intense concern about sharply falling standards of living, especially among those who are already poor. Much misery was caused by the early policy framework and its inappropriateness to achieve the targets of a rapid switching of resources to more profitable lines of production and a more efficient allocation of resources. Commentators have argued that, far from the poor being obstacles to the new economic efficiency, their mobilisation could actually contribute to it.

A small group of writers associated with UNICEF's *Adjustment with a human face* (1987) have argued a set of policies which enfranchise the poor in new economic structures on the grounds of "production not welfare" (Cornia et al., 1987). They point out that standard policy packages, through changing producer prices, have an impact mainly on restructuring production *between* sectors. To mobilise the resources of the weak requires restructuring *within* sectors. The new approach includes:

(a) more expansionary macro-level policies entailing a different timing of adjustment and more gradual correction of imbalances;

(b) meso policies (see below) designed to meet certain established priorities among the needs of the vulnerable and entailing prioritisation, selectivity, redistribution and restructuring, while holding to broader economic targets;

(c) sectoral policies to facilitate restructuring within productive sectors, resting on promoting opportunities and encouraging factor mobility; and

(d) compensatory programmes to protect health and living standards.

New allocatory practices under *(b)* and *(d)* are largely to do with the most effective investment in human resources within budgetary limits. However they are designed, the need for, and benefits of, the range of facilities offered are bound to be felt differently by women and men. Conversely, if it is thought desirable to invest in women's and men's productivities differently then the range of these facilities can be appropriately designed. The main arguments about the impact of gender on the efficacy of adjustment strategies (and, by extension, of growth strategies) lie with the workings of factor and product markets. Tackling the impediment of gender stratification of these markets should be one purpose of allocatory practices which can touch not only factor productivities but also institutional infrastructures. This introduces the idea of meso policies.

Meso policies have been described in different ways. They are designed to maintain the basic living standards of the poor as well as sustain conditions for growth (Cornia et al. 1987). Another description points out that macro variables can be associated with a variety of sectoral or micro implications which are called meso implications to distinguish them from both macro aggregates and micro projects (Stewart, 1987, p. 153):

> Generally, conventional adjustment packages take a broadly neutral view of meso implications, allowing them to occur as determined by the normal workings of the system. Adjustment which combines growth and the human dimension, in contrast, is predominantly concerned with meso implications.

Each meso policy is tailored to improving the impact of a given macro variable on the allocation of resources and/or the distribution of income, the better to achieve the priorities laid down.

Meso policies include the direction of credit, subsidies and taxes to priority uses (to improve the supply of certain goods from the public or private sector) or to priority target groups (to influence the pattern and level of demand). This type of meso policy uses financial instruments. But Stewart also sees meso policies in the form of institutional changes, including land reform, which advance the twin objectives of improving the efficiency of resource use and helping the poor to raise their incomes. These latter reforms change the terms on which people engage in economic activities. The main aim is to improve the bargaining position, or terms of trade, of those with relatively weak access to resources. Meso policies are intended to empower the poor to engage effectively in economic activities. Implicit in them is the assumption that empowering the poor will raise the overall level of efficiency in the economy. Depending on the package of meso policies and the selection of target groups, this should be true. But to design the package it is necessary to have some idea of how markets are rigged at present and what are the immediate constraints on the poor.

By stating that meso policies can be introduced within the set macro targets the implication is that they are cost free: the turnstiles in resource and product markets are just tinkered with so that pre-ordained resources flow in new channels. That may be so, but the question naturally arises: "If these meso policies are so effective, why should they not be allowed to influence the macro targets themselves?" If, for instance, credit to the poor provides a good return in terms of supply of goods, then there is a case for allowing this credit absorptive capacity to influence macro credit policy.

Meso policies have been seen as the means to combine growth and poverty eradication. If they allocate resources on the basis of where they have the highest potential for growth and poverty eradication, a natural reaction is to question whether these two objectives are always fortuitously compatible. Is there a trade-off somewhere? There is one obvious answer. There may be a trade-off, hidden or visible, but with numerous different possible resource allocations to achieve a sustained and high level of growth, who can be sure that one holds superior guarantees to all others? It should always be remembered that meso policies operate within laid-down macro targets. Since economies is not an exact science and predicted trajectories for the economy are never achieved, an approach to growth which emphasises empowering the poor to become more productive has as much claim to acceptance as any other. And empowering only men merely sets up a new set of distortions.

Women depend on meso policies to reduce the burden of their reproductive work and to make them effective actors in markets. There is nothing in the armoury of planners than can match the influence of meso policies in eliminating gender impediments to medium-term efficiency and longer-term growth.

Conclusion

This chapter described the reasons for planners' reassessment of earlier adjustment packages and indicated the kind of broader, more selective thinking that this had led to. There is now a wide-ranging debate over the primary issue of how to moderate or reshape the adjustment package to make allowance for obstructions to the eradication of internal and external imbalances and to growth. It is now some years since "just getting prices right" was exposed as a badly flawed approach to sustainable growth. Today the desire for finer tuning through a discerning sequencing and phasing of possible policy levers has ushered in a discussion on the subjects that should be reviewed in such improvement of the planning process. The way women's economic role and status, relative to men's, has an impact on the result of different adjustment packages is properly one of these subjects. What remains is to set out the way gender can affect the result of these packages and what are the implications for planners.

Gender in the published commentary on structural adjustment 8

General comments

The great bulk of articles and books on stabilisation and adjustment make no reference to gender, or women, in either their diagnosis of the economic malaise or their policy analysis. This is as much true of the writings of academia as of World Bank country papers. Jolly (1988) has offered the explanation that the economics of recession and adjustment have been tackled by economic and financial specialists within a traditional framework which makes no direct reference to the human situation of people. In other words, economics has been discussed at such a macro and aggregated level that it has been difficult to interject a class, let alone a gender, dimension.

But Jolly also suggests a further explanation for this lacuna which reflects on the women-in-development (WID) lobby. While issues relating to women have, in other contexts, received increasing attention and analysis, the particular hardships of the "lost decade" of the 1980s for women have been neglected. The problems of the 1980s have not appeared in studies of women in developing countries. What is more relevant and could justifiably have been pointed out was that these studies have rarely placed their analysis in the context of any policy environment, new or old, or of the economic problems of any decade.

The first exception of real note was the project "Development Alternatives with Women for a New Era (DAWN)" (Sen, 1985), written for the International Conference on the End of the Decade of Women in Nairobi. The author reviewed the possibility of women doing well in new employment in export agriculture and export-oriented industries created by adjustment policies, but also tackled the issue of basic needs particular to women and the concurrent cuts in social service expenditure. Yet it was only in 1987 with the publication of UNICEF's *Adjustment with a human face* that the particular impact of recession and adjustment on women entered the dialogue on adjustment, together with the first intimations of what might be done for the poor, especially women, without impairing the new economic strategy.

Although these early pointers have been taken up and recycled by others, many of the most telling analytic points that have been made anywhere were made in the UNICEF publication. Essentially the problem has been that the WID literature all along has described and analysed "what is" and what specific assistance women, as a separate interest group, need in order to be more productive, mindless of what else was occurring in the economy and what other claims on resources were being made. By the time stabilisation and structural adjustment arrived on the scene there was still no established means to "mainstream" gender issues in policy analysis and formation. The small body of seminar papers and notes that have circulated in the past 18 months have for the most part summarised the likely or actual effects on women. In this respect Elson (1987) has been careful to distinguish between women in different parts of the economy. Some women will gain in terms of employment and income from the end of certain subsidies and the development of the market; others will lose. The contraction of the State's role will also have a mixed effect on women. Certain actions of the State have perpetuated women's subordination while others have aided women.

There is one other introductory point to make about the commentary on adjustment. Gender issues have mostly been expressed in terms general to all developing countries. This global approach to gender issues is partly due to the universality of the way that economic upheaval and worsened poverty impinge on women's multiple roles in delivering sustenance to their families and partly because the evidence of the impact of the new policies on women tends to be anecdotal with continental cross-references. Some of the speculation about the effects on women is obviously made with Asian and Latin American situations in mind. The notable exception to this generality is the treatment of women and adjustment in agriculture. Typical situations of women in sub-Saharan African agriculture are used as reference points again and again in the commentary, particularly when likely effects of adjustment policies are mentioned, sometimes to the exclusion of references to women farmers in other regions. There are two plausible explanations for this: *(a)* more has been written in the WID literature on women's roles in agriculture in sub-Saharan Africa than in any other region, and *(b)* the food crisis in Africa has given a high profile to women because of their dominant role in African food production.

The emphasis on consumption and welfare

The impact of stabilisation and adjustment programmes on consumption levels quickly became apparent in a number of countries. The reductions in real incomes from loss of work or frozen wages and from the steep rise in prices of essential consumer goods have been undoubtedly severe. It is true that living standards had already fallen during the economic decline which necessitated these radical strategies. But it is the abrupt harshness and the particular inequitable distributional effects of the economic remedies which have caused so much concern. Health surveys have produced some alarming data on increases in child malnutrition and mortality. Other social indicators have supplied widespread supportive evidence of a serious slippage in welfare, and at the same time as demand for social services is increasing social sector budgets are being cut.

UNICEF's role in sounding the alarm bells and arguing for a more merciful passage of stabilisation and structural adjustment finally gave the cue to those in the WID lobby. A great deal of the commentary on gender and adjustment can be reduced to the depiction of women as a particularly vulnerable group in the face of declining real incomes and public sector supports. They bear the brunt of falling living standards because they have majority responsibility for ultimately delivering sustenance and care to the family. This means that it is mainly up to them to find compensatory means to uphold consumption and welfare. The household budget, or that part of total household income that women have access to, has to be eked out more carefully. More time has to be spent on finding the best bargains, or cash expenditure has to be displaced as far as possible by substituting an additional female labour input such as walking farther distances for fire-wood or cooking in a different way. But whatever women do their labour cannot substitute completely for money, food and health services. And when ill health strikes in the family women have to spend more time on yet one more of their occupations. On top of this, as several writers properly point out, intra-household distribution of income and food aggravates the situation for the least empowered members of the household, namely women and children. Not all household income is pooled and allocated in a rational welfare way. And the irrationality can increase as income declines. The argument here is essentially that husbands and fathers transfer only part of their income to the household budget. When men's income declines they do not necessarily transfer higher proportions of it to the active household budget dispensed by women. It is a fair conclusion that in these circumstances women's front-line role in family welfare places them under greater personal stress.

This explains the two themes which run repeatedly through all the written material, and which do much to characterise the commentary on the impact of adjustment on women. (See, for instance, Joekes, 1988; Joekes et al., 1988; Elson, 1987.) The first is the greater work burden and more severe time constraints imposed on women. The second is the importance of intra-household income (and sometimes resource) distribution. Both are mostly discussed in relation to women as consumers and upholders of welfare. But they have also been mentioned in relation to women as producers in the case of peasant agriculture because they have a potentially profound effect on women's production incentives. Indeed, this applies to women in any family-based enterprise.

The Commonwealth Secretariat's *Engendering adjustment for the 1990s* (1989) places the points variously made in other publications in the logical order of describing women's roles, the impact that adjustment has had on them and what attempts have been made (in the context of adjustment and in general) to help women. But apart from a few very succinct pages on women's gains and losses in employment, their weakly felt agricultural price incentives and inferior access to resources, and a listing of some desirable interventions in infrastructure and markets which lend substance to the publication's references to women's production potential, the report focuses on the non-economic roles of women and on their welfare and well-being.

The notion of women being responsible for the reproduction and maintenance of the family (or the social and economic rearing of children) is given repeated emphasis in the written commentary. If there has been a common framework for analysing the impact of adjustment policies on women, it comprises the listing of the main occupations of women—producers/earners, providers of goods and services of immediate use value, consumers/budgeters and child carers—and a study of changed conditions in each of these occupations. The approach of the Commonwealth Secretariat's report is a little different. Women's roles, contributions and situations are discussed under women as *(a)* producers, *(b)* home managers, *(c)* mothers, and *(d)* community organisers, and this categorisation is used as the basis for an explanation of the impact of adjustment on women. It is not easy to see the reason for separating home managers and mothers, unless it is to view women's burden of allocating a smaller real economic wage (home management) differently from the consequences of eroded public provision of education and health (mothering). But the latter is also shown to impose budget management problems when women are forced, as depicted in the report, to decide whether to pay new school fees or put children to contributory work.

In all the literature so far, majority attention has been on women's unremunerated and invisible work.

Poverty alleviation measures and meso policies

There is a noticeable tension in the commentaries between the impact of adjustment on women and the impact of women's activities on the adjustment process. This is nowhere more in evidence than in *Engendering adjustment for the 1990s.* In places the report seems poised to develop arguments about the economic and demographic costs of ignoring women's other roles, but then it reverts to lengthy commentary on welfare. In addition, while pertinent references are made to the importance of women's access to resources for incentives in agriculture to work, on balance the report does not relate support for women to the success of adjustment programmes or demonstrate how it is a necessary ingredient to sustainable growth. In fact, it rounds up the analysis with a section on "structural adjustment and women's well-being". There is a danger that policy-makers will see this kind of engendering of adjustment as a plea for social sector expenditure to make women's lives more tolerable.

The tension between the impact of adjustment on women and the impact of women on adjustment is similar to that between the need for poverty alleviation measures, on the one hand, and the need for the adjustment package to include measures to empower the poor to make an economically efficient contribution to adjustment, on the other. The former measures have been called fire-brigade actions which pick up the human casualties of an adjustment strategy. These measures include employment creation schemes not closely related to the main economic strategy, or compensatory schemes on the social sector budget. But it is the latter which give credence to the case for there being more than one path to successful stabilisation and adjustment, and that respectable economic arguments of long-term release of resources from inefficient use, creation of valuable external economies, more effective competition for resources and altering existing comparative advantages, can be mounted in support of gentler and more prolonged, but still economically effective, paths.

Two interesting things emerge from this. Both could be turned to resolve the tension mentioned above. The first is the focus on investment in human resources, and the second is the nature and direction of very recent or impending research surveys on household income and expenditure.

No publication puts the economic case for investment in human resources better than *Adjustment with a human face*. Indeed, some of the other writings cited here give it only tangential or implicit recognition. Planners implicitly assume that greater economic effort can be expected from women while government expenditure on water, sewerage, health services and local communications is being reduced, causing women to spend more time, or not being able to reduce time spent, on providing goods and services of immediate use value to their families.

Elson has placed the possible consequences of this in focus for economists. She warns of what could happen to policy objectives if it were assumed that unpaid tasks by women would continue regardless of the way resources are reallocated (1987). Elson is concerned that a breaking-point could be reached or a collapse of women's capacity could occur as a result of "gender neutral" policies. One of her most telling points is that what planners might see as higher productivity or efficiency is in fact a shift of costs from the paid to the unpaid economy. It is but a short step from this to ask: Which resources' allocative efficiency are adjustment policies concerned with? In later, as yet unpublished papers, Elson goes further by taking up the theme of a gender bias in macro-economic policies due to the limited range of resource allocation distortions so far considered in economic analysis.

The expert group on women attached to the Development Advisory Committee of the OECD states the same point in a different way. "There are important cultural and socio-legal barriers to the effective expansion of women's economic activities in many sectors of national economies. This will directly hinder the efficiency of the factor shifts implicit in the process of economic adjustment" (1988, p. 5).

This interdependence of economic and social sectors leads to the need to invest in human resources. Social sector policies influence economic performance through the level of investment in human resources. Because of additional demands made on women's time, particular support services and investments for them are necessary if they are to contribute to economic growth. Implicit in this are two things: capitalising women's work processes to raise the productivity per unit of their labour time, and the provision of external economies from resources above the household level.

There are some loose ends in the arguments. Assumptions are made that improved human stamina translates into higher labour productivity, and that investment in displacement of unpaid drudgery will transfer labour time to activities which offer an economic return. The validity of these assumptions may depend on other policies, affecting individuals' opportunities and incentives, being in place. But that investment in human (particularly female human) resources is a crucial ingredient of the "package" of policies cannot be doubted.

One of the most valuable contributions of *Adjustment with a human face* is the discussion of meso policies (Stewart, 1987), which were referred to in the previous chapter. Meso policies have been described as the selection and directing of resources to fulfil priorities in meeting the needs of vulnerable groups and promoting economic growth. Many such policies are essentially about opening up factor and product markets to the influences of equity and efficiency. Therefore the framework of the interaction between macro and meso policies helps to make the gender dimension explicable to policy-makers who wish to put a more sensitive package of policies together.

The World Bank/UNDP Social Dimensions of Adjustment Programme in Africa has taken up these ideas. The programme is a package of activities with a core of strengthening the poor in order that they can share in the benefits of structural adjustment when they come. There has been debate in World Bank/UNDP circles as to how poverty alleviation measures can be combined with this objective.

Formal sector employment

The relevance of tracing relative changes in women's and men's employment in the formal sector rests with the implications that these changes hold for the wage labour market and especially for the supply of labour for gender-typed employment in the informal sector.

The immediate effects of demand management and trade reforms are usually found in the formal sector. All commentators agree that the formal sector is badly hit, at least in the short term, by demand management and market liberalisation, and all the gender-focused literature leaves it an open question how women are affected relative to men. It is obvious that the outcome depends on the gender division of employment by industry and occupation. None of the literature so far has included an examination of data, disaggregated by industry and gender, for a particular country. Instead a generalisation is put forward in the form of a list of points to look out for.

The threat to public sector employment from budget cuts is a common theme. The public sector has consciously been a leader in adopting the kind of labour legislation which offers particular benefits to women. Women have enjoyed minimum wage legislation and job security provided in this sector in the past. Elson (1987) makes the valuable point that the public sector has provided more jobs and job security for skilled and professional women than the private sector. It is feared that the typical policies of freezing the numbers employed or cutting costs could threaten women's employment especially. Moreover, if fiscal retrenchment induces more severe cuts in the public sector than foreign and domestic market liberalisation induces in the private formal sector, then women could lose out disproportionately in terms of access to both employment and relatively high wages (Joekes et al., 1988).

The essential economic ingredients of a change in employment conditions are that tradables will enjoy direct price incentives but that a product with a high import content will suffer reduced net incentive because of a simultaneous rise in costs. In addition, fiscal and monetary retrenchment will deflate demand through the negative action of the employment and income multipliers.

There is an implicit assumption in some of the material on gender and adjustment that import-substituting industry would suffer more or gain less than export-oriented industry. Women's employment will suffer along with men's in the decline in production for the domestic market. However, women are likely to benefit more than men from a successful expansion of export-oriented industries because their presence here is often dominant (Sen, 1985). Nevertheless, as pointed out earlier, which subsector of industry gains or loses depends on changes in protective tariff levels, different degrees of import content and the extent of domestic demand contraction. Fast conclusions, even per product, cannot be drawn. For instance, in one country the textile industry might be import substituting, with or without a high import content, and in another country partly export oriented, with or without a high import content. Therefore even if the gender division of employment by industry or occupation were the same in all countries (which it is certainly not), the relative impacts on women and men would be influenced by how each industry stands in relation to domestic markets and foreign trade regimes. Anything beyond generalities will have to emerge from country cases.

Export processing zones (EPZs) are often given a mention because wages tend to be higher in them and women workers are frequently in the majority. EPZs often have a high import content, but also privileged access to foreign exchange. However, they are more typical of other regions of the world than of Africa.

Despite the difficulties of trying to predict the relative impact on women's and men's employment, some noteworthy observations have been made. There may be a shift in the age or gender composition of employment as a consequence of generally declining employment opportunities. Joekes (1988) points out that rising unemployment means that all workers now show greater commitment to their jobs. Where previously men and younger women might not have accepted low pay and onerous conditions, now employers lose no advantage in employing them. It has also been suggested that where there is a high import content this may lead to reduced wages rather than reduced numbers of employed workers. If this were true then it could be said that, in an area of mainly male employment, numbers will generally be maintained, but wages reduced. It is interesting to note that both Joekes and Jolly mention a more rapid rise in open unemployment of women than men in reference to some Latin American countries. Jolly refers to a widening of "the rift of occupational segregation", and Joekes to the fact that declining men's wages means that more women are actively seeking work and therefore are in the labour force. However, this is a case of economic contraction leading to an increase in the female labour force rather than a fall in women's employment.

With it being generally more difficult to find a job in the formal sector during stabilisation and adjustment, it may be that women face bigger obstacles than men in finding a new job. Men are now more committed to a job, and not all the protective employment legislation applies to them. Joekes reports that there is some evidence that "once women lose a job in the formal sector they are less likely than men to gain another". The risk appears to be greatest, moreover, for female heads of household. The alternative to trying to make a re-entry into the formal sector is to try to find a niche in the informal sector. However, there are conflicting opinions about the opportunities for this during the adjustment process.

Employment in the informal sector

The debate on the outcome of adjustment policies for the informal sector can be reduced to different views on:

(a) the impact of reduced real demand in the economy via both income and price substitution effects (bearing in mind that the informal sector often supplies cheaper and inferior quality close substitutes of formal sector goods);

(b) the share of tradables among informal sector goods and the direct effect of devaluation and foreign trade reforms on domestic demand for them; and

(c) how far market deregulation measures remove obstacles to fairer competition between the informal and formal sectors.

The knock-on effect of reduced activity and incomes in both formal manufacturing and the public sector could affect the informal sector disproportionately. Part of this sector supplies goods and services to formal sector enterprises and to their employees. Reduced real income or lower employment participation rates in the formal sector will reduce demand for these goods. There are, of course, also parts of the informal sector which will be directly affected by devaluation and tariff reform.

Women are not usually more numerous than men in the informal sector. However, female participation rates are much higher in the informal sector than the formal sector. The ease of entry, flexible working conditions and, in the case of the self-employed, small initial capital requirements, help to explain why women, especially female heads of household, are more strongly represented in this sector than in the formal sector. Moreover, it is precisely falls in low-income purchasing power that affect particularly the women in the informal sector. Supplying cheap garments and snacks, for instance, to the low-income formal sector workforce is typically a woman's informal sector activity. But falls in high-income purchasing power can also affect informal sector services. Reduced earnings of professional women, or their loss of jobs, will, in turn, reduce demand for female domestic servants and child carers.

The references to gender in the commentary on the impact of stabilisation and adjustment on the informal sector are sometimes confusing, particularly over service employment. It is not always clear whether it is the formal or informal sector that is under consideration. Jolly (1988), seemingly referring to the formal sector, states that demand for labour in services has often suffered less than that in manufacturing industries, and even that income-generating women's employment in the informal sector has often grown. Sen (1985) argues that reduced demand for many goods will lead to a switch to the cheaper products of the informal sector and therefore that women's employment may increase with structural adjustment, but under the negative conditions of that sector. Joekes, on the other hand, argues that "because adjustment measures increase the profitability and production of tradables versus non-tradables, they discriminate against services . . . Since women tend to be heavily concentrated in services, there may be a negative effect on their employment opportunities and/or wages" (1988, pp. 27-28). Elson seems to agree with Jolly but on the grounds that women's resourcefulness in survival strategies will involve them more in the informal sector. This last seems to be the most plausible explanation. There is cumulative evidence that women's participation in the informal sector has increased in the past decade. Yet there must have been a contraction of demand for its goods and services in aggregate unless there has been a price substitution effect shifting demand to inferior products. In the absence of hard information to the contrary, this crowded sector must have become even more crowded. Labour productivity and average earnings must be even lower than before. This says nothing about the effect of changes in price relatives on the composition of goods and services.

Overall it is fair to say that the nearest that the commentary on stabilisation and adjustment gets to gender issues in the response of the formal and informal sectors is to deduce speculatively how women's employment and earnings will be affected. There is almost nothing about relative changes in women's and men's employment. It has been said that women's enterprises in the informal sector are on a smaller scale, less capitalised and therefore of lower productivity than men's. Gender aspects of the short-term and longer-term adaptability of the labour and capital markets, which (meso) policy-makers might seek to influence, are not raised.

Agriculture

Not only is the commentary on gender in structural adjustment most extensive for the agricultural sector, but for this sector it is also most specific to African contexts. This is the sector which is alleged to benefit clearly from price incentives and market deregulation, and to act as a new engine of growth to the whole economy. Yet Jolly can write ". . . although increasing attention has been given to agriculture in adjustment policies, it is far from clear that women have gained much, or at all, in the process". The reasons are twofold and are echoed in one way or another by other commentators. First, simultaneous increases in both food and cash crop production are likely to increase the work burden of women. Second, cash crop income is likely to accrue to men. There is, therefore, a massive contradiction at the heart of the macro policies directed at the agricultural sector.

References to the problem of competition for resources within peasant households are usually made at an abstract level. For instance, a close analysis of the adjustment experience in Malawi drew the following conclusion:

> With the benefit of hindsight, the objectives of rapidly increased peasant exports and of food self-sufficiency appear excessively ambitious, probably not jointly achievable in the short term. The short-term aggregate supply response to price of Malawi's peasant agriculture is likely to be positive, but not at the high magnitude which would have been necessary to bring about the result sought by the Bank's planners (Kydd and Hewitt, 1986).

Elson moves closer to what this competition imposes on the farm household. "While there is evidence that rural producers do switch from one crop to another in response to changing relative prices, it is far less clear that they will be able to increase output of a wide range of crops in response to a general increase in crop prices" (Elson, 1987, p. 20). She goes on to include a gender dimension by stating what it means at the micro level for women's choices of labour deployment. "There is a limit to the extent to which women can switch from human resource production and maintenance to crop production . . . children will not be left unattended because another crop becomes more profitable". This point made by Elson, and others, about women's labour time is a crucial issue. What is worrying is that so much other general commentary on structural adjustment stresses the importance of research on packages of higher-yielding crops and accompanying chemicals for small-scale farmers, yet higher-yielding crops and chemicals will raise land productivity only if more labour inputs, notably female labour inputs, can be applied. Rarely is labour technology mentioned in World Bank and government documents on structural adjustment, and even then sometimes only technology for land preparation. There is an implicit assumption that more labour time can be squeezed out of women for the more labour-intensive practices which result from these increases in (potential) land productivity.

In the gender-specific commentary the portrayal of women's work covering self-provisioning activities, cash crop production and wage labour precedes the impact of selective increases in cash crop prices on demand for women's labour. The common viewpoint is that women will be asked to work more hours on cash crops. With women's labour time limited, the claimed outcome of the impact of adjustment (that is, a change in producer prices) is therefore either a fall in food output or what Joekes calls compensating labour strategies, specifically the greater involvement of schoolchildren (especially girls). If some food production is forgone this could threaten family welfare. The diversion of women's labour resources thus has implications for national food security and, therefore, the long-term success of structural adjustment. This extra burden also comes at a time when there are fiscal retrenchment and public expenditure cuts to health services and water supplies. This makes it even more difficult for women to redeploy some of their time towards more cash crop production. The logic of the argument is that public expenditure on enabling services for women provides an external economy, or a complementary resource, to the supply response to price incentives. This is the *raison d'être* behind some of what UNICEF calls "meso policies".

The World Bank is well aware of these arguments. When identifying supply-side issues of the response of agriculture to adjustment policies in sub-Saharan Africa it emphasised the biases in services against women farmers (World Bank, 1989, p. 74). It also saw that productivity improvements were linked to reducing demands on women's time.

At a theoretical level, economics would decree that profit from cash crops would be invested in means to reduce this damaging competition for women's time. The small body of literature under review gives absolutely no consideration to this because of the second major determinant of both the impact of structural adjustment on farming women and the impact of women's roles in agriculture on structural adjustment. This is the influence of intra-household distribution of cash income. Even if women had some slack labour capacity, they might not be willing to work more on cash crops because this work is not remunerated (or there is an unsatisfactory amount of "transfer income" from cash crop revenue made available for expenditure on household maintenance). So little transfer income might be forthcoming that women (and the family) might be worse off than before the price incentives because less time is now spent on self-provisioning. Women's refusal to be redeployed to unremunerated work on export crops weakens the efficacy of price incentives for export production. In Mali, for instance, women refused to grind the increase in men's maize output because they saw no return and had to give up some self-provisioning work to do it (Joekes et al., 1988). Even where there is nothing to prevent a woman shifting resources ostensibly under her control to better-priced cash crops, she might refrain from doing this because she fears she will lose control of the market transaction and consequent income. Thus "... in Zambia the high price of maize (a man's crop) led many men to increase the size of land planted with maize, but their wives continued to cultivate groundnuts, despite its heavier labour requirements, because they could sell it on the informal market and control the resulting income" (Commonwealth Secretariat, 1989, p. 59).

Alternative sources of cash income to farm women are agricultural wage work and the sale of food surpluses. There is broadly negative comment on the benefits to women of the impact of structural adjustment on wage income. There might be an increase in employment (Elson, 1987), but nominal wages would have to be devalued by the price increases in food and consumer manufactures resulting from devaluation and price decontrol (Joekes et al., 1988). As a result women may see wage labour as too risky and choose to remain in low-productivity self-provisioning agriculture to underwrite the survival of their families. The handling of agricultural wage work in the commentaries is surprisingly cursory. Larger farms are bound to benefit from price increases and it is difficult to see how women would actually lose from a more active female rural labour market. The main disadvantage of wage labouring would probably be loss of income from sale of food surpluses. But this loss has to be set against wages gained.

The marketability of food surpluses might be affected (negatively) by contracting demand or (positively) by market deregulation (as reported from Senegal and Zaire). Credit deregulation is also seen as a possible gain to women in that it should release more credit supplies. More plausibly, however, it will have no effect on women without major institutional reform governing access.

There are, on balance, real grounds for fearing that women's access to household income and enabling resources from the public sector is weakened by the usual adjustment packages. It is not obvious where the resources to capitalise women's production methods will come from. More than one writer concludes that women will remain in low-productivity agriculture and that this will lead to problems of supply response to adjustment measures and doubt over the long-term success of the strategy. Certainly there are reasons to suppose that adjustment will turn the terms of labour exchange and other trade against women farmers. Reversing the urban bias to increase efficiency in the economy is a major plank of structural adjustment. Reversing the gender bias has not yet reached the agenda.

There are two major omissions in the commentary. The first is the impact of structural adjustment programmes on women's access to land. The general literature on structural adjustment in agriculture (particularly World Bank documents but also some academic material) refers frequently to the need for reform in land tenure. The argument that security of tenure is required to encourage private investment in land is well known. But there is no mention of a gender division of leasehold or of secure usufructuary rights. When land reform or land adjudication is mentioned as one element of structural adjustment, there is never any following comment on what this will do for women's incentive to invest in higher productivity. The issue of women's security of tenure does not seem to have been raised at all in the commentary, except by Sen (1985) and, briefly, Longhurst (1987). In the other papers that focus on gender, or women, the closest references to land are to "women's access to resources", and this often in the middle of a discussion of intra-household income distribution.

The second omission is the impact on women's own-account farming. The implicit model of the material reviewed here is one of women's food production with a little sale on the side, otherwise labouring on husbands' crops for uncertain returns. This is a model common in eastern and southern Africa. Elsewhere the situation is different, with women sometimes growing tradables (or quasi-tradables) on their own account.

A third omission should be mentioned. There is a complete silence on women household heads as farmers, producers and earners, except for a brief mention in *Adjustment with a human face* (Longhurst and Cornia, respectively).

Strategic and practical gender needs

Following this short review of how gender issues, or rather women's interests, are perceived to be affected by adjustment strategies and the introduction of new policy concepts, it is of interest to end this chapter by referring to a pithy exposition of women's policy needs. Moser (1989) delineates "strategic gender needs" (to overcome women's domestic handicaps and structured gender discrimination) and "practical gender needs" (a response to an immediate perceived necessity which does not challenge prevailing forms of subordination). The first represents a sea change in women's command over resources. The second merely allows women to cope better in a continuing situation. The welfare approach caters to practical gender needs.

Although Moser declines to go so far, there is much in the concept of strategic gender needs that is relevant to achieving market efficiency and the elimination of biases. But strategic gender needs must penetrate beyond markets. All resources, not just those in market exchange, must be properly costed and their utilisation rationalised. The question is, does structural adjustment do this, or does it exclude a huge subsector of resource absorption? Moser cautions that the efficiency approach (read structural adjustment approach) to development need not improve the condition of women. It may simply amount to a shifting of costs from the paid to the unpaid economy, through further exploitation of women's reproductive work.

It is precisely this point which questions whether adjustment programmes, as presently conceived, can empower female human resources to participate in new opportunities and causes apprehension over the long-term population implications of the new strategy.

Implications of the theoretical framework for the economic success of adjustment programmes

9

In this chapter we are concerned with the relevance of gender constructs in markets to the outcome of the adjustment strategy in terms of changes in material production. The validity of planners' expectations of supply responses will be examined from the viewpoint of gender issues framed in previous chapters.

It will be helpful to recapitulate briefly the main contradiction that has arisen in practice. The basic weakness of stabilisation policies is the difficulty of reducing demand without reducing supply as much or more, thereby accelerating economic decline without influencing inflation. In this situation market liberalisation will be less effective. Structural adjustment has its own set of difficulties. The root of the problem is the weakness of supply response. Assumptions about the workings of domestic factor and product markets have proved optimistic. Optimism has also surrounded investment in higher productivities whose prioritisation would be signalled by the movement of prices in liberated markets. Part of all this optimism relates to the past implicit assumption that gender is irrelevant to the outcome of adjustment strategies.

Because this study is focused on the outcome of adjustment in terms of sustainable economic growth this chapter is devoted to the agricultural, manufacturing and directly productive services. The civil service, teaching and medicine are, of course, facilitators to this growth. But as facilitators the result of their influence is not normally felt over the short to medium term. Reference to their relevance to supporting and further developing resources for these main economic sectors will be made, particularly from the viewpoint of long-term moderation of gender inefficiencies. The primary concern is whether agriculture, manufacturing and services, which have to return a net monetised profit from market operations in order to continue, can deliver the goods on which all else, notably funding government services, depends.

Agriculture, on the one hand, and manufacturing and services, on the other, are discussed separately.

Responses of the farming sector

Chapter 1 mentioned that this study set out to gain recognition for gender-based distortions, at both above and below the farm household level, in the appraisal of adjustment strategies.

The response of farmers is determined by the net effect of felt incentives and supply possibilities.

Felt incentives through prices and purchasing power

There are three aspects of incentives to consider: first, incentives from new prices and improved market outlets; second, the strength of alternative sources of income currently pursued; and, third, new real purchasing power and new opportunities to exchange cash income for desired goods. To be fully operative these incentives have to be felt by individuals, that is women as well as men, otherwise the effectiveness of policies will be weakened. With so few material incentives directed to women in the past, the latent response has been largely uptapped. Few now doubt women's appreciation of personal disposable cash income, as well as social sector investments in their immediate environment that particularly help them. That they have done so well in the market-place on so little assistance attests their desire to gain from specialisation and exchange. There can be little doubt that the developmental returns to opening up markets to them and giving them more equal access to all necessary resources should be substantial.

Taking the first aspect, of price changes, devaluation and market liberalisation will have a direct effect on export crops and crops that have been on the import bill. The theory of stabilisation and adjustment heralds significant price increases for these crops. The practice has often been in the order of 50–80 per cent devaluation. Locally marketed foods, surrogates for non-tradables or even tradables, are unlikely to experience the same price increases. Chapter 3 supplied illustrations of the great variety of crop mixes in women's and men's own-account farming, for both own consumption and sale. There will be situations where women's own-account crops that constitute tradables will enjoy price increases, while those of men's crops which are locally traded will not. Notwithstanding, the balance must be that all other things being constant, there will be greater encouragement to increase the output of men's production accounting units. It is widely the case that where foods are considered prestigious they are grown by men. In addition, the leading tradables, as distinct from the potential or surrogate tradables, are very largely managed by men. However, there are several reasons why the net outcome of relative incentives is unpredictable.

Women and men may produce the same "tradable" from their respective accounting units, but sell it in different markets. In this case they will experience different price changes. For example, female farmers have mostly sold their surpluses of staples—such as maize or rice which are also exported or imported—in local or district markets, or to small traders at the farm gate. Prices received have, therefore, always been subject to free market forces, albeit in confined zones and under monopsonistic conditions. If national marketing structures were improved sufficiently to integrate local and national markets these prices would gain directly from devaluation and price liberalisation. In the short term, or even medium term, this is unlikely to be the case without investment in the rehabilitation of the infrastructure and an extension of co-operative and parastatal clientele to women—or a successful entry of private traders. In some countries co-operatives and parastatals do accept produce directly from women, but this is far from being universal.

At such time as the private sector is capable of purchasing the main crops that were once the monopoly of parastatals, female farmers should gain because private traders do not discriminate among sellers other than for reasons of profitability. But a private trading sector cannot be created, or resurrected, in a short period. Realistically, the new price incentives will arrive well ahead of the unification of local and "foreign sector" markets. To the extent that this argument is valid women's output, be it of the same crop as men's, will not receive the same price incentive. Felt incentives will be different because of the continued differentiated market.

But there are difficulties of reaching even male farmers with new prices. The physical and institutional infrastructures might be so run down that devaluation and release of urban prices do not reach the farm gate at all. In the past male farmers have been much more affected than female farmers by official market outlets which freighted export crops to ports and staple foods to deficit or urban areas. It is these outlets that ought to enjoy new price signals. However, one obstacle commonly found during structural adjustment is that official marketing structures suffer a new liquidity squeeze (the phasing out of subsidies) and are unable to buy, transport and store their usual procurements at higher prices. In this case either part of the crop rots or the price increases that are experienced are smaller than expected.

Women who do not raise crops that have ever been traded externally may still experience derived price incentives through cross-substitution price and income effects. Because of these effects there may be said to be "surrogate" tradables. When they enjoy a clear price increase, this has to be at the expense of a more moderate price increase of the usual tradables. Frequently comprising secondary staples or different qualities of main staples, they can represent a significant part of women's crop portfolio.

A further reason why the shift in relative profitability to men's farming might not be so great is that in better times male farmers enjoyed subsidised credit and fertilisers. In some countries they might have continued to receive these benefits for strategic export crops during the years of economic decline. Female farmers, on the other hand, have not generally been direct recipients of subsidised inputs, which have normally been obtained by farmers through marketing boards and co-operatives that have not directly addressed women's agricultural accounting units. Women have generally obtained credit in the private rural market and physical inputs from local stockists, usually at free market prices, although use made of these inputs has been very small. The withdrawal of subsidies should not then change the calculations of their accounting units.

Given the many different combinations of common and separate fields in the household, the new prices that do get transmitted through parastatals are bound to make resources under the control of men more profitable notwithstanding the mitigating influence of cross-substitution effects and withdrawal of subsidies. Women receive no direct incentive, only an indirect one dependent on husbands corporately sharing additional income. If women feel this is quite tenuous, they may experience no incentive at all.

What all this means is that new producer prices will be experienced directly or indirectly for a wide range of crops. There will be a mosaic of felt incentives by crop. But so long as there are market imperfections this mosaic will not lead to the goal of allocative efficiency. One major imperfection is gender based.

The second aspect of felt incentives includes how individuals experience new real purchasing power. There is a dimension to the gender division of this felt incentive which could be affected by the redeployment of household resources as a consequence of price changes. Any fall in the profitability of women's farming relative to men's raises the question of the insecurity of women's own-account farming. Should the balance of profitability tip strongly in favour of men's crops, women's usufructuary rights to land could be jeopardised. Just as worsening rural-urban terms of trade reduced the real purchasing power of farmers, so worsening terms of trade for women in labour and other exchanges with men within the household could reduce women's real personal disposable income. But if, at the same time, much greater profitability of large commercial farming encouraged an increase in demand for wage labour, women would have alternatives other than working more on their husbands' land for uncertain returns.

In Chapter 3 some indication was given of the other gainful activities of farming women. The economic opportunity cost of women's farming is rarely zero or near zero. But these activities are not only valued for their returns relative to own or joint family farming; the income from them is more assuredly under the control of women. Women may seek to retain these other gainful activities in the face of improved agricultural prices because of the risks of losing control of resources or returns to labour they perceive as emanating from exploiting new agricultural profitability. The nature of these risks is outlined below. But what needs to be understood is that farming women may feel that their maximising position is unaltered by price changes because responding to those price changes would worsen the gender terms of trade in resources and income within the household. Clearly this does not represent the most efficient use of resources in economists' terms, but it is the most efficient survival strategy from women's viewpoint. This has even more serious implications for longer-term transformation because the desired realignments of agriculture and new comparative advantages, which would involve heavy commitment of resources, could be utterly frustrated.

Intra-household distribution of resources, including income, has been raised repeatedly in the literature on gender and adjustment. Its significance for planners is that it affects incentives, especially when the employment market beyond the household signals an economic opportunity cost to women of working on their husbands' or "household" land. Structural adjustment programmes can be expected to increase the socio-economic stratification of farm households and, with that, to expand the agricultural wage market. Farming wives will, increasingly, "have somewhere else to go". If they do go, smallholders' main cash cropping will no longer enjoy what is effectively a family labour force subsidised by women. The very survival of the smallholder sector may be at stake if women do not share equitably in the direct farming incentives of adjustment programmes. What could be done to secure their incentives belongs under supply possibilities because it relates to securing them high productivity, and professionalised own-account farming with control over resources.

Another dimension of this second aspect of felt incentives was raised in Chapter 7. The immediate availability of consumer goods, especially if inflation is a reality or an expectation, is the *raison d'être* for striving for higher earnings. But a first question is: "Whose consumer goods incentives are we talking about?"

One interesting feature of the illustration of lack of consumer goods incentives taken from the United Republic of Tanzania is that the argument was phased around coffee production, a likely candidate for male control of earnings. Maize production, on the other hand, did see a significant response in that country. Part of the maize output was traded locally, with women no doubt having an active financial role. The essential consumer goods that women purchase may not depend so much on availability of foreign exchange but might be quite easily produced from local raw materials. Cloth, for instance, might be especially favoured by women, while semi- or non-essentials might be a relative priority with men. The image in the literature of the peasant demanding imported consumer goods does not fit so well with peasant women. The expenditure pattern from maize income could be quite different from the expenditure pattern from coffee earnings. Which consumer goods are still available in rural areas and for how long should influence the felt incentives of women and men, respectively.

Supply possibilities

The implicit assumption made about the beneficial impact of increases in producer prices is that small farmers' supply is price elastic. Leaving aside the land question for the moment, this elasticity depends on farmers' ability to mobilise variable factors of production. This has led to much debate about the period required by farmers to mobilise for greater output, and what prerequisites were unavoidable. Any conclusion would have to draw heavily on a gender analysis.

There are basically three ways to increase output. The first assumes that there is current capacity which is brought into production when demand (that is price) increases, essentially a Keynesian unemployment situation. This is the shortest term response. But a condition of its plausibility is that either *(a)* there is idle capacity of all necessary complementary factors of production, or *(b)* the factors with idle capacity can be put to work without increases in the use of already fully employed factors.

The second means to increase output is by mobility of the existing stock of currently fully employed factors of production between uses. The third, improvements in productivity, has received most attention but requires a gestation period.

In exploring gender issues of the first way to increase output, a useful approach is to ask the questions: "Which factors of production at the household level are currently unemployed or underemployed?" and "What are the possibilities of technical substitution between them and the fully employed factors?"

Land is not generally regarded as lying idle (apart from necessary fallow periods in a shifting cultivation cycle). However, unused land is a characteristic of female-headed farms. Land requires labour to be applied to it to yield output and, as we have noted, women in these farming households need a significant increase in farm profitability to persuade them against off-farm work. Moreover, the crops they usually grow are unlikely to benefit directly from price incentives arising from devaluation. In the cases where tradables are cultivated, some extra attention to these households may be necessary to reap a good outcome from price adjustments. Otherwise, land in these households may remain unused.

Is there idle labour capacity? If there is, could it be applied to good effect on yields, through more careful cultivation practices without the need for complementary factors? If there is not, what can a medium-term adjustment programme expect to activate? If the answer is nothing, everything must wait upon investments in productivities, which often have a gestation period.

The agricultural timetable and the gender issue of labour must be brought into any analysis of idle labour capacity. Labour is demanded in different amounts at different times of the year. There is certainly excess capacity of men's labour in certain periods. In off-peak periods women find they can reduce their total "double day" to a moderate six to eight hours of not much more than household-associated work (including fetching water and fuel). But if the tasks that are critical for higher yields do not occur when there is this seasonal labour slack, there is no point in discussing idle capacity for other tasks.

Of all the field tasks, one stands out as offering an opportunity to raise yields in the short term before investment in higher productivity can take effect. That task is weeding. If more weeding cannot be done, then stabilisation and structural adjustment programmes for agriculture are in jeopardy. A second weeding might raise yields by 20 per cent or more, while a third weeding would offer a significant further improvement of yields.

Extra weeding does not require complementary factors of production, but it is the most female of all tasks. Although there are instances of men weeding, they are far from common. However, the weeding period—the period of the rains and declining food supplies—is the time of year when women are most stretched, as maternal and infant health indictors show (Dyson and Crook, 1981). Further weedings on main cash crops could only be undertaken by forgoing weeding on other crops.

If women somehow cope with the ordinary weeding period, this suggests that there is "excessive female labour" at other times of the year for planting and harvesting. Yet there is no point in applying more labour to harvesting if the standing crop is not more abundant. There might or might not be a greater abundance of the early standing crop if planting were done more carefully. But if weeding practices cannot be improved there may be little point in trying it. In short, applying more weeding labour raises the marginal product of labour on planting and harvesting, respectively, which in theory ought initially to be zero. It is, of course, only to be expected that the most productive application of increments of labour occur just when there is no slack labour capacity to bring into play. The weeding factor, taken in conjunction with the enormous role of agriculture in successful adjustment strategies, is the most important single influence on the short- to medium-term production outcome of adjustment policies. Neglect of the crucial gender dimension would be folly in the extreme.

The second way to expand output is by rearranging a given endowment of factors of production. The new price incentives operate directly on major traded crops. Therefore one can expect women who also farm other crops on their own account to be under pressure to surrender more of their labour time and perhaps some of their land for the cultivation of the major traded crops. This may, or indeed may not (because men insist on claiming more resources for their newly profitable crops), be moderated by the indirect effect of cross-substitution effects on "surrogate" tradables. A switch of resources to male production accounting units is much more likely to be the first response of farmers to producer price increases since idle capacity is a dubious reality. How much of resources currently used by women for their own production accounting units will be withdrawn from them will depend on the size of the price increases, and the determination of men to shift resources from their wives' accounting units and/or men's promises to recompense their wives (directly or through assuming more of basic household expenditures) for working on their more profitable tradables. The status of women within the farming household is a determinant of the outcome. Chapter 3 listed causes of women's insecurity of land tenure. Two of them, increased crop profitability and land reform, are principal goals of adjustment.

Does it matter that women might lose land use rights after the reshuffle of cropping incentives? There are two objectives of adjustment that could be affected. The first is food self-sufficiency and the second is the efficient allocation of resources. Official documents usually refer to this at the national, not the household, level. The consequence of not aiming at rural household or village self-sufficiency will probably be felt through health indicators, and therefore determinants of population variables. Chapter 3 supplied grounds for concern about what happens to household food security if women lose land use rights, not necessarily because they always grow own-consumed food but because in the great majority of African situations women are by custom responsible for underwriting the cooking pot from one source or another. In plain economic terms, women are responsible for labour reproduction and maintenance, thus freeing men to pursue "maximising profit goals". In this scheme of things there is no mechanism for assessing the profitability of self-provisioning food production (or women's cash crops) relative to that of men's accounting units. The profitability *to women* of supplying immediate use values in the shape of food could be greater than the cash profitability *to men* of marketing tradables. It depends entirely on the regimen and weighting that go into imputed prices of self-provisioning food farming. Therefore, pursuing a maximising position of tradables (or even locally traded crops) says nothing of the allocative efficiency of the *overall uses of resources,* including labour's reproduction and maintenance. It merely returns us to Streeten's question: "Adjustment of and for what?"

The whole subject of the alienation of production from reproduction and maintenance is a matter for the inter-personal utility analysis of welfare economics. Planners concerned with adjustment policies have moved from mere macroeconomic analysis to micro-economic responses and the social dimensions of adjustment. But they have yet to incorporate welfare economics.

Even in cases where men grow both food for self-provisioning and tradable crops, family maintenance could be threatened by the switch of resources between these. Men's contribution to the family's food requirements might be expected to come through purchases made from the new increments of cash income. In practice this substitution is likely to be less than perfect. Of course, where women also grow both self-provisioning foods and tradable crops they will face similar choices. However, it is more likely, outside parts of Muslim West Africa where men assume much greater responsibility for finding the family's food, that women will ensure the necessary food purchases or hold more firmly than men to a self-provisioning objective within their overall production objective. The latter would not be because of an innate aversion to specialisation and the market but because women may believe that their control over resources is threatened by a move to tradable crops away from the agriculture which confirmed usufructuary land rights on them and because the terms offered them by the market have been so abysmal in the past.

What this suggests is that household food self-sufficiency could be threatened by dependence on a rearrangement of household resources for a supply response to price increase, while household food self-reliance (the ability to purchase food instead) may not be a perfect substitute because, inter alia, women lose control over resources.

The only way this can be avoided is if, in the process of rearranging resources, factors of production are combined more efficiently. But it is difficult to see how this can be done without some new investment. If factors can be combined more efficiently without investment, why has this not been done before? One reason might be that gender, or the subordinate status of women, stands in the way of an efficient recombination of the existing stock of resources. Economic instruments of adjustment may have little effect on this anomaly, or on any other which is determined by the social fabric of the household. The only way to remove this gender obstruction to a more efficient combination of resources is through the kind of intervention which meets strategic gender needs affecting women's status in the household (see Chapter 8). But this would be a long haul and entail measures which would more correctly come under the rubric of economic transformation.

Finally, if one crop is not to enjoy an increase in output at the expense of another because of competition between resources then investment in higher productivity is essential, whether it be of the crop earmarked for output expansion or the crops with which it competes for resources. The success of agricultural adjustment and transformation, therefore, does not rest solely with policies which promote principal tradables as an engine of growth that may raise the productivity of non-tradables in its wake. This outcome did not occur in colonial times with the development of cash crops. There is nothing to suggest that it could happen automatically from the standard adjustment package to date. It is only when barriers to free competition of productivity improvements are eliminated that the true potential of comparative advantages can be revealed instead of the engineered comparative advantages we see today from the male bias of past promotions. This release of competition for resources above and below the household level will, in the process, move the allocation of household resources to a more optimal position. It is difficult to see what there has been in adjustment programmes so far that would help to channel or counter gender influences to a better outcome for adjustment.

But competition for resources is based on the technologies or production functions that are applied. Relative profitabilities, were they measurable, would merely reflect the present technologies used. Chapter 3 gave evidence of the as yet untapped yield potential of women's own-account farming. Had women enjoyed equal access with men to the information and inputs of higher-yielding technologies, the current relative profitabilities of their farming would doubtless be very different.

What this amounts to is that static efficiency can be quite different from dynamic efficiency, and dynamic efficiency can take any direction depending on the commitment to eliminating or countering discrimination in markets and making up for lost time and wasted opportunities. This is a subject for Chapter 11, but here it should be pointed out that if security of land tenure is seen as a precondition for men investing in land, it should be true of women too.

Left to market forces, the impetus to invest resulting from devaluation would lead, in large measure, to raising further the productivity of male accounting units only, continuing the long neglect of the productivity of women's accounting units. There is nothing in the WID literature to justify optimism that profits earned by men's accounting units are invested in the productivity of women's accounting units.

The obvious response to this is that it might be better for adjustment to encourage men's accounting units to absorb women's accounting units so that all household land enjoys investment opportunities. This solution does not address the problem of misallocation (super-exploitation and chronic low productivity) of female labour, unless there are absolutely no impediments to women in the household taking off-farm employment. If those off-farm employment opportunities do not exist, then the best chance for improving the efficient use of female labour is for women to have the bargaining counter of secure access to their own land. But adjustment programmes have not yet addressed the means to either of these solutions. There must be fear that female labour resources will not be used according to static efficiency, and not invested in according to dynamic efficiency.

The outcome of adjustment programmes for production of women-headed farm households is difficult to predict but is unlikely to be as straightforward as the theory of adjustment supposes. Members of women-headed households and polygamous households may not benefit much directly from adjustment policies and may wish instead to participate more in the rural wage labour market. It needs to be borne in mind that a general rise in the profitability of farming should raise the demand for hired labour, and with that wages. Against this gain women heads of farm households must set their expectations of greater profits from own-account farming bearing in mind that they will have to hire (ploughing and other) labour to cover their labour deficit. Risk avoidance looms large in the strategy of these households. It would be very understandable if they responded by profit-taking from higher prices, rather than expanding production, and supplemented their income from the more buoyant wage labour market. Policy-makers might have to consider that encouraging an ordered labour market might be one way of facilitating the best contribution of these women to the outcome of adjustment; and in the process helping them.

To raise the private profitability of cultivating the whole acreage of female-headed farms will entail a social cost in terms of research into their priority problems and economically optimal crop mixes, and possibly subsidising ploughing services and the capitalisation of other field tasks. The social profit will be the value of the output from the increment of cultivated acreage. The social benefit-cost ratio could be substantial. Governments have to decide how much they value the economic and social gain of full land utilisation. An alternative is to depend on greater production from more viable small farms and from large farms which can then offer wage employment to women heads of farm households.

Differentiations in the response of manufacturing and services

This section examines the presence of gender issues of felt incentives and supply possibilities in manufacturing and services. Chapter 6 indicated the likely cost squeeze impact of devaluation and reduction of subsidies. These must be considered as givens of the context in which possible gender influences are examined: they reduce profits in some enterprises and increase them in others. But there are no obvious gender influences in them, nor is the supply of raw materials expected to be influenced by gender except in so far as they emanate from the agricultural sector.

What is of predominant interest here is the operations of the labour market from the point of view of employment and income (effective demand as an input of felt incentives) and availability of appropriate labour in the right places (supply possibilities).

Unlike the agricultural sector, manufacturing and services face labour redundancies and lay-offs. There is no doubt that women share in this as much as men, perhaps more so because of cultural attitudes to defining main breadwinners and because of employers' expectations of extra costs in employing women in their reproductive years. Here we are interested in gender-differentiated changes in employment only in so far as they bear on demand for goods and services.

Adjustment is supposed to encourage the deployment of labour in uses where its returns are highest and equal across all uses. For that there should be ease of mobility of labour in free and open markets to respond to new relative incentives. What happens is different. Here we are concerned with gender as one influence on the outcome.

Labour is not the only factor of relevance here. The goal of efficiency demands that capital, entrepreneurship and raw materials should also flow freely through markets. In fact gender influences this outcome too.

Felt incentives through effective demand

When income changes, the income effect alters the pattern, as well as the level, of expenditure. Were women and men to be represented approximately equally in the employment of these sectors but affected very differently by redundancies and lay-offs (or new employment opportunities), consumer demand patterns could also change owing to gender differences in patterns of expenditure. However, Chapter 4 indicated that female employment in the formal sector was only a small fraction of male employment so that gender disparities in employment retrenchment in this sector are unlikely to influence the pattern of domestic demand for final products, or producers' felt incentives.

The effect of employment changes in the informal sector is likely to be different because women and men are much more equally represented, although men usually remain in the majority. Also personal disposable income generated in the informal sector may total many times the total wages bill of the formal sector. What happens to gender-differentiated employment and income in the informal sector could affect producers' felt incentives. Which producers' felt incentives is another matter.

The way gender influences patterns of expenditure is through women's cultural role of being much more responsible than men for budgeting for day-to-day essentials. These goods must be found for survival. If real purchasing power falls, then cheaper sources of them or close substitutes for them are sought out. If we can suppose for the sake of argument that men's disposable income supports demand for non-essentials, the purchasing choice may be between one non-essential good and another, or between purchasing now or later. Even if cheaper sources were to be found in the small-scale or informal sectors, the non-divisibility of some of these expenditure outlays would force choice on the consumer.

To the extent that essentials can be found from a variety of sources ranging from small scale, bordering on the informal and formal sectors, to the very informal, and non-essentials from the more formal, the greater the fall in employment and income of women the greater the shift of demand for essentials towards more informal outlets, and the greater the fall in employment and income of men the sharper the reduction in demand for non-essentials from all outlets. To these patterns of expenditure of non-agricultural income earners must be added the changes in expenditure of the farming community. The gender-differentiated increments of income and patterns of expenditure have been dealt with in the previous chapter.

All in all, then, gender-differentiated reductions in personal disposable income could make some difference to the respective felt incentives of the formal sector, the small-scale and the more pronounced informal sectors.

Supply possibilities

The more important impact gender could have on the outcome of the adjustment process comes on the supply side. There are two aspects of supply response to be taken into account. The first is gender in access to factor markets and the second is gender in labour market adaptability.

In the case of the first aspect, capital and raw materials are obtained in the formal sector by means normally unaffected by gender influences. Owners or managers in this sector usually operate in a business stratum where gender has little influence.

Increasingly the informal sector is being looked to in order to shorten the period of supply disruption and to alleviate the worst shortages. If planners assume that the informal sector is adaptable and flexible enough to fill the breach in supplies for new demand patterns, are they relying on male or female entrepreneurs, and what influence has the gender of the entepreneurs on the elasticity of supply response?

The greater dependence of the formal sector on capital and raw material imports places it at a disadvantage to the informal sector. However, although small-scale enterprise production does not usually have as great an import content as larger formal enterprise production, a foreign exchange crisis can affect the former quickly and cause them to close because they are last in the queue for any foreign exchange. Logic dictates that those with ease of entry and appropriate production functions should do better out of this import liberalisation than those working with fixed and high-cost factor ratios. But import licences may be awarded directly to user enterprises or to traders obliged to sell to them, or the large-scale and formal contracts of importing enterprises might operate agaisnt distribution to many small outlets. In this way quantitative restrictions operate against the smaller and more informal enterprises, sometimes to their exclusion in all rationing of imports. Under adjustment reforms in the foreign trade sector, foreign exchange should go to the highest bidder and the imported goods should be passed on to those processors who can offer the highest prices.

From the little information that we have we might suppose that male informal sector employment has closer relations with formal sector activity through supplying it with intermediate materials. However, women in the informal sector do have one special link with the formal sector in urban areas, and that is catering to the demand for snacks or groceries in small quantities. If anything, the impact of demand management policies will be to shift demand from more formal eating establishments and shops to smaller informal ones. Thus, where informal sector activity is directly dependent on formal sector activity, female entrepreneurs are likely to gain more or lose less from stabilisation and adjustment than male entrepreneurs. This conclusion is based on the assumption that market liberalisation includes removing the mark of illegality from all these informal activities.

But as one visualises the informal sector moving to small rural towns or the rural areas, if our modest information serves for other countries, then the enterprise becomes smaller, more specialised in one line of activity and is characterised by more manufacturing than servicing. Of these local rural enterprises, blacksmithing and repairs, and processing of primary produce should gain most from the new policies. Both male and female self-employed are involved and will tend to be one-person enterprises. The closer this informal sector activity is to the farming community, the more it is likely to gain from increased demand if structural adjustment in agriculture is successfully pursued. In the case of blacksmithing an apprentice or wage labourer might well be taken on because of the skills required of new entrants. However, in the case of value-adding processing the technologies are already widely known by rural women so that it is more likely that there will be more female self-employed entrants than new assistants or apprentices to meet the greater demand.

If we can assume that in general women's participation in manufacturing and servicing rises steadily with the degree of ruralisation and informality of production methods, the gains from the anticipated impacts of stabilisation and adjustment policies should fall disproportionately to women in terms of demand for their goods and services. Therefore women will enjoy new opportunities in the informal sector, particularly in rural areas. Conversely, women have an important role to play in expanding some lines of production or switching resources to others in order that the adjustment process is successful. But their ability to do this might be more impaired than men's because of gender-based impediments in factor and product markets.

Identifying the potential beneficiaries of this increase in demand is important. But there may be a particular difficulty in identifying potential female entrants because they tend to have a mixed portfolio. The study of small rural enterprises in Zambia indicated that it was just women's contributions to the rural informal sector that tended to be part time. These women are also involved in own farming or work as seasonal farm labourers. There will be fine gradations of women's situations between the margins of own-account farming and wage labouring. How women finally deploy their time will also depend on the impact of adjustment on farming incentives. It might not take much of a shift in relative profitabilities in favour of the rural informal sector for a greater interest in non-agricultural activity to emerge. Overwhelmingly, the increase in employment will arise from new self-employed entrants.

After the exercise of trying to identify the gender of entrepreneurs in the most likely new growth areas comes the analysis of how the gender of the entrepreneur affects the ability to respond, particularly in the changing environment brought about by adjustment programmes.

In the informal sector where owners of capital and/or managers are more dependent on the local culture for these factors of production, gender will have the greatest bearing on access to inputs. Women may be assumed to be less creditworthy than men because they start endowed with fewer assets or because of restrictive cultural attitudes to women making contracts outside the family. They may also have less information about credit and raw material sources, being confined to smaller geographical and social territories than men. Where women and men tend to undertake different lines of economic activity the success of adjustment programmes is more heavily dependent on gender equality in factor markets than when either sex could produce a certain good or service. But even in the latter case economic efficiency is promoted when all aspiring or existing entrepreneurs share equal terms of participation in factor markets.

One obstruction to informal sector activity that figures importantly in some countries is illegality. If a mode of supply is illegal (often because it competes with formal sector supply), there is an impediment to efficient movement of factors of production into informal sector supply. Gender enters this because the question of illegality tends to focus more on women's informal sector activities than on men's.

A separate issue is entry barriers. As the informal sector moves to more rural areas, increases in employment in existing enterprises will become less important in providing the supply response. The nature of the activity will lead more appropriately to self-employment. But there may be gender biases in the way women and men gain entrance to their respective self-employment. It is important to identify the relevance of gender in dealing with entry barriers because overcoming them may need gender-specific treatment.

The Lusaka case study pointed out that women's very informal economic activity could respond to intermittent need or a particular shortage in urban areas. This adaptability should be just as easily demonstrated when demand and cost changes present new opportunities. In the 1980s, after many years of young female migration to towns, there should be no shortage of women who have experience of urban settings, and are "street-wise" in dealing with bureaucratic obstacles and obtaining input supplies. The greater dependence on capital and raw material imports of the formal sector should intensify this shift by adding a price cross-substitution effect.

To assess the impact of the second aspect of supply responses, labour market adaptability, it is necessary to see how gender might influence retraining, the process of recombining labour with other factors of production and the relocation of labour either geographically or by type of job. Non-homogeneity of factor markets was discussed in Chapter 7. In the case of the labour market, gender-based causes of non-homogeneity easily come to mind. They arise because of employers' choices or because of imperfect substitutability of female and male labour inherent in reproduction arrangements and culture. But the process of adjustment can alter the way gender influences non-homogeneity, in many ways exacerbating it to the detriment of economic efficiency.

In situations of much unemployment and little gender specificity of jobs, the particular problems of reaching women with training facilities are not relevant to the economic outcome of adjustment: employers will train those who do not present special problems. But gender specificity means that employers must find female labour to meet the requirements of the production functions. If new skills have to be acquired, then unless the special problems that women face as trainees are not met, the outcome of adjustment for production could be less than expected.

Retraining upgrades the job. In the process difficulties can arise or employers' attitudes may be activated such that the job passes from women to men. This will not promote efficiency if women with inherent talent are cast aside. Retraining is usually conducted on site when it constitutes practical application and is needed in an existing enterprise. When it involves working extra hours, or requires higher levels of basic education and special courses, some women—who could successfully be retrained—are automatically weeded out. Women as mothers have a second job to do and cannot meet the times specified by men for male role models. They usually have fewer years of education. Unless the facilities and conditions for retraining are designed to meet women's lesser availability and to pitch basic education requirements at levels which realistically keep the door open to real talent instead of rationing out trainee places by a simple method, there will be discrimination against potential female trainees. This must mean a loss in efficiency.

Job upgrading is reinforced by new production technologies. Recombining labour with other factors of production is often the follow-up to retraining and usually means dealing with capital of a higher technology. When this happens the job is seen as upgraded. Again, cultural influences may depict the new job as male specific, thereby excluding female candidates no matter what their aptitudes and regardless of the fact that a very similar task might have been performed by women formerly.

But recombining labour can also mean new forms of specialisation within an enterprise, or merely a rationalisation of labour deployment because past practices led to overmanning in some departments. The ratio of administrative workers to manual workers could be altered, or a recombination of factors of production might entail a significant redistribution of manual workers amounting to relocation within the enterprise. When this happens, efficiency would demand that workers are directed to where their abilities and comparative advantages lie. However, Chapter 4 revealed that there is much gender specificity of jobs, which will make this difficult to achieve.

Relocation within an enterprise is less likely to alter existing gender specificity of tasks when it arises from economic rationalisation than when it arises from a change in the technological underpinning of the production function. A new production function carries its own inherent inefficiencies when jobs upgraded through technology pass from women to men because of cultural perceptions of suitable jobs.

Of course the end of gender specificity of jobs in itself is a means to greater efficiency in labour use. However, what is much more likely to happen is the substitution of one kind of gender specificity for another.

Related to this is employers' antipathy to hiring women because of generalised expectations of absenteeism, maternity leave costs, and so on. This is the fact of "statistical discrimination" mentioned in Chapter 4. With the rising urban unemployment that is so characteristic of the first years of economic adjustment, employers are in a strong position to apply the statistical factor, so rejecting some women who are more able than some men who are hired. This short-term approach will make it more difficult to develop the numbers of skilled people required in the long term.

This discussion has offered illustrations of how adjustment programmes which do not include measures to reform institutions or raise labour productivities, but depend merely on short-term gains can make long-term dynamic efficiency more difficult to achieve. There is a natural antipathy in stabilisation and structural adjustment policies to countering gender-based non-homogeneity in the labour market. Moves to a homogeneous market must await a programme of economic transformation.

The foregoing analysis of employers' reactions is easier to apply to the formal sector. While something is known of the gender division of labour in the informal sector along the lines of subcategories (handicrafts, repair services, food processing, clothing, and so on), too little is known about how the informal sector labour market works when *(a)* new entrants cause overcrowding, *(b)* there is a redistribution of production of a certain good between near formal, intermediate and very informal sectors, and *(c)* the composition of demand for goods produced by the informal sector changes. Because female labour is less mobile and female entrepreneurship faces greater problems of developing assets, it is likely that men will enter fields previously regarded as women's province. While this can be seen as promoting efficiency within the static context of women being confined by domestic roles and being regarded as less creditworthy, it contributes nothing to the concept of dynamic efficiency when time allows these parameters to be modified. There is a real danger that the pressure to achieve short-term gains from the adjustment process will reinforce these gender influences by cutting back on supporting services to mothers and granting credit on customary discriminatory terms. If this happens the context within which the labour market operates will exacerbate inefficiencies and postpone long-term investments in a more efficient allocation of labour resources. But there are other supporting facilities which can particularly affect the adaptability of the female labour market.

If the data on Zambia are relevant to other sub-Saharan countries, then there is likely to be a gross underestimation of official figures of informal sector employment there too. With that there will be misrepresentation of the adaptability of those with a little skill operating at the margins of the economy. Their potential response to new absolute and relative prices and to market liberalisation could be enormous. Since such informal enterprises are noted for greater scope for capital-labour substitution, the value of their potentially high incremental employment-to-capital ratio to the new strategy would be great. But to realise this potential they will in all probability need financial assistance. That is to say, the adaptability of the self-employed labour market is influenced by other factor markets. The rise in interest rates will not represent a worsening of their position because they will not have enjoyed cheap credit before. But finding working capital remains a problem. It usually comes from retained profits or loans from friends and relatives. The initial contraction of real savings from all sources resulting from demand management should cause some drying up of this source of capital. Women and men are likely to be affected differentially by changes in source of capital.

On the question of geographical relocation, there are two points of consideration: whether the same labour units can move to new locations or whether employers are able to find qualified workers in their new locations. The flexibility and adaptability of the labour market might be strongly influenced by how great a distance from former employment centres qualified labour is expected to be found. The gender issue on the first point is fairly clear. When women and men have settled their domestic situations, women have greater difficulty commuting much farther or undertaking some semi-migration. That is why, as mentioned in Chapter 4, it is probably true of most countries that women's participation in non-agricultural activities rises fairly steadily, moving from urban areas to small rural towns to rural areas. Should adjustment programmes shift the balance of these activities to smaller communities, the preparedness of a female labour force could be critical. The notable example of this is the new profitability of processing primary produce, which being bulky is more economically undertaken close to sources of raw materials. It can be expected in many countries that employers seek a female labour force in semi-rural areas which can adapt to new modes of processing primary produce. These newly relocated enterprises will, in many cases, compete with the local self-employed. But it is not yet clear from the literature on adjustment whether new economic activity is expected to be located in quite different areas.

Conclusion

There must be serious questioning of whether adjustment policies for agriculture improve or worsen, through gender influences, the efficiency of resource use. Women's land status is crucial to this. But their equal access to farm support services is also very relevant. Notions of efficiency are suspect when different farmers in the household have different financial responsibilities for household maintenance. In addition, a history of neglect of women's farming technology invalidates the use of static efficiency criteria for success except in the case when only quick short-term gains are expected. Dynamic efficiency entails correcting long-established discrimination and neglect as a prelude to seeing where fresh improvements in productivity can be most efficiently designed. If considerations of long-term dynamic efficiency are not borne in mind at the start, then resources will have to be found later to undo what structural adjustment has done to markets.

Product for product the informal sector should be able to survive and prosper better than the formal sector during adjustment. But for a fuller contribution to the success of adjustment policies, its long neglect by government should end. Much has to be done in terms of redesigning programmes and undertaking institutional reforms to assist those not normally in the front of the queue for government assistance and to improve the homogeneity of labour and other factor markets. If the goal of dynamic efficiency is not borne in mind at an early stage, it could be more difficult to achieve later. One reason for this is that gender-based market structures become more pronounced during stabilisation and structural adjustment, even though other market features are being liberalised.

Implications of the theoretical framework for the population outcome of adjustment programmes

10

Here we are concerned with the likely outcome of adjustment policies for population variables. This is viewed in the following way. First, the probable outcome for population variables is summarised on the assumption that the intended results of the programmes for the economy and economic institutions were achieved. Second, likely characteristics of changes in population variables are examined on the basis of a more realistic assessment of the actual socio-economic results. In the case of the latter these assessments must incorporate not only the gender influences on actual results as described in Chapter 9, but also the more fundamental weaknesses outlined in Chapter 7.

The chapter is constructed around the main determinants of population variables, as gleaned from the review of theories in Chapter 5. These are: income, workloads, health and educational investment in human resources, socio-cultural factors and the status of women, and migration.

Agriculture-based families

Income

One of the major goals of adjustment programmes is to improve rural-urban terms of trade to provide income incentives to farmers. Much of the solution to external and internal imbalances depends on the growth of production prosperity of farming households.

The higher income should improve nutrition and family welfare leading, in particular, to lower infant mortality rates. This should help to moderate fertility rates. But at the same time there will be an income effect on fertility which the literature on population research in sub-Saharan Africa deems, on balance, to be positive, at least for lower bands of income. This should result in maintained or even higher fertility rates. The net outcome of these two opposite influences is difficult to predict. Improved infant health depends on more per capita resources being spent on mothers and children. If greater income is simply seen as a means of supporting more children, then the primary population variables which are expected to favour a demographic transition will not change.

However, if the increment of income is largely appropriated by men the ability to support more children on the part of women, who in most African situations are the major funders of day-to-day consumption expenses, will be unaffected. It may even be weakened if women lose access to factors of production for their own accounting units in the process of adjustment. Therefore the income that matters could decline as a result of improving the rural-urban terms of trade and giving absolute price incentives to farmers. According to the theory of the income effect, fertility should also decline. But research in Africa is not conclusive on this point, and the observed positive income effect might well be based on men's visible earnings while women's more invisible earnings might be moving in the opposite direction. If this were true, the income effect would more accurately be described as negative.

In the absence of data some judgement has to be made about the probable changes in women's and men's personal disposable income resulting from adjustment policies. Chapter 6 indicated that products which are potentially exports or import substitutes would gain most from the new price relatives. Chapters 3 and 9 revealed that these were generally managed by men but that a few women also produced them, while others produced surrogate tradables enjoying cross-substitution income and price effects. The general conclusion must be that the impact on resource and income distribution in the household would be similar to the impact of any increase in profitability of the major cash crops. On the basis of what is known from the WID literature of similar colonial and post-colonial changes, women will be obliged to surrender land and/or labour from their own-account activities to men's. The welfare effect will depend on the change in size of the household's budget for consumer essentials, which in turn depends on cultural and inter-personal differences.

The reality is that agricultural incomes for either sex have been slower to improve than intended. Differences between past and current profitabilities or (given the rise in price of urban products) real purchasing power, and between women's and men's accounting units may not be so great. Intended producer prices are weakened by the time they reach the farm gate because of marketing difficulties. The phasing out of subsidies on production inputs, previously almost exclusively benefiting male accounting units, will act to reduce the net price incentive.

All in all the agricultural income effect of adjustment programmes on population variables is not likely to be significant, or even clear. A much more important effect is that of demand for labour.

Workloads and children's assistance

The new prices will generally encourage farm households to try to produce more, despite or because of urban product price rises and regardless of the intra-household distribution of income. The background is one of government sending strong signals to farmers that they are now to be favoured. The imperfect transmission of intended prices is not likely to totally discount the influence of these signals.

In the short term there is not likely to be much slack labour capacity. There are already commonly found seasonal labour bottlenecks. The worst is usually at the critical time of weeding, a task which could increase yields with the application of labour alone. Weeding is mostly or exclusively undertaken by women. Therefore this labour bottleneck relates to the deployment of women's labour. Labour bottlenecks that are only a little less significant can occur at planting or harvesting times. In the absence of a change in the gender division of labour or of investment in higher-productivity work processes, these bottlenecks can only be forced by women cutting back on their other tasks. This they may be unwilling to do because of the cost in terms of family welfare.

But structural adjustment is supposed to promote the efficient working of markets. If the supply of a factor of production proves inelastic when confronted with an increase in demand for it, its scarcity is reflected in its price relative to other factor prices. There is an incentive to spend resources on raising its productivity first of all. The expectation, if not the arrival, of higher income will finance increases in the productivity of a factor of production which is found to be in short supply. Two writers, commenting on the impetus to investment in higher productivity, present this as the theory of induced technical change:

> When increases in factor demands are confronted with different elasticities in the supply of production factors, the result is changes in relative factor prices . . . In agriculture, the constraints imposed on development by an inelastic supply of land may be offset by advances in biological technology; the constraints imposed by an inelastic supply of labour may be offset by advances in mechanical technology.

Or again:

> A rise in the price of labour relative to land induces technical changes that permit the substitution of capital for labour and at the same time induce institutional changes that enhance the productivity of the human agent and increase workers' control over the conditions of employment (Ruttan and Hayami, 1989, pp. 394 and 409).

But the WID literature makes it clear that a rise in demand for female labour in the past has not led to investment in mechanical equipment for female-specific tasks. Chapter 3 made it evident why the deployment of farm household labour does not follow the principles of a free market. While social values can oblige women to work so much harder than men, and men would be the direct beneficiaries of even harder work, the notion of a point being reached when it pays to invest in the productivity of one's labour force is misplaced. Because so much of women's labour is un-monetised, scarcity prices have to be imputed, and imputed prices do not have the same force in market terms as actual prices paid.

In theory if husbands cannot obtain more of their wives' labour, then acquiring mechanical implements ought to be cheaper than hiring extra labour. Cultural factors might make husbands reluctant to invest in work methods for women's specific tasks. Taking other employment or migrating might be preferred alternatives for men. Women themselves can feel the need to purchase implements. But apart from the fact that they probably would not receive the full return to their outlay of funds, they lack the immediate liquid assets to attempt it. The terms of their tenancy of land does not allow them to operate in factor markets in ways assumed by micro-economic analysis. Their stream of cash income is usually small and already fully committed. An anticipated higher income does not solve the problem of lack of present assets.

While it could be argued that investment in any productivity improvement, however simple, is not possible in the short term, the impediment to a resource-efficient response to a scarcity of female labour within the farm household is such that that response is unlikely to take place even in the longer term. It might take many years for the necessary cultural and/or institutional changes to occur. The alternative is targeted and specific subsidies.

But changes in agricultural prices are not the only means of adjustment programmes having an impact on workloads. Cuts in social sector budgets mean that safe water supplies receive less investment or maintenance funds, while reductions in health services mean more days of sickness of family members to attend to. All this amounts to more work for women.

Because water supplies and health services can be planned only at the community or national level they tend to be financed in this way too. It is unrealistic to believe that individual production profits can substitute for this source of funding. There is an alternative means of funding them, but this has dimensions that go beyond women's work.

There are different ways in which women can relieve the work pressure on them, but all of them entail costs. One is to reduce work in their own-production accounting units, but this is likely to mean less self-provisioning food agriculture which assumes that cash purchases of food must come from the greater profits of men's accounting units. A second way is for women to cut down on reproduction work, but this may be cut back so far that the health and welfare of young members of the family are threatened. If this limit has already been reached, then women maximise their position by doing what they did before adjustment programmes were launched. The new price relatives do not affect their current optimality. Women could only alter it if they gained directly from producing tradables, or their surrogates, and might thereby be tempted to work for less for the same former personal income, or if their husbands shared enough of their income increment to provide women with a direct incentive. A third way to solve the labour shortage is to apply children's assistance.

Far from there being an opportunity cost of children, women have a newly confirmed need for a large family.

The costs of these resolutions to the problem are therefore variously food self-reliance, family welfare, weakened supply response to adjustment policies and maintained or increased numbers of children. The alternative to all these is endangered health through super self-exploitation.

There are a number of primary, intermediate and final population variables involved. Wherever health and family welfare are affected, there are dangers such as low birthweight, loss of weight during pregnancy, prematurely reduced or terminated breast-feeding, reduced washing and feeding care of infants, and reduced post-partum amenorrhoea. Intermediate variables could be more sickly infants and higher morbidity rates. Owing to the probable imposition of heavier workloads on women and the absence of proper market mechanisms to increase their labour productivity, the final population variables of mortality and fertility could experience continued high levels or even rises.

Health and educational investments in human resources

Stabilisation and structural adjustment aim, among other things, to reduce the government budget deficit through phasing out subsidies and reducing total social sector expenditure. These policy packages essentially contract the role of the State by throwing more of the burden of reproduction of the labour force and investment in a better future on to the private citizen. Following closely on this philosophy of personal responsibility is one of accountability of the suppliers of social sector services to those who use them. Both are gratified by "user charges"; that is to say, people contribute to the cost of health services and their children's schooling and are thereby in a position to render health and education officers accountable to them. This, it is alleged, will improve the quality of the services. Accountability leads to better value for money.

In practice this intended outcome is undermined by the poor not using these services as much as in the past because they cannot afford to pay for them. This must have predictable results for the primary population variables of infant health and mortality, and literacy. User charges are bound to roll back the advances made in sub-Saharan Africa on female education because those families that have limited resources will tend to invest in their sons' education first since they lose their daughters on marriage. Although some studies quoted in Chapter 5 revealed that the influence of the education factor was not clear, that only applied to primary schooling. The point that needs to be made is that primary schooling is the door to, or precondition of, secondary schooling which undoubtedly makes a difference to fertility. If girls do not reach their previous primary school achievements, what hope is there of society moving on to mass secondary education for girls?

This is an example of short-term adjustment policies jeopardising longer-term objectives.

The application of user charges also raises the question of which parent—or relative—should pay them. Planners of adjustment strategies may not go beyond thinking that higher agricultural incomes can be spent on health and educational investments in children without great hardship. But if the mother is left to fund part or all of these expenses, this assumed happy net outcome of two important aspects of stabilisation and structural adjustment may not be realised.

Socio-cultural factors and women's status

Adjustment packages do not formally incorporate cultural factors. It is either assumed that policy instruments are "neutral" in this matter or that it is simply not the province of economic planners to be concerned with cultural interactions. But adjustment packages do have an impact on the socio-cultural organisation of production and reproduction, and therefore inevitably on the status of women.

The stronger paramountcy of tradable crops can be expected to cause more household-based land and/or labour to be applied to their production. Where land is scarce this means surrendering land used for other crops and therefore, for women, losing rights to control the produce from it (Youssef, 1988). Women's economic autonomy diminishes with the stock of resources managed in their economic accounting units. This autonomy is important for women's ability to take decisions, including decisions on their reproductive practices.

There are two other adjustment policy instruments which are intended to have favourable material outcomes but which can reasonably be expected to have a negative effect on women's status and not to favour a demographic transition. They are the privatisation of land (through registration or adjudication) and measures to intensify production on small-scale farms. The model idealised by adjustment planners is the family labour force working its own private farm for its own exclusive profit.

Some (including the World Bank) see private registration of land and a land market as a pillar of longer-term adjustment in agriculture. There is the hope that this will encourage enterprising, commercially minded nuclear families, and therefore (if economic planners ever think about it) presumably lead to new lifestyles and rising expectations of success which would be followed by a fall in fertility. However, if past land adjudication practices proliferate in future, this is not likely to be the outcome for several reasons.

In practice this land reform means men's private ownership of land and less secure access to land by women than under traditional lineage practices described in Chapter 3. Customary laws were the foundation for women's separate economic accounting units to feed the family. Land privatisation can sweep aside these customary laws. In particular, land privatisation accompanying a programme of intensification of small-scale plots in the hope that they become emergent commercial farms places a question mark over self-provisioning and, in fact, over all of women's own-account agriculture. Women's ability to deliver the means of sustenance to the family, and with that the prospect of healthy children, may be diminished.

How are wives apportioned land for own use after privatisation of land by male members of the lineage? If the acreage of "household plots" for self-provisioning agriculture incorporated in typical resettlement schemes is to be emulated by the new private male farmer, then the traditional resource base for women's traditional economic responsibilities disappears and until new norms of responsibility corresponding to access to resources appear, the maintenance and reproduction of the family could be in chaos.

Moreover, if women are given the use of some land now owned by their husbands, their chances of using this land as any kind of surety in dealings with institutions or private suppliers could be weakened. Where before lineage practices did not confirm land titles, it was possible to consider that anyone given traditional usufructuary rights had an effective collateral. Land privatisation cuts through any vagueness to make it clear to financial institutions that collateral powers rest with the owner, not the user, of the land. Women's access to and control of resources are impaired and with that their status in the family and society.

But land under the control of women favours a demographic transition for reasons other than assuring the healthy maintenance of children and the chance for women to find the resources to mechanise work processes. As indicated in the previous section and contrary to assumptions usually made, women did not feel that the amount of land owned by the household (or its head) influenced their sense of old-age security. Both divorce and widowhood could reduce a woman's access to land to zero. Land privatisation means that women can no longer appeal to their husbands' lineage in the event of divorce, widowhood or, now, sale of land. Women do not have direct "asset status", in the jargon of the demographic literature. Instead they bond themselves to assets through affective relationships with those who do have this status. In patrilineal societies a better bet for old age is surviving children, preferably sons who will inherit the land and allow their mothers to benefit from it. And this entails multiple motherhood.

Land privatisation would modify another determinant of fertility, although it is unclear how. Tribal affiliations and more immediate kin ties would wither if land were no longer disposed of through the lineage. It is difficult to see which flows of money and assistance and which affinal expectations would survive the privatisation of land resources and output revenues. Crucially, net surpluses will also be privatised. Production, consumption and reproduction units can be expected to coalesce more on the conjugal unit. Ostensibly the costs and benefits of children will fall on the conjugal pair. More specifically, some will accrue to the mother and some to the father. The wider network assisted the mother in some of her tasks: there was no economic opportunity cost of children in her occupation. Now that support is gone. There may now be some opportunity cost but her demand for children's assistance will most likely become greater as she is distanced from the support networks.

There are grounds for believing that nuclear farming households on modest incomes will be at least as pro-natalist as sharing groups of kin. After all, historically women had lower total fertility yet were able to satisfy the social demands of patrilineal groups with their numbers of children and so assuage their own fear of insecurity. With the nuclear farming household, on the other hand, there is a driving need for a large family labour force for marketed and all immediate-use production. Moreover, a woman's security is now heavily dependent on family patriarchy, one man, whereas formerly her status would be determined by the checks and balances offered by a group of men of the lineage patriarchy. The necessity of a woman to have children to prove her worth to, and make her passage through, the patriarchial lineage has now been succeeded by her necessity to bond herself to nuclear family patriarchy and to surviving sons.

It is a misconception of women's lives to assume that creating small-scale emergent farmers out of land adjudication and support services will bring about a demographic transition. The only possible anti-natal tendency would come from the proletarianisation of rural women through the abandonment of small-scale family farming for a more remunerative rural wage labour market.

One senses that structural adjustment should leave a mark on polygyny, but it is not clear what that mark might be. These households usually have large acreage and one might suppose on this basis that they are in a position to gain more than the average from price incentives. However, they tend to consist of separate farming entities, to use less labour per unit of land and consequently to experience lower land yields. To the extent that this is true there is a suggestion of an additional inefficiency in polygynous farming households which would render them especially vulnerable to the competitive pressures of structural adjustment. Apportioning land resources to each wife, who must share adult male labour or hire it, might be less viable in free market competition than monogamous women's own-account farming with its exchange of labour resources within the monogamous households. A successfully "structurally adjusted" polygynous household would mean a very large family labour force under the control of the head of combined wives' households. Fertility might then become more closely comparable with monogamous farming households. At a later date these polygynous households might be among the richest farm households. Hired labour may therefore come to displace wives' and children's labour sooner in them.

The increase in costs of children and a decline in their utility should signal lower mortality and fertility rates, more because of the affluence that the resource base polygyny provides than any social attributes of that kind of marriage. Affluence, of course, can operate in the same way on monogamous households. But with larger total resources polygynous households could well lead the way.

The forces released by stabilisation and structural adjustment will inevitably help to shape the long-term transformation of agriculture. It can be argued that the long term will bring increased economic autonomy to women.

Some countries which have experienced structural adjustment to the stage where government budgets are being prioritisised and patterned to be more effective in their impact are promoting research to raise yields of non-tradable crops, especially sorghum and millet. Already a number of countries have turned to innovative extension services and there are isolated cases of credit schemes to reach women farmers. But the tradables will have received better support services and will have demonstrated a new comparative advantage long before the research results on subsidiary crops are ready. By the time an effective package has been put together to reach women own-account farmers, there may not be much acreage remaining to this farming, except among female heads of household who have not given up farming or in ecological areas where tradables do not have a comparative advantage.

There are various potential scenarios for a transformation of agriculture. The starting-point for any discourse must be the development of new comparative advantages away from the colonial legacy towards supplying viable export and import-replacing industries with raw materials, and towards funding a concerted food security policy, nationally or together with neighbouring States. Industries will generally require what are known today as tradables. But there are also potential export markets for women's higher-value foods, which currently make their way to local, indigenous markets. If, within the framework of transformation, free-lancing co-operatives (selling to the private sector) could offer a hard and viable economic base to many female own-account farmers near a tarmac road, many women farmers could begin a process of surplus accumulation under their own control.

The elevation of women's marketed produce in this way is not yet firmly on the adjustment agenda. Until it is, after the rhetoric of intensifying small-scale farming during the latter stages of structural adjustment is spent, long-term transformation is bound to mean giving large-scale farming its head. While physical yields per unit of land might be higher on small farms using labour intensively, net monetary profitability per unit of land is likely to be greater on large-scale farms. The power to create paid jobs, and to accrete land through purchases, lies with such farms. What has been overlooked in the literature on adjustment is that large-scale farming competes with small-scale male farmers' tradables, while small-scale female own-account farming mostly escapes competition from large-scale farming. In the great majority of cases it is the current tradables, rather than future high-value tradables, produced under contract, that will be first monopolised by large scale.

Therefore the view taken here is that agricultural transformation means the demise of small-scale male own-account farming and the expansion of a rural wage employment market based, according to the current gender division of labour, largely on female labour, concurrently with some interesting developments in female own-account farming.

If we can assume that the predictions of long-term transformation of agriculture are correct, then the long term leaves rural women with at least as many economic opportunities as rural men. Their participation will be desired both in own-account farming and in the rural wage market. Their income-earning capacities might even become greater than their menfolk's. They could increasingly take on the role of main "cash income" breadwinner, a crucial transformation from being "self-provisioning" breadwinner. With this comes the possibility of surplus accumulation (multiple economic reproduction) to supersede the goal of supplying child labour and old-age security (multiple biological reproduction).

Non-agriculture-based families

Income

A reduction of domestic demand for resources is the initial intended result of stabilisation and structural adjustment. This translates into lower real incomes. Rising unemployment and reduced purchasing power in urban areas where the bulk of non-agricultural employment is found are among the first consequences of adjustment packages. The economic theory of fertility (ETF) would decree an income effect of reduced demand for all consumer goods, as well as for children.

One of the first responses to new price relatives in urban production is expected to be some movement of resources into the informal sector. But adding to an overcrowded sector will cause a fall in average income. Therefore there is unlikely to be relief on the side of income effect on population responses. Furthermore, the latest entrants to the informal sector might have already depleted their assets so that, with adaptable production functions, work processes in the sector will tend to average greater labour intensity and lower labour productivity than before.

Diminishing income and asset status in theory leads to more concern about old-age security and therefore pro-natal decisions. On the other hand, some empirical evidence indicated that urban parents expect less from their children in old age than rural parents. Also, in the new intensified daily struggle to survive such a long-term objective of having children might receive no consideration.

Looking beyond the immediate reshuffling of the non-agricultural economy is of much greater importance. Of particular relevance is whether the new developments in formal secondary industry which are beginning to take place in a number of countries are replacements for the same capital and management of previous formal sector industries, or whether they are emerging from successful parts of the informal sector. For instance, are domestic resource-based industries being built on the skills and more suitable technologies of the informal sector, holding out the promise of much employment creation? And are women poised, through their familiarity with the transformation processes implied by this new industrial product mix, to gain more equitably with men and therefore proportionately more from this new formal sector employment? Plausibly, yes. Thus role conflicts for women should re-emerge, especially if new employment is in formal sector enterprises. Theory suggests that this is opportune for further advances of the demographic transition.

The longer-term transformation of manufacturing implies quite new comparative advantages revealed after factor productivities have been invested in and new markets depended on. The product mix of secondary industry will change. New technologies, not necessarily capital-intensive, will be applied. Much of them will depend on increased supplies of raw materials and consumer demand from the agricultural sector. Because of the active employment and income multipliers involved, transformation is much more likely to generate continuous increments in demand for labour than the past industrialisation of one-off import replacement. This time round, then, women will not arrive in urban areas only to find that industrial development has tapered off. They should gain more than the present small fraction of formal sector employment. The future product mix, favouring consumer goods, should also be in their favour.

Work and opportunity costs

The tertiary sector includes government services, which now face stricter budget limitations. Government employment has, in the past, carried the best security and conditions of work for women. Because it is very formal employment it is arguably the occupation that presents the strongest case of women's economic opportunity cost of children. Therefore, to the extent that government employment of women is reduced, a number of women will experience less of an opportunity cost of children. The same will be true of decreases in private large-scale formal sector employment, which is particularly affected by rising import costs and more exposure to competition. The type of employment for women that was most likely to offer an opportunity cost of children will see the greatest proportionate reduction.

But the principles on which structural adjustment rests lead to the assumption that factors of production will switch to new uses when price relatives change. Because of its greater flexibility and adaptability the informal sector is expected to benefit first from this resource switch.

Depending on what informal sector activities women do, and where in proximity to their homes, there may or may not be an opportunity cost of children. Chapter 5 indicated that women who are employed in the informal sector are able to benefit from the assistance of children. The assistance children can give over a very wide range of informal sector activities could be an influence.

On the count of what is expected to happen in both the formal and informal sectors, adjustment programmes will encourage the maintenance or an increase in fertility rates.

Health and education determinants of population variables

But the other major short-term outcome, less public expenditure on social services and public amenities, is hypothesised to move fertility rates in the opposite, higher, direction through less favourable indicators of the health and education determinants of population variables. The social wage, always larger in urban areas and one of the former attractions to migrants from rural areas, is reduced. User charges for education and health are introduced or increased. Hygiene and sanitation measures in municipal slum settlements are cut back. The effect is likely to be a rise in infant morbidity and mortality rates. The children of the poor will enjoy less education. Apart from a lack of development of skills, user charges for education are bound to mean sharpened discrimination against girls. All in all, for the next generation of young mothers there will be a loss of health and family planning attributes. Investing in the quality of children will now be a more direct burden on parents and will come at a time when real income has fallen. Furthermore, women will have to spend more time "covering" for the loss of public services (carrying water farther, more nursing of the sick, walking to save on higher bus fares, etc.).

There is also doubt whether urban people are moved to make population responses to changes in economic and health circumstances in the short to medium term. It is possible that the economic and health determinants of fertility choices do not have the same impact when their numerical values move in the opposite direction to former experience and when a psychological threshold on reproductive behaviour has already been reached. These are all factors which mitigate against altered fertility rates.

If the current debate on budget reform leads to more cost-effective prioritisation, linkages and targeting the real value of the social wage bill will increase. Therefore, given adequate time for more careful fiscal planning and for improved quality of services and lower prices of public amenities and welfare services, the second-generation effects of adjustment programmes on population determinants should be more favourable to a demographic transition than the first-generation effects.

Migration and household formation

The reduced urban economic and social wages represent a new push factor for migration. If rural areas do not suffer so much, or even gain, the relativity of situations gives rise to a "pull" factor back to rural areas. The pull factor will work a little later and may grow in force over several years. Whether the (mainly male) migrants reverse the step-migration (proceeding from village to rural town to large urban area) or return directly to farms will depend on how the new growth poles are distributed between farm, village and rural town, and on the gender division of labour at these growth poles. It will also depend on whether the new farm production requires the presence of adult male household members (not just to supply labour but to negotiate and apply intensified farm extension services).

The evidence of reverse migration is meagre. But one report (ILO, 1988) states that in sub-Saharan Africa the steady narrowing of the gap between rural and urban incomes, and the fall of urban wages below the level required to acquire a basic food basket, has led to the phenomenon of reverse migration back to villages of origin. But the overall trend towards increasing urbanisation persists because the rural-urban income gap is still wide and combines with other factors—such as the clear advantages of urban areas in public amenities and social services—to attract large numbers of the rural people to the towns (p. 32). Who is moving, which way, and what their age and land asset status is, are subjects of considerable importance.

But return migration does not only cause a new dispersal of population. The new urban refugee can bring back to rural areas some lifestyles and attitudes which, though not rooted historically in the rural economy, are not necessarily antagonistic to the rural resource base.

One effect of this reverse migration will be to alter the distribution of female-headed households. There will be fewer in rural areas and more in urban areas. These latter women will have to seek work anywhere. Some might receive remittances. But for years to come a growing number of female-headed households, with their characteristics of lower per capita income, intense role conflicts for mothers and hazardous childhoods, will be seen in large cities.

Strictly speaking, these changes in the fortunes of urban areas do not represent a situation of different generation effects of the same phenomenon, adjustment, but one consisting of a succession of quite different packages of economic policies to which, in theory, there ought to be a corresponding succession of fertility responses. But this implies a proposition that is a little ludicrous: three alterations in reproductive decisions in, say, less than ten years. What is missing in this display of modelling is a regard for people's opinion, right or wrong, of economic trends over a good number of years. If people believe an economic resurrection is only a few years off, they may not change their reproduction decisions in the short term. On the other hand, if they believe that any upturn in the economy, when it comes, is temporary, they will take decisions now for assuming continued economic depression. Or, given the impossibility of divining the chances of adequate employment within ten years, they will continue "as usual".

Finally, there must be some unease about blithely assuming that reproductive relationships work the same in reverse fashion. The ETF is based on a one-way demographic transition. If the new environment in terms of urban employment and social amenities is a return to the previous status quo, does the memory of recent reproductive behaviour have no influence? If families passed a cultural and psychological threshold in better times, do they step backwards over that threshold in hard times? Or should we not consider new coefficients binding population determinants together? This is basically the question of new ideas "forever planted". It has so far only been introduced into the ETF in terms of migrants bringing ideas back to rural areas and is, for that reason, more important for the impact of new terms of trade favourable to agriculture. But it is plausible to argue that if economic determinants are so uncertain for urban people, then cultural and psychological determinants become more influential. This is particularly true for women who have enjoyed relief from constant reproduction through the adoption of family planning.

Conclusion

In the past rural and urban populations have tended to exhibit different demographic characteristics. Adjustment policies treat them quite differently. The rural population with the pre-demographic transition features of high fertility and, in most cases, high mortality is accorded favoured economic treatment under adjustment with the promise of some means to modernity. The urban population, emerging from the demographic transition, is thrown into a state of economic disequilibrium. But in both cases the ramifications, in terms of personal income and asset status and of physical welfare, are likely to be different for women and men, but similar for farming and non-farming women. The usual adjustment programmes would not meet women's strategic needs to alter their socio-economic status, while previous standards of services to meet their practical needs to cope with their working lives would be put under threat.

The conclusion of the analysis on farming women must be that adjustment policies in agriculture are pro-natalist. This is strongly reinforced when one goes beyond the determining variables of the ETF to look at the elements that go into women's background "status", or the socio-cultural environment of gender relations. There is no indication that adjustment programmes as they are packaged at present would reverse the flow of wealth from children to the chief responsible parent.

As far as can be predicted, structural adjustment in agriculture will impose more work on women but grant them less control over a resource and income base for some years to come. The only relief is in the proclaimed new research and extension interests in non-tradable foods. But this may only be realised after tradables have been fully exploited and therefore after the resource base for non-tradables has been reduced or rendered less secure. This is a recipe for demographic disaster. A package of programmes and policies which improves and secures women's own-account farming stands a good chance of altering this outcome. But it is difficult to see it occurring in the measure required. It is to the longer term and structural transformation that one must look for relief.

The farm household could experience a new crisis of poverty and welfare, keeping it in a high mortality-high fertility frame while agricultural income is significantly rising.

What is most worrying is that this modernisation of peasant farming, through first concentrating on tradables, could draw African farming women away from own-account farming which alone provides the possibility of reinvestible surpluses available for capitalising women's work. Instead, farm women could be confirmed in the role of low-productivity labour with uncertain returns to family upkeep. Boserup (1970) and others have noted how the introduction of cash crops and plough technology weakened female farming systems and women's status. It is highly plausible that a second round of this weakening is being launched with adjustment policies. If so, it could contribute to a more parlous state of maternal and child health.

If structural adjustment policies lead to the demise of female own-account farming on a significant scale, the demographic transition in rural areas may have to await developments other than high-income, small-scale farms. Those developments seem to be twofold: the rise of a well-off farming bourgeoisie and the expansion of a female rural wage labour force. At present this seems a long way off. The literature on African agriculture still mentions kin and affinal ties, and lineage land allocations, But structural adjustment policies and land privatisation could make rapid inroads into these relationships. Contract farming to new agro ("resource-based") industries and a new emergent class of farmers could transform large areas.

This is a sombre picture of the population consequences of adjustment. Yet it is just not credible that governments and international agencies, with their record on gender issues, are capable of putting on the agenda soon enough what is required to make agricultural modernisation compatible with a demographic transition.

For urban populations the signs are, according to the ETF, that adjustment policies will, in the short to medium term, raise the value of children's assistance. At the same time more widespread and intense poverty will, for many families, delay further the chance of investing in the quality of their children. Tighter government budgets for health and social services would make young life more precarious among the poor, and at least not reduce the need to replace deceased children. The net outcome of budget reforms and user charges is unpredictable. Adjustment programmes so far do not ostensibly help larger proportions of the urban population towards a demographic transition.

Part III

Policy implications

In this part of the book implications for policy formulation of the foregoing analysis are drawn out. Throughout the manuscript so far, two main topics have been pursued: first, the terms on which women gain access to factor and product markets and, second, the impact of adjustment policies on population variables and the demographic outlook. By posing gender issues in this way, the question "What is the economic and demographic cost of inaction on women's status?" is implicitly asked. This turns around the far more common question "What is the cost of economic adjustment to women?" It also provides policy-makers with direction when applying a gender approach to improving the efficiency of resource allocation and to consideration of the requirements for long-term sustainable growth.

Gender equity and promoting economic efficiency

11

It is assumed here that monetary stabilisation is about the immediate goal of recovery in external and internal balance by a contraction of domestic demand for national resources, and that *structural adjustment* is about opening up markets to competition to discover the true economic use and value of resources given current technologies. These two programmes should make the present underlying economy function more efficiently. Without any *structural change*, this would represent a state of static efficiency. Structural adjustment should do something else as well. By properly costing resources (that is, reflecting their relative scarcity in the face of prevailing demand) the free market indicates where investments in higher factor productivities should be placed if new comparative advantages are to be sought for long-term transformation of the economy. In other words, true static efficiency points to where investments should be made for dynamic efficiency. The outcome of structural adjustment, as it is narrowly defined in this study, is supposed to bring about this benchmark situation, but not to proceed to dynamic efficiency (as other definitions might have it).

Dynamic efficiency essentially means that, in the process of growth and transformation, resources are allocated efficiently over a long period taken as a whole, without necessarily appearing to be efficiently allocated in any single snapshot analysis. Thus, for instance, a dynamic is achieved by forgoing some profit today in order to invest in higher productivity, with those investments being targeted to achieve the long-term objective at minimum cost to resources. This involves a rearrangement of resources.

Long-term objectives will shape the path of dynamic efficiency, and this path will have a great influence on the interim short-term resource allocations. But adjustment programmes demand that there are also short-term efficiency objectives. There is therefore a conflict between the objectives of the long and short terms. Economic transformation will call for compromises of short-term objectives.

The relation between static and dynamic states has always been difficult for economists to analyse. It has to be pointed out that, conceptually, dynamic efficiency can be achieved without any of the successive static states being very efficient. Why then is the goal of static market efficiency sought here? One reason is that the misallocation of resources through government intervention has been so great in sub-Saharan Africa that some substantial initial convergence on market efficiency must be a preliminary to targeting large investment sums. For the purposes of this study it is also useful to demonstrate how gross are the continuing gender biases in markets after structural adjustment, and how much they could compromise dynamic efficiency if dealing with them were postponed.

In Chapter 9, while exploring the likely influence of gender on the successful outcome of adjustment, it was found that the customary adjustment policies to eliminate market inefficiencies did little to weaken gender-based distortions and might even strengthen some of those described in Chapters 3 and 4.

This chapter begins by looking at the possibility of improving on the level of static efficiency by correcting gender biases in factor and product markets in the time span, five to six years, assumed for stabilisation and structural adjustment programmes. A range of policy instruments and their likely impact are looked at briefly. This is followed by a review of the subjects that planners would have to contend with if gender issues were to be incorporated in plans for dynamic efficiency.

In Chapter 2 three main gender considerations were put forward: discrimination in access to resources and outlets for produce, markets within the household and the additional responsibilities of reproduction and family welfare that women face. The first two are subjects for static and dynamic efficiency policies. But the third is held back for a separate review of policy options. This is done to encourage planners to think in bolder terms than would be suggested by grafting reproduction issues in an ad hoc way on to production issues.

Governments need to keep a sense of proportion on the gender dimension of their economic strategies. Not all the other sources of distortions will have been eliminated by adjustment programmes, and new ones might have crept in. Demanding the instant elimination of gender distortions, which would be virtually impossible anyhow, would be to revert to the former practice of producing a shopping-list of women's demands regardless of the merit of other claims on economic resources. Nevertheless, as one source of market distortion the question "What is the cost of ignoring the gender bias?" is as valid as the question "What is the cost of ignoring the urban bias?" Previous chapters have indicated how important is the misallocation of resources arising from gender-based distortions. Planners need to know what countervailing measures are appropriate and feasible if the obvious solutions are not realistic. At the beginning of this study it was stated that its purpose was to help policy-makers think systematically about gender. Here the issues concerning drawing up an agenda for policy formulation are presented in an order which should help that process.

Gender policies for static market efficiency

The influence of structural adjustment programmes on discrimination in markets

Structural adjustment programmes have affected both female and male employment in the formal sector. Although it is not possible to obtain information on this, it is very likely that employers took the opportunity to discard female employees disproportionately, either because they could incur maternity leave costs or because of the latent statistical discrimination mentioned in Chapter 4. Either way this does not augur well for the uptake of the most effective human resources. Some of these female human resources will move to the informal sector where their skills should make a valuable contribution if they have access to complementary factors of production.

Adjustment programmes so far have not obviously weakened gender discrimination in the distribution of public resources. The design and delivery of public facilities, such as information, extension, training and credit, which have given men privileged access, have not been changed except in isolated cases such as agricultural extension in Kenya. Training programmes are drawn up with male-typed employment in mind. Credit schemes are still widely based on orthodox banking practices which, requiring fixed collateral, discriminate against women because they inherit less and have less chance of accumulating assets. The access points of credit and information services are still more elusive to women because of their greater immobility, illiteracy, and so on. Structural adjustment programmes have not yet dealt with these issues of design. The danger is that by reducing budgetary resources for these public goods and services past privileges have become even more exclusive, so worsening the gender bias and lowering the cost-effectiveness of any supply response from the now more important small-scale and informal sectors.

A separate issue is entry barriers to the informal sector. We cannot assume that it is only existing enterprises that can provide the supply response. Some parts of the intermediate and informal sectors will experience a bigger increase in demand than others, and it is in these that new entrants might beneficially be encouraged through facilitating measures. One costless measure is to legalise these activities. This is only beginning to occur. Most of the legal prohibitions, affecting market stalls, concern female entrepreneurs.

It is in the agricultural sector that the greatest gender biases occur. Those that emanate from both above and below the household level are aggravated by a particular part of the structural adjustment armoury. The standard texts on agricultural development advise policy-makers who are interested in the efficient allocation of resources to ensure that small family farms enjoy at least equitable access with larger commercial farms to extension, credit and inputs because small family farms are more efficient in terms of land yields. This argument is behind the adjustment policy of land reform (between households) and support services going to heads of small farms. Assuming that *(a)* land is the scarcest resource, and *(b)* land is used between crops within the small-scale farming household in some overall maximising way, then this definition of what is most efficient is approximately valid. But in the African agricultural context neither of these assumptions holds good.

The reason why land yields are higher for small farms is because of the more intensive application of female family labour through the gender division of labour and the ultimate authority over land use of the head of household. But this labour, more often than land, is the scarcest of all factors of production. Its lavish use makes no economic sense (and, as seen in Chapters 5, 10 and 12, no demographic sense either). So much female labour is applied on small farms that its productivity (product per unit of labour applied) is very low. It will remain so until women's work processes are capitalised. But this will be most unlikely to occur while women have weak control over productive resources and their general socio-economic status is low. This is basically because of discrimination in the land market due to patrilineal inheritance and custom. The permanent solution to this lies in the long term. But here it is relevant to note that structural adjustment programmes, as practised so far, must have worsened this misuse of resources.

The second assumption defines the family farm as one homogeneous enterprise acting corporately to internalise, and maximise, the rate of return. The theoretical framework showed that this is not valid. Separate accounting units frequently exist in the African farming household, each having its own rate of return. Equalising access to factors of production among heads of farms would be no guarantee of the efficient use of those factors below the household level. One bias could be swapped for another.

There is nothing in structural adjustment programmes for agriculture which corrects or takes into account these gender biases in agricultural factor markets. On the contrary, what is entailed in ending the urban bias, and promoting tradable crops and encouraging the small farm suggests that the misuse of farm family resources, patricularly female labour, will worsen. It is difficult to see what else could be the result given the way access to land is divided between women and men in the predominantly patrilineal lineage system. Were all household land to be brought, under land reform, into one economic accounting unit family labour would effectively be bonded; and thus being partially "free" to the employer it would be utilised in a way which increased the difference between the value of its marginal product and its economic opportunity cost. This assumes that female family labour is not mobile in the locality.

But another consequence of structural adjustment programmes might counter this. If, at the same time, alternative rural employment were expanded, women would be encouraged to take employment off their own family's farm. If female family labour did take this alternative employment, it would be reducing the misallocation of labour resources below the household level by forcing a proper costing of labour on the family farm manager who would now have to hire labour. In the circumstances small family farms may not be more efficient in terms of either land yields or profitability. The encouragement to male members of farming households to assert their reserve powers over family land and labour deployment is likely to be greatest in the fertile, line-of-rail areas. But large commercial farms in the same area will gain as much or more, so countering with greater incentives to female wage labour. The final outcome of adjustment programmes for the efficiency of female labour deployment could be determined as much by the social fabric as by market forces.

Gender equity in access to product markets in all sectors complements what occurs in factor markets. If there are privileged and underprivileged operators in product markets, discriminatory returns are being made and this has its effect on factor markets through backward linkages. Gender inequalities in product markets arise from biases in sources of information, marketing channels and socio-institutional structures. These have not been redressed through adjustment programmes.

One product of labour is income, in cash or kind. The theoretical framework described the asymmetry of exchange and reciprocities of women and men in family-based production. This is applicable to all sectors, not just agriculture. In effect, women are not always able to control the returns to their labour. De facto, then, they have restricted access to a product market. This is the problem of intra-household income distribution so frequently raised in the published commentaries on gender and adjustment and mentioned in Chapter 8. The fear is that the array of orthodox adjustment policies designed to offer incentives to producers to expand or switch production may offer little incentive, or even disincentive, to women to co-operate because they anticipate that they will not see much of the new income. The intra-household distribution or disposal of income is one of the most difficult distortions to correct. It rests on the unequal access of women and men to resources and the socio-economic status of women. As such its permanent solution lies in the very long term. But Chapter 9 showed that structural adjustment programmes would probably have made this bias in product markets worse, and with that aggravated gender biases in factor markets.

Feasible solutions in the short to medium term

What can be done in the short to medium term to eradicate gender biases? The answer is "very little". Many of the gender constructs of markets are not amenable to treatment over a few years. The ones that are would be those affecting access to public resources, which is what makes the public sector so important in reducing gender distortions. In the climate of government trying to save on expenditure it might be supposed that these innovations have to be postponed. Yet some of the more effective innovations to improve women's access to public resources require only legal and institutional reforms.

Some public resources, such as training and health, give rise to human resource investment which can offer dividends in the medium term. But public resources supply other variable factors of production such as working capital, technical information and marketing outlets. Feasible solutions to gender discrimination in their distribution would consist of redesigning the nature of these services and their access points to make them of greater relevance to women. Criteria for granting credit could be altered to give women a better chance. Co-operatives, credit societies and marketing societies could all be obliged to open their doors to women and ensure wide access points to services. If these measures are to counteract a tendency in past designs to favour men's needs and access, then they can be regarded as permanent reforms, not as holding actions. They simply constitute more successful means to reach the intended targets. Therefore there are a number of reforms that could become new permanent fixtures in a short time.

What characterises these solutions is that they entail legislative or institutional reforms governing the absorption of public sector resources. The private sector, in which the great bulk of resources lie, is not amenable to institutional changes in this limited period. Because so many of the causes of gender discrimination in the private sector are rooted in social attitudes the range of solutions achievable in five to six years is not great. For this reason it is most unfortunate that some aspects of economic adjustment policies act as catalysts to a more pronounced role for these causes. Therefore, if there is any way to limit these causes of gender discrimination in the medium term, they must rest in a modification of stabilisation and structural adjustment programmes. The chief means is slowing or weakening the new production incentives to give time for public sector redesign and some institutional reforms to take effect. But governments may not wish to postpone new production incentives, in which case something stronger than searching around for medium-term solutions is called for.

Counterbalancing policy instruments

If it is not possible to reduce a market distortion, overall efficiency can be raised by inserting a counterbalancing distortion. Because withdrawal of government intervention from markets is a cardinal principle of adjustment, some relaxation of the economic rules is required. Among Stewart's list of meso policies are all kinds of counterbalancing policy instruments. These comprise subsidies, taxes, allocations and some further institutional reforms representing positive discriminations.

A counterbalancing distortion can comprise more than one policy instrument. For instance, the allocations of credit may be at low subsidised interest rates. Or sales of men's agricultural produce may be taxed to finance any investments in women's higher labour productivity. Allocative intervention can be used as a counterbalancing distortion to one that exists in the use of training facilities. The more the aggregate training and education budget has to be cut, the more imperative is it to design the facilities so that resources reach intended target groups. Quotas for female entrants is one measure. Discrimination against males in user charges for both education and health facilities is another. There is also a case for making women a priority group for small and informal sector employment support services, such as information, training and credit lines. One of the most important inputs of any production is credit. There are near costless ways of overcoming access problems of those who could make efficient use of it. If the design reforms mentioned above prove inadequate in the medium term, then targeting priority groups with subsidies and quotas are other possible policies. It goes without saying that credit should be made available to individual women, and therefore credit reform should go below the household level.

Although these meso policies need not affect the macro targets of stabilisation and structural adjustment programmes, they do have to win over planners to the idea of new subsidies, taxes and allocations. To the strict free marketeer they will be anathema and will have to be argued on the grounds of one distortion countering the effects of other, inherent, distortions which cannot be dealt with in the medium term.

Counterbalancing actions do not resolve anything. They provide space and time, and can hold back worse things. But like all counterbalancing actions they are not expected to last for ever. What distinguished meso policies from the feasible solutions of the medium term mentioned above is that the former should be seen as temporary solutions. Prioritising and positive discrimination can be only a means to an end if the ultimate objective is long-term efficiency of resource use. In the context of this chapter, they constitute a holding operation against some market imperfections until more permanent reforms are possible. They cannot be a permanent feature of long-term adjustment programmes.

What is worrying is that application of the full range of meso policies may not be able to prevent a worsening of gender-based static inefficiencies during structural adjustment. It could be argued that this is the price that has to be paid for more substantial gains in market efficiencies in other directions, and that dealing with gender inequality in markets must wait for wealth to be created by these other improvements. However, the overall economic strategy of adjustment and transformation depends heavily, in the sub-Saharan context, on women becoming much more economically effective than they have been in areas such as agriculture, agricultural processing and the informal sector. Planners are drawn back to the question: "What is the cost of ignoring gender biases?" There are two further calculations to be made before conceding the case that nothing must impair progress on eliminating other sources of market inefficiency.

The first is that other gains in market efficiency need not be forfeited by a modified stabilisation and structural adjustment package which seeks to prevent a worsening of gender-based inefficiencies. As was pointed out in Chapter 7, if the success of some of these meso policies is very great then there might be a case for moderating macroeconomic targets if these stood in the way of even greater efficacy of meso policies. That is to say, if counterbalancing distortions are effective but would require an easing of macro targets (mostly monetary and fiscal) to be even more effective, there is a case for reshaping the overall adjustment package in the light of gender's contribution to structural adjustment reaching static efficiency. This is another means to give time and area for manoeuvrability to bring more meso policies into force to balance gender effects. But the situation will only be eased, and the gender structured markets will probably be little affected. There are other reasons why policy-makers are thinking of modifying macro targets. Gender can now be added.

The second calculation is that if gender biases are not restrained during the structural adjustment process towards static efficiency they could add problems, unnecessarily, to an already lengthy long-term agenda.

Unfinished business

It was earlier suggested that the flushing out of static inefficiencies reveals where investments are necessary for dynamic efficiency. But it looks now as though this promise cannot be kept as far as gender-based inefficiencies are concerned. Continued gender bias will make sure that true scarcities are not revealed by free market prices, and some gross resource misallocations will remain hidden from market view. Completing this unfinished business through an extended structural adjustment programme is not the answer. A modified adjustment programme can only be ameliorative and palliative. Gender structures in markets will still be there.

What this means, in effect, is that gender-based barriers to static allocative efficiency are eliminated only in the very long term, which allows for the possibility of novel solutions. Some of these barriers are so deeply rooted in the way society is organised that they will not succumb to the usual price signals and reforms, let alone to withdrawal of government intervention and liberalisation of markets. The nature of gender biases is such that to reduce their influence, intervention of one kind or another may have to be spread over a period of time sufficient to see substantial changes in society. So this is the contradiction: static gender efficiency can only come after socio-economic transformation.

Gender requirements for dynamic market efficiency

Economic transformation and dynamic efficiency

Dynamic efficiency means allocating resources to where their returns are maximised over a term long enough to release their potential through reforms and investments. This maximising position is not obtained immediately. Present dividends have to be forgone to invest in higher-yield potentials. The preconditions of dynamic efficiency will be determined by the transformation that is undertaken. That transformation will not be entirely objective. Governments have their own ideas of what future comparative advantages should be and what the best internal economic dynamic is. They will want to diversify out of a few critical exports, and so on. These decisions will require a futuristic outlook. Earlier in this chapter the possible decline of the small family farm in the face of an expanding female rural wage labour market was mentioned. If labour is properly costed by small farms, it is difficult to see how these farms will survive the virtually inevitable rise of commercial farms emerging from the top end of the small-scale sector. If governments wish to secure the future of the small-scale agricultural sector, economic transformation might have to include some novel changes in economic relations between the sexes.

Whatever path and direction of economic transformation is chosen, there will be a corresponding set of gender issues to reach that transformation in the most efficient way.

However, governments are bound to see gender issues in the economy also in a subjective light. It may be that they are not willing to face the transformation of socio-economic relations between women and men that the most cost-effective shift to new comparative advantages or the desired internal dynamic would entail. The view that (very long-term) economic evolution is preferable to economic revolution (change forced through within, say, ten to 15 years) is perfectly valid. But it is the duty of economists to point out the economic price of this preference.

Nevertheless, it is proper that economic planners should be able to present options for eliminating long-term inefficiencies in markets caused by gender influences, and to indicate the consequences of rejecting them.

Long-term aspects of gender efficiency in markets

There are two aspects of long-term gender efficiency in markets. The first is dealing with the underlying causes of the inability to reach static gender efficiency. The second is the new business of ensuring that new gender biases are not developed during the process of economic transformation. The latter is made more difficult because the true costing of resources is not possible in the medium term. And yet both are so closely related to the status of girls and women, and to women's access to and control of resources, that the agenda for dynamic efficiency is really a matter of laying down the necessary preconditions to achieve this equality.

In formal sector employment the relevant issues are education and training of girls and boys to prepare both equally for new work practices and techniques. Without this, non-homogeneity of the formal labour market will continue to be extensive.

This human resources development will also both strengthen women's relative access to other variable factors of production for informal sector entrepreneurship and self-employment, and give teeth to institutional reforms. But it has a gestation period which means that it takes effect only after a time lapse. If it is supposed to deliver increasing levels of efficiency in resource allocation towards a state of dynamic efficiency, then gender equity in human resources development cannot be postponed.

In agriculture, reaching the necessary preconditions involves much more fundamental socio-economic change than human resources development and reform of public facilities. Raising the productivity of women's farming efforts requires distinctive action on the part of government. Subsidies for better implements, with or without taxation of sales of produce, only tinkers with the issue of lifting women's very low labour productivity to its much higher potential. Unless the problem is addressed, the drive for transformation of agriculture through capital investments could bring about the misuse of capital, as well as labour. In other words, capital spent on new agricultural research and technology could be wasted if there were not accompanying action on female labour productivity. On the other hand, if capital were directed to raising female labour productivity while using the same quantity of captial on technical inputs, the yield on both capital and labour could increase.

Raising the productivity of women's uncommoditised farming is also essential if dynamic efficiency is to penetrate a large block of primary resources. But doing this will present difficulties, especially in an era when the pressure is on to show direct monetised returns to any public outlay. It must be stressed that this is not an argument for gender equality. It is about how the whole agricultural economy can expand and move forward. Present low productivity of uncommoditised agriculture is a constraint on the successful outcome for all agriculture. Investment in higher-productivity methods of uncommoditised production can offer external economies to commoditised production through the release, or more efficient use, of resources.

But there is only one way of raising women's agricultural productivity, and that is to give them assured control over the resources they manage.

Realistic restrictions on gender reforms

Reforms cannot be planned devoid of reference to social or cultural opposition. Some will be easier to implement than others because of social factors. But the postponement of one important reform because of this kind of opposition could leave a hole, or a weakness in the tension holding other reforms together.

Opposition to reform will arise in cases where it leads to units above the family level encouraging women to conduct autonomous economic lives. This may be in the area of personal financial contracts or provision of technical advice and business planning.

But the most important policy reform is women's rights of inheritance, marriage settlements and land. This cuts deep into men's authority over women, and there is no question that it will be resisted. Yet it is crucial to economic transformation and dynamic efficiency. Women must be able to raise capital as easily as men if capital resources are to be efficiently distributed. Dynamic efficiency is not compatible with non-homogeneity of the capital market.

In the past economic planners have ignored the issue of women's land rights because they have mentioned the friction of a Western nuclear family model. Their advocacy of the small farm has drawn on research findings (mainly from Asia) that these farms are more efficient in land use than large ones because they use family labour more intensively. Now, in an era when a stronger spotlight is on allocatory inefficiencies, African economists are confronting the truth. The ECA's *African alternative framework* . . . makes this plain. The World Bank is also in general agreement with the importance of women's land rights in raising agricultural productivity. The economic case for women's equal land rights is overwhelming. But there should be no underestimating the opposition to any attempt to implement them in a direct manner.

In Asian centrally planned economy countries women's rights in the land reform legislation were given added teeth through reform of the marriage law (child custody and retention of personal assets on divorce or widowhood). Although the way the two were linked in Asia may not be appropriate for sub-Saharan Africa because of the seeming impossibility of direct land reform between women and men in Africa, the principle of the linkage could be adapted to the African context by guaranteeing women lifelong tenancy of certain assets they came to manage at marriage.

If securing long-term land tenancy rights for women is not possible, then the same is true of an agricultural transformation strategy based on the small family farm, in which case dynamic efficiency has to be planned with some other ultimate objective in mind.

If social opposition to gender equity in markets is very strong, then what is required is a reformulation of dynamic efficiency around what remains of gender equity. In doing this, the means to compensate for deficient equity might be sought by stronger emphasis on one or more gender reforms in the form of meso policies or modified macro targets. In the final analysis, then, gender efficiency in markets may have to be simulated for decades by policies that ought really to constitute merely holding operations.

The reproduction labour tax

So far gender imperfections of markets have been treated as though women are merely units of productive labour or entrepreneurship which are discriminated against. This ignores the quantum of daily hours women put into the supply of immediate-use goods and services for domestic maintenance and child care.

The different domestic maintenance and child-care tasks of women are well known. What has to be pointed out is that these extra unremunerated tasks act as a labour levy, or tax, on women to be paid before they can join in marketed activities. Like all taxes it distorts. Thus women's reproduction activities distort the "production" labour market. Any labour market entrant who is tied for periods of her/his working life to other responsibilities is unable to compete equally and for an equal length of time on the basis of intrinsic merit. But what happens in one market has a derived influence on other markets. Therefore a distortion in the labour market has a knock-on effect in other factor markets; and distortions in factor markets create distortions in product markets. In this way the reproduction tax on women sends ripples of inefficiencies throughout the economy.

There is already an implicit recognition of this tax, and the response has been, effectively, a countering subsidy. When governments ameliorate conditions in the domestic sector through social expenditure, it enables women to cope better. Meeting this practical gender need is often motivated by the fear that women's domestic work threatens "economic" output. But this intervention need not improve the underlying efficiency of resource allocation. This depends on how the released labour of women is channelled and, in turn, influences the allocation of other factors of production. An obvious outcome is that female labour is used even more intensively (lavishly for a scarce resource) in production. The only guarantee that resources in the domestic sector are absorbed and used efficiently is when these activities are exposed to market forces. And this can only be done by strategic gender changes which allow women equal access with men to resources.

Essentially the misallocation stems from the fact that the non-biological elements of this reproduction labour tax which could be subject to market forces are not. This cannot be corrected by changing prices or by institutional reforms in present markets. Until it is opened up to market forces, the cost in terms of national resources used and economic production forgone can only be guessed. But by the same token this is an area of work in which labour productivity improvements are not generated from within. It does not give rise to a reinvestible surplus. An obligation on women to fund such improvements from a surplus on any of their own market-oriented activities amounts to a tax on those activities and therefore jeopardises their further development. Any strategy to give women new income-generating activities, such as vegetable gardening, to fund a new domestic water supply comes under this category.

The subsidies that are effectively used by women, through the social sector budget, are visible to planners. Some planners no doubt view these subsidies merely as a means to supply basic needs and therefore do not expect them to produce an economic return. Presumably such diversion of resources is allowable on political or social grounds. What is far less visible is the diversion of resources arising from the reproduction tax on women's labour time. Quantifying this tax runs into enormous methodological and definitional problems. But a conservative estimate must put it well in excess of any social sector subsidies enjoyed exclusively by women. This digression is made in order to point out that there is a wider economic cost to the country (as distinct from the immediate financial cost to women and their families) of women's labour-intensive, non-commoditised housework and family welfare work. Its relevance to policy formulation springs from the need to develop a view on what amount of prioritisation of budgetary provision is justified by the gains from reducing market distortions arising from this labour tax on women.

What is the impact of structural adjustment programmes on this labour tax on women? Cuts in social sector expenditure increase it. And this occurs at a time when women in agriculture will be expected to work longer hours in the fields and when urban women seek and carry out any gainful employment in increasingly time-consuming ways. Most recent changes in the policy environment allow other possible scenarios. Budget reforms, extra resources and further meso policies in "social dimensions of adjustment" packages will counter the impact for some women.

But these are ameliorations of crisis conditions. They do not answer the question: "What is to be done to reduce this huge labour tax on women in the long run?" Tap water and electrification of homes would bring about the greatest reductions but they require large capital investments which have a long gestation period. At the very least, however, they should find a place on the agenda of economic transformation.

In the shorter term the distorting effects of the labour tax can be reduced by counterbalancing taxes. In effect, this would amount to using fiscal measures to award transfer payments to a group which starts in market exchange with a handicap. Transfer payments in the form of child-minding facilities in villages, in formal sector enterprises and even in localities where there is a concentration of informal sector activity is one possibility. Maternity leave legislation can be added. The funding for all this could come from an employment tax on all enterprises listed on the companies register, to be paid into a national provident fund. This scheme will carry its own distorting effects, such as weighing on the formal sector and more heavily on labour-intensive production. But these are minor compared with the continued drain of resources resulting from role conflicts of women. In rural areas the funds could be raised from a sales tax on selected main cash crops as a form of redress for the poor remuneration of female labour. This would constitute a small disincentive to priority production under stabilisation and structural adjustment, and therefore involves a modification of a macro target.

All this might be seen as helping women to cope better. But it is more than this if women's greater activity in market exchange brings them direct increments of produce or cash income.

What has been argued here is to bring as much as possible of the reproduction labour tax on women into market exchange: tap water and electrification of homes means a paid workforce in public utilities. Crèches mean professional, paid child-minders. All this amounts to new sources of officially recorded "personal disposable income" instead of women's unrecorded burden. The significance of this should not be lost on African governments now trying to reform fiscal practices to raise more revenue. Without any net cost over the long term it can release women's labour, correct a massive distortion in the labour market and raise revenue through sustainable channels.

This chapter has outlined an agenda for debating policy instruments to counter persistent, or worsening, gender distortions in markets. It draws on previous chapters to show that the goal of static efficiency of structural adjustment as it is narrowly defined here, and as it has been practised during the 1980s, is not achievable in terms of gender. This means that an agenda for economic transformation is inevitably burdened with this "unfinished business" of structural adjustment, and that prevailing market prices cannot be assumed to reflect relative scarcity of factors of production, especially female labour. Separate from this is the question of what boldness of strategy is required to reduce the log jam on sub-Saharan African development caused by women's reproduction work. One way of looking at it is presented here.

Influencing the demographic outcome 12

The issue

This study began with the supposition that the ultimate goal of economic planning was an improvement in per capita income. To that end economic growth must outpace population growth. Moreover, because resources are in finite supply that process must also, inter alia, bring population growth rates to a level which in the very long term converges on zero. This is not to say that populations should be fixed at their present sizes. Resources can be made more productive through technological adaptation and some areas can carry a larger population. But there are already indications of the future limits to the production-bearing capacity of the environment. It is prudent therefore to plan population growth now on the assumption that high rates of aggregate economic growth cannot be maintained indefinitely.

The humanistic way of reaching a supportable population growth trend must be through a demographic transition. This can be assisted by relating as much of economic planning as possible to achieving goals for population variables which should steer the population through a demographic transition.

The analysis in Part II of the impact of adjustment policies pointed to changes in some of the more important primary and intermediate population variables which would, on balance, not encourage a demographic transition. In particular, there would be little hope for more restriction of family size than takes place now. When these determinants are examined from women's particular viewpoint, the prognostication for the short and medium term appears worse. The issue for planning, then, is to design population and economic strategies which are compatible with each other's objectives.

Present population policies

Research on demographic relationships has achieved some understanding of the influences on population variables such as mortality, fertility and migration, and an appreciation of the respect that must be shown towards cultural and social variables if apparently conflicting conclusions are to be explained. But the influence of research on a population policy has been limited. Two writers have summed up the situation well:

> The basic point is that if researchers want to contribute to the policy process, they have to recognise that variables such as infant mortality are not policy instruments in themselves, and that in order for research to be very helpful to the policy process, it must go one step further and build in a careful examination of all steps from the decision or the potential decision to undertake the programme to the ultimate objective, which is to change fertility (Simmons and Farooq, 1985, p. 117).

The initial obstacle to the translation of research into policy lies with the limited goals of much that has passed for a population policy until recently. This policy has rested largely on trying to influence a narrow range of determinants, mainly health indicators, by means of resources directed to social sector budgets. Consequently, only a few specific policy instruments were under consideration.

In sub-Saharan countries what might be termed active population policies have focused on family planning. But this can be regarded as another ingredient of health, and anyway has limited coverage of the population. A bigger weakness in tying a population policy to health policies is that health indicators have been treated in isolation and without any accompanying policy on the underlying determinants of health. Family planning, as a health measure, is partly one of practical containment, and it can be defeated by more primary influences. But factors such as women's literacy and socio-economic status, which would make up a strategic population policy, cannot be addressed in this way. They call for a wider application of research findings and a place on the agenda of economic planning.

Even within the social sector, population policies are sometimes viewed as exogenous, ad hoc components which end up making demands on social services without being fully integrated with them. The selection of other social policies may not include consideration of their consequences for demographic variables and processes. Where this is the prevailing policy environment it is understandable that population programmes can amount to no more than additional maternal and child health and some preventive health measures.

Farooq and Pernia (1988) have pointed out that, in spite of a consensus on the importance of the inter-relationships of the population dynamic and economic development, the treatment of population variables in socio-economic planning remains rudimentary, with population factors still being treated as exogenous planning components. "The state of the art seems restricted mostly to an examination of population projections in relation to the demand for social services" (p. 11). The failure to integrate population and economic planning is both an institutional and an intellectual failure. Government units with responsibility for population policies are usually located in non-economic ministries and do not have access to economic ministries and their planning mechanisms. An agenda for a dialogue between demographers and economic planners does not exist. The conditions for the success of a strategic or population-influencing, as distinct from a reactive, population policy are not present. The weak institutional framework in government machineries is obvious. But this will not be corrected until the conceptual and methodological framework and the objectives of population policy units are better established.

Population planning units in government machineries invariably commence their work by gathering baseline data on population variables and extrapolating the demographic future (mostly for manpower and social sector planning purposes). So far population planning seems to have rested passively on planning for the numbers to come rather than trying to plan those numbers. "Since the early 1980s an increasing number of countries have recognised the need for an active population policy, but concrete action programmes are yet to be devised" (ILO, 1988a, p. 62). The units have not yet developed a framework for arguing a different economic strategy to make population goals more feasible.

Current activity towards achieving this concentrates on training. This includes training in utilisation of data and research for policy analysis, and techniques of making demographic projections and their utilisation in sectoral and subnational planning (ILO, 1987a, p. 53). All UNFPA/ILO projects and training activities are directed towards this goal. Behind this is the objective of "creation of awareness of the impact of population variables on development goals and processes". However, this does not fully represent what those who want to take population policies further have in mind. In the same reference it is mentioned that the major problem area remains in the development of the means to evaluate the demographic impact of the more pertinent development policies and programmes so that socio-economic policies can make their due contribution to the objectives of population policy.

New moves to broaden the analytical framework included a 1986 inter-country training workshop for senior development planners drawn from 20 sub-Saharan African countries, which addressed concepts and analytical techniques for comprehensive population, human resources and development planning. Its agenda does not indicate any substantive treatment of economic and demographic relationships apart from "Population and development planning: Before and after Bucharest—The significance of human resource development", which was given introductory status (ILO, 1987a, p. 57). A later, international in-service training workshop took the discussion further but fell short of a debate on an agenda for inter-departmental dialogue (ILO, 1989c).

Making demands on the planning process

A fundamental difficulty of formulating an adequate population programme is the ongoing separation of economic and social planning. Population policies have, effectively, become a claim on social sector budgets because of the major role given to health and welfare variables. As long as this state of affairs continues population programmes will be totally dependent on the fortunes of the social sector budget, and there can be only a fortuitous reconciliation between economic and population objectives. On the record of the past, and on near-term predictions of the impact of adjustment strategies, this is unlikely. Both welfare and population programmes have had the distinct air of fire-brigade actions trying to quench the emissions from hegemonic economic policies.

Before discussing what the integration of population and economic planning could entail, it is necessary to indicate what it means. What is not meant here is integration of a component of integrated area development, as has sometimes been the case. Farooq and Pernia (1988) suggest the following definition of integrated population and economic planning: "The explicit and direct consideration of socio-economic and demographic interrelationships in the design (and implementation) of policies, programmes and projects, with due regard to potential conflicts and complementarities, to achieve a country's social and economic goals (p. 5)." This will allow a progression over time from the selective intervention of corrective planning to full economic-demographic modelling: a cumulative process rather than an instant achievement in the short term.

The definition of the final goal is comprehensive enough. But the progressive path to it is not yet fully elucidated. The problem is that "intervention and correction" could be taken to mean the same as ad hoc fire-brigade action at worst, or redesigning a few separate economic policy instruments at best; and if there is no sense of urgency about reaching full economic-demographic modelling, what starts as an interim means of raising population issues could become a permanent fixture.

The model of progressing from corrections to full integrated economic and population planning is associated with the step-by-step training curriculum and activities development of the population planning units that exist. The first steps comprise putting together the stock of known research on demographic and socio-economic linkages, followed by an inventory of socio-economic data and demographic estimates and projections. The next step is to identify further research questions, especially those related to current economic planning practices. Then comes the task of developing selective intervention and corrections to economic planning, as for example: "Demographic, labour market and income distribution subsystems, based on the results of partial studies on specific demographic/economic linkages, could be developed for grafting on to the existing economic models" (Farooq and Pernia, 1988, p. 15). Thus we have stages of activities and a grafting on to existing economic models. Full integrated modelling is not yet in sight.

There is nothing in this "corrective planning" which might question the appropriateness of the economic policies themselves for an economic strategy which is deemed cost-effective when its demographic harvest is finally reaped. That kind of cost-effectiveness can only be assured when demographic issues become part of:

(a) the identification of the economic problem that planning is to solve;
(b) the clarification of development objectives; and
(c) the consequent policy packaging.

Anything less than this means that integration starts after certain options for the economic strategy that are favourable to a demographic transition have been closed off and demographers have to do as best they can with corrections of population policies, while population and development policies remain basically at cross purposes.

In bolder relief, integration must mean the institutionalisation of joint population and economic planning, from the settlement of overall objectives to the design of sectoral policies and budgets. Economic development and population dynamics will each have contradictions between their respective short-, medium- and long-term objectives. The integration of economic and population objectives will mean dealing with a matrix of contradictions. But there will not just be contradictions. Some population objectives will reinforce some economic objectives; and vice versa.

It will not be easy for population analysts to establish a role in the early formulation of economic strategies. The weight of post-1950 tradition has been that economists are the high priests of development planning, while practitioners of other disciplines are the supplicants. This has given rise to the hegemony of economics. It will require a sea change in thinking about development to place economic planners in the role of facilitators of demographic objectives. One approach is to commence immediately with a dry run on integrated population-economic modelling using a particular and narrowly defined economic strategy. In effect this jumps over the stage of corrections and "grafting on". It should indicate the potential of population objectives with more complicated economic strategies.

A proposed modelling exercise

Structural adjustment and economic transformation provide a suitable background development strategy to such a dry run on modelling because of the realism they introduce into planning in general and because they are directed against misallocation of resources and lost opportunities, including those arising from the current status of women.

It is therefore proposed that this modelling exercise is confined to the particular type of economic development based on goals of efficiency and transformation to higher factor productivities and new comparative advantages for strategic purposes. The economic framework and its ultimate purposes are therefore assumed. But the policies are not. This study provides ideas on what is to be negotiated between population and economic planners. Chapter 5 concluded by questioning how economic adjustment and transformation policies could be designed to bring about desired population variables. Chapter 10 taken together suggested that demographers' first task might be to persuade policy-makers to modify current adjustment packages because, arguably in the light of population theories, they encourage undesirable changes in population variables.

Confining the economic model to well-defined adjustment and transformation strategies is the first of two differences between the exercise proposed here and the fully integrated population-economic development modelling alluded to above.

The second is that the development of human resources is not the centre-piece of the proposed modelling exercise, as it seems to be for the population planning units. Instead of holding a brief for human resources development and making supplications to economic planners to get the best deal for human resources by arguing a convergence of interests, the approach here is to turn economic planners into supplicants wishing to obtain cost-effective labour and entrepreneurial contributions to the economic strategy and to secure per capita income benefits. Much of the discussion would be the same as that pursued in future by the units, but the presentation of arguments and immediate objectives could differ.

The basics of an agenda for a dialogue

Relating objectives

If economic planners become the supplicants, then the hegemony of economic objectives comes to an end. The door is open to negotiating economic objectives in the light of population objectives. What is of concern here is how to move to two final developmental goals: dynamic economic efficiency and a demographic transition. It is likely to take decades to achieve these goals. That long period of time needs to be divided up into shorter, more manageable periods. A first step is to establish realistic packaging of successive immediate objectives. There are several issues here.

Short- to long-term objectives and policies

Chapter 11 took up the point that gender gives rise to one of the contradictions between the objectives and processes of static efficiency and dynamic efficiency. Reconciliation of this contradiction will require acceptance of trade-offs and restrictions on short-term efficiency, and above all the imposition of short-term counterbalancing biases to contain the inefficiency until investments and reforms required by dynamic efficiency can be made.

A strategy of population adjustment does not experience contradictions in the same way. That is to say, achievements of the short term should not present problems for the long term. However, while some primary and intermediate variables are easier to change than others, without change in certain crucial variables they could lack the force of impact. For instance, health indicators and the infant mortality rate can be improved through resource allocation to social sector budgets and economic policies might be able to deliver on family incomes, but without achieving the objective of an increase in the socio-economic status of women (and particularly women's workloads) these changes might contribute little to moving the population to a demographic transition. Thus some short-term (easy option) achievements might not add up to much if other (more difficult) achievements are not in place. The issue then becomes one of putting objectives and their associated policy instruments in an ordering of different time horizons which contains internal consistency and feasibility.

Because improving the socio-economic status of women includes altering social parameters it might be viewed as involving a long haul and therefore a long-term objective. But there are aspects of women's status which can be dealt with in the short to medium term. These involve some institutional reforms. But, in addition, economic planners who are concerned with efficiency of resource allocation will not let pass arguments that social sector budgets cannot be utilised most efficiently until women's status is improved. They will want something to be done about women's status straight away, even if it presents a challenge to their own array of economic policy instruments and to social practices.

Thus far we have the beginnings of separate agendas for the objectives and policies for economic adjustment and for population. Where population planning units aim to integrate human resource development with economic development, this study holds fast to the goals of economic efficiency but adds the goal of a demographic transition. This is reiterated here because in what follows it could mistakenly be assumed that a fully integrated economic/population model is being pursued. Even though this study is not concerned with such models, its concern with the impact of adjustment policies on population variables means that those adjustment policies have to be questioned.

Economic adjustment and transformation include development objectives with a very long-term view. They must embody a futuristic image of a viable relation between population and their own processes. But immediate objectives should incorporate two aspects: *(a)* a staging of the long-term demographic-economic objective into shorter time spans, and *(b)* some changes constituting preconditions for others.

The first aspect makes what is a new and speculative exercise more manageable and offers the opportunity for stocktaking and revisions of packages. Since adjustment and transformation will be planned in stages anyway, it is appropriate that changes in population variables are reviewed over the same time span. If these time spans cover limited periods there will be opportunities to monitor and correct economic policies. In addition, governments can gauge the amount of resources at their disposal only for a few years at a time.

The second aspect is the substance of relating population variables to planning structural adjustment and transformation. The challenge rests in judging the waste of resources in attempting some economic targets while primary and intermediate determinants of population variables are operating as they do; and judging the waste of resources in attempting some demographic targets without first laying down favourable economic and social conditions. For instance, rural maternal and child health might be so bad that it would not be cost-effective to provide incentives and farm support services for intensified production methods before something was done about it. Or targets of lower fertility depending largely on family planning facilities would incur waste unless couples, and especially women, saw reason, through economic changes, to reduce fertility. The concept of some changes opening the door to others also means that the demographic transition need not be expected to progress steadily and uniformly across a range of population variables and their determinants. If this is understood, then the immediate economic and population objectives could appear to be out of step with each other while contributing to a consistent longer term.

Practical and strategic gender needs

Moser's distinction between strategic gender needs and practical gender needs is useful here. Strategic means a permanent structural change from which flows a new stream of social or directly economic resources. Practical means a response to an incapacity to function well within a given set of structures. The first opens the door to new things; the second provides easier coping with the old. To achieve both dynamic efficiency in the economy and a demographic transition meeting the strategic needs of women is indispensable. Of course, meeting a practical gender need, such as providing safe water supplies, can lead to a permanent structural change by releasing women's labour resources for other activities. But then the end result is meeting a strategic need of women. To constitute an immediate objective for changing the socio-economic status of women it must be cast as a strategic gender need.

The issues involved in placing the treatment of practical and strategic gender needs in some order include:

- selecting what is necessary to at least hold the line on the circular deterioration of women's lives mentioned in Chapter 1, when adjustment policies start to take effect;
- identifying aspects of adjustment programmes which make it less likely that strategic gender needs will be met; and
- identifying meso policies and modifications of macroeconomic targets that would correct the above.

There is also the issue of dealing with social and cultural opposition to gender reforms. This was taken up in the previous chapter in relation to the influence that gender reforms had on progress to dynamic efficiency. There it was pointed out that postponement of these reforms had an economic cost. But it is the impact of social and cultural opposition to gender reforms on primary population determinants that brings the issue even more to the forefront of policy. The solutions rest much more with new economic policy instruments than with social sector programmes.

The choice of policy instruments and their packaging will emerge from the formulation of the immediate objectives and judgements about the relative contribution of strategic and practical gender needs. Past research findings will provide the arguments for selection, prioritisation, sequencing and design of those policy instruments.

Outline of an agenda

It has to be admitted that this invasion of economic planning processes is not going to occur overnight. But something more than *post hoc* corrective action could be demanded at the start. If it cannot be agreed that objectives must combine economic and demographic dynamics, because of the uncertainty surrounding relationships, one line of action would be to check every objective and every statement of intent of economic adjustment and transformation for its population implications—not after publication of a Five-Year Plan but when the Plan is still on the drawing-board.

In incorporating population planning in stabilisation and structural adjustment programmes, one has to accept that these programmes have been pursued for some years and that they will have settled into an institutional groove. They will also have left a legacy of population determinants in flux for the next stage of adjustment to cope with. Many of the budget reforms now being undertaken include an element of countering the fallout from the recent severe economic programmes that earlier went unchallenged by population planners. This is indicative of the fact that the population-economic agenda is thus more crowded than it would have been had population considerations been taken into account at the start of adjustment.

An outline of the agenda might be drawn up around the following inquiries:

1. Does the absence of consideration of determinants of population variables in the early years of adjustment call for a revision of intended economic policies?
2. What effect will the implementation of macro-level variable targets have on sectoral (and spatial) labour markets and, inter alia, on primary and intermediate determinants of population variables? Should other measures accompany the implementation to promote a more positive relationship?
3. What effect have the present health status and demographic profiles of households on the ability of workers and the self-employed to respond to intended economic incentives? How might these intended incentives be appropriately reduced or augmented in the light of this effect?
4. What market, legal and institutional reforms should be selected, and how should they be packaged, to ensure women's access to new gainful opportunities under their autonomous control?
5. Is there a case for postponing certain aspects of macro-level policies to allow time for economic, legal and institutional reforms to take prior effect at meso or sectoral level in order to promote a more positive economic-demographic relationship?

6. What is the future cost, in terms of economic resources, of postponing the rendezvous with the determinants of the demographic transition? How much of which of these resources can be expanded by giving paramount consideration to structural adjustment and transformation of the economy?

In the process of a population-economic development modelling exercise like this, data and research requirements will suggest themselves. Engaging demographers and economists in a dialogue around investigative issues could arouse the intellectual curiosity of economists about the consequences of their decisions for population variables. Otherwise population planners will find themselves knocking on the doors of economic ministeries after options have been reduced and none of the remaining is favourable to a demographic transition.

Conclusions 13

In no other region of the world are gender issues more critical to economic and social development than in sub-Saharan Africa. This rests on two premises. Women have a prominent position in production, especially in the most populous sector of agriculture, but they lack control over resources and are discriminated against in markets for private and public goods and services.

Past efforts to rectify the gap between women's responsibilities and resource endowment have taken the form of projects to create income-generating opportunities. There have been criticisms of this appproach, not the least being that the projects do not always represent an effective allocation of resources. In recent years there have been calls to "mainstream" gender issues in economic planning, but so far little progress has been made because of the failure to place these issues in the context of planning the efficient allocation of resources giving due regard to the relative merits of other claims on resources. Chapter 8 showed that analysts of gender in adjustment packages are still not ready to enter into a dialogue on the impact of gender on economic policies. The discussion always reverts to the impact of economic policies on women.

Of equal concern have been the persistent high rates of population growth. Unlike in other parts of the Third World, there is little sign in Africa of an impending slowing of the rate. It is highly plausible that this has to do with women's socio-economic status and therefore must be addressed through economic policies.

This study has taken the opportunity presented by the new planning creed of economic adjustment and, latterly, economic transformation to lay out both a framework for analysis and a procedure for policy formulation which relate gender issues to the goals of cost-effective development and a demographic transition.

Apart from drawing on the women in development literature to illustrate the nature of gender constructs in markets, the study is a theoretical piece which reaches conclusions didactically since the emprirical base for assessing the outcome of adjustment is far too weak to be of much use.

Part I sets out the theoretical framework for the relation between gender, on the one hand, and economic and population outcomes, on the other. Buried in the mass of description of the situation of women relative to men in the WID literature are clear implications for a strict economic analysis and, with that, pointers to what might be changed to advance the goals of economic planning. It is considered that there is enough baseline information on sources of gender-based market distortions to go on. More of this empirical research is not required. The WID literature was also seen to lend substance to some of the theories of fertility. Reviewing characteristics of women's socio-economic status makes it easier to understand why sub-Saharan Africa is not yet in a demographic transition.

The overwhelming conclusion of Part II, which deals with the likely influence of gender on the economic and demographic outcomes of adjustment programmes, must be that the influence is negative in both cases. The basic problem is that the macro and sectoral measures taken so far in customary adjustment packages to liberalise markets and eliminate distortions do nothing to improve gender equity and reduce gender biases in markets; and may well make them worse. The most disturbing aspect of all must be the fate of resource allocation within the farm household. Adjustment, by giving price incentives to tradables, essentially exercises the same forces as the colonial promotion of cash crops. The result of that experience was the misuse of women's labour to the point where children's labour was more intensively used. There is nothing to suppose that adjustment programmes will have a different effect. Nor do the social relations of production and exchange between women and men of the farming household guarantee an optimal use of land.

In manufacturing and services market liberalisation does little to eradicate or counter gender biases. The way public sector services are realigned suggests that this resource entitlement of women is under threat, resulting in an intensification of the present gender biases.

The corollary to these trends in gender equity in markets has to be that women will continue to cleave to the only security over which they have control, their biological reproduction.

The suggested procedure for correcting gender biases along the route to a cost-effective economic transformation is presented in Chapter 11.

The goals of static efficiency and dynamic efficiency are taken in succession. The array of instruments to overcome gender obstacles to static efficiency are *(a)* feasible permanent solutions (design of services and some institutional reforms), and *(b)* counterbalancing meso policies (taxes, subsidies, quotas and positive discrimination). The first seem to be largely confined to questions of access to public sector facilities because the private sector is not open to such remedies. There are more opportunities for counterbalancing measures but these cannot be any permanent solution to inefficient market structures and misallocations of resources. This means that at the end of a medium-term programme of adjustment, when it is hoped that corrective policies have done their job, there will be much serious unfinished business on tackling gender biases. Much of this has to do with meeting strategic gender needs, as distinct from practical gender needs to help women cope better with the present economic order.

This unfinished business has to be borne by the agenda for dynamic efficiency. This is not to say that it is to be postponed. It is rather that the seriousness of what it entails and the length of time required for its implementation involve the approach to economic transformation of the Economic Commission for Africa rather than structural adjustment as defined here and as hitherto practised. The goal is economic transformation; the means should be subject to the discipline of dynamic efficiency.

Dynamic efficiency constitutes the most cost-effective pattern of investments and reforms to achieve very long-term objectives. The path will depend heavily on what those objectives are. Therefore the path to dynamic efficiency in gender terms must incorporate a view of future social and economic relations between women and men.

What is primarily at issue from the planners' viewpoint is women's low productivity—of all the resources they use as well as, but particularly, their labour. Are governments prepared to continue with this powerful brake on economic development? If not, then taking a view on what has to be done becomes inescapable. Are governments prepared to meet the precondition of releasing this brake, which has been argued here to be women's direct access to and control of productive resources and, in the case of women's reproduction work, investment in the means to commoditise their work? And if not this solution, then what?

If the gender bias, the weakest link in sub-Saharan economies, is not resolved these economies may have an absolute advantage in no product and a comparative advantage only in lines of production based on the super-exploitation of women and a demand for children's labour assistance.

The new thinking on economic development that has emerged from the crisis in Africa and from the failure of early attempts to remedy it offers a unique opportunity to introduce gender issues into the planning process. What this study shows is that unless recognition is given to gender-based biases in markets, they could become worse through policies ostensibly designed to make markets more efficient.

Bibliography

Addison, Tony; Demery, Lionel. 1985. *Macro-economic stabilisation, income distribution and poverty: A preliminary survey*. Working Paper No. 15. London, Overseas Development Institute.

—; —. 1987. "Stabilization policy and income distribution in developing countries", in *World Development* (Elmsford, New York), Vol. 15, No. 12.

Adeokun, Lawrence A. 1989. "Population growth, migration and development in the African context", in United Nations: *Consequences of rapid population growth in developing countries,* Proceedings of an Expert Group Meeting, New York, 23-26 Aug. 1988.

Allen, J. M. S. 1984. *Baseline survey report (1980-82), Chinsali.* Zambia, Integrated Rural Development Programme.

Anker, Richard; Hein, Catherine. 1985. "Why Third World urban employers usually prefer men", in *International Labour Review*, Vol. 124, No. 1, pp. 73-90.

—; —. 1986. "Introduction and overview", in R. Anker; C. Hein (eds.). *Sex inequalities in urban employment in the Third World.* London, Macmillan.

—; Knowles, James C. 1977. *The determinants of internal migration in Kenya: A district level analysis*. Population and Employment Working Paper, No. 56. Geneva, ILO.

—; —. 1982. *Fertility determinants in developing countries: A case study of Kenya.* ILO/UNFPA. Liège, Ordina Editions.

Barres, Victoria et al. 1976. *The participation of rural women in development: A project of rural women's animation in Niger, 1966-1975.* Paris, IRAM.

Bevan, D. L. et al. 1987. "Peasant supply response in rationed economies", in *World Development*, Vol. 15, No. 4, pp. 431-439.

Boserup, E. 1970. *Woman's role in economic development*. London, George Allen and Unwin.

Bukh, Jette. 1979. *The village woman in Ghana.* Copenhagen, Centre for Development Research.

Burfisher, M. E.; Horenstein, N. 1985. *Sex roles in the Nigerian Tiv farm household.* West Hartford, Connecticut, Kumarian Press.

Caldwell. 1982. Theory of fertility decline. London, Academic Press.

Chipande, G. H. R. 1987. "Innovation adoption among female-headed households: The case of Malawi", in *Development and Change* (London, Institute of Social Studies), 18 (2).

Colclough, Christopher. 1988. "Zambian adjustment strategy—With and without the IMF", in *IDS Bulletin,* Vol. 19, No. 1 *(Stabilisation—For growth or decay?).*

—; Green, Reginald H. 1988. "Editorial: Do stabilisation policies stabilise?", ibid.

Commonwealth Secretariat. 1989. *Engendering adjustment for the 1990s*. Report of a Commonwealth Expert Group on Women and Structural Adjustment. London.

Cornia, Giovanni André et al. 1987. "An overview of the alternative approach", in UNICEF: *Adjustment with a human face*, Vol. I. Oxford, Clarendon Press.

Date-Bah, Eugenia. 1977. *Women in an urban setting of Ghana: Ghanaian women in factory employment*. Paper presented at a Policy Workshop on Women and Development. The Hague, Institute of Social Studies.

Dey, Jennie. 1981. "Gambian women: Unequal partners in rice development projects", in Nici Nelson (ed.): *African women in the development process*. London. Frank Cass.

Dieckermann, Nicki; Joldersma, Rita. 1982. *Cultivating the fields and plaiting mats: The changes in the situation of women in a Bamileke chiefdom, Cameroon*. Wageningen University, the Netherlands, Department of Home Economics.

Dixon-Mueller, R. 1985. *Women's work in Third World agriculture: Concepts and indicators*. Women, Work and Development, No. 9, Geneva, ILO.

Due, J. M.; Mudenda, T. 1984. *Women's contribution made visible, from farm and market women to farming systems and household incomes in Zambia*. Illinois Agricultural Economics Staff Paper No. 84 E-285. University of Illinois at Urbana-Champaign, Department of Agricultural Economics.

Dyson, Tim; Crook, Nigel. 1981. "Causes of seasonal fluctuations in vital events", in Robert Chambers et al. (eds.): *Seasonal dimensions to rural poverty*, London, Frances Pinter.

Economic Commission for Africa (ECA). 1989. *African alternative framework to structural adjustment programmes for socio-economic recovery and transformation*. doc.E/ECA/CM.15/6/Rev.3. Addis Ababa.

Elson, Diane. 1987. *The impact of structural adjustment on women: Concepts and issues*. Paper presented to the Development Studies Association Annual Conference, Manchester.

—. 1989. "How is structural adjustment affecting women?", in *Development* (Lavoro, Society for International Development), No. 1.

Evans, Alison; Young, Kate. 1989. *Gender issues in household labour allocation: The transformation of a farming system in Northern Province, Zambia*. A report to the (British) Overseas Development Administration's Economic and Social Research Committee for Overseas Research. Brighton, Sussex University, Institute of Development Studies.

Fapohunda, Eleanor R. 1987. "The nuclear household model in Nigerian public and private sector policy: Colonial legacy and socio-political implications", in *Development and Change*, 18 (2).

Fapohunda, Olanrewaju. 1977. *Employment and unemployment in Lagos*. Occasional Paper No. 60. The Hague, Institute of Social Studies.

Farooq, Ghazi M. 1981. *Population, human resources and development planning: Towards an integrated approach*. Geneva, ILO.

—. 1985. *Population and employment in developing countries*. Background Papers for Training in Population, Human Resources and Developing Planning, No. 1. Geneva, ILO.

—; DeGraff, Deborah S. 1988. *Fertility and development: An introduction to theory, empirical research and policy issues*. Background Papers for Training in Population, Human Resources and Development Planning, No. 7. Geneva, ILO.

—; Pernia, Ernesto M. 1988. "Need for and approaches to integrated population, human resources and development planning", in *Population Bulletin of the United Nations*. (New York), Nos. 23/24, 1987.

Fortmann, Louise. 1984. "Economic status and women's participation in agriculture: A Botswana case study", in *Rural Sociology* (Bozeman, Massachusetts, Rural Sociological Society), 49 (3).

Garenne, Michel; van de Walle, Etienne. 1989. "Polygyny and fertility among the Sereer of Senegal", in *Population Studies* (London, London School of Economics), Vol. 43, No. 2.

Gathee, J. W. 1980. *Role of agricultural research in assisting women small farmers in Kenya.* Ford Foundation Seminar on Women in Agricultural Production in Eastern and Southern Africa. Nairobi.

Goldschmidt-Clermont, Luisella. 1987. *Economic evaluations of unpaid household work: Africa, Asia, Latin America and Oceania.* Women, Work and Development, No. 14. Geneva, ILO.

Green, Reginald Herbold. 1986. *The IMF and stabilisation in sub-Saharan Africa: A critical review.* IDS Discussion Paper No. 216. Brighton, University of Sussex.

Haalubono A. K. 1983. *The expected impact of a maize production project on the economic activities of men and women: A case study of the Adaptive Research Planning Team Project in Chipapa, Lusaka District.* Research report. Lusaka, University of Zambia.

Hansen, Karen. 1975. "Married women and work: Explanations from an urban case study", in *African Social Research* (Lusaka, University of Zambia), No. 20.

International Crops Research Institute for the Semi-Arid Tropics. (ICRISAT). 1980. *Profile of farm units in two villages of central Upper Volta.* Progress report. West African Economics Program 1. Burkina Faso, Ouagadougou.

ILO. 1987. *Background Document.* High-Level Meeting on Employment and Structural Adjustment. WEP 2-46-04-03 (Doc. 3). Geneva, 23-25 November.

—. 1987a. *Population, human resources and development planning. The ILO contribution.* Geneva.

—. 1988. *Distributional aspects of stabilisation programmes in the United Republic of Tanzania 1979-84. Report of an ILO Mission.* Geneva.

—. 1988a. *Rural employment promotion,* Report VII, 75th Session, International Labour Conference. Geneva.

—. 1988b. *Substantive and operational aspects of Population, Human Resources and Development Planning Programme activities.* Report of an In-Service Training Workshop, 3-7 October. Geneva.

—. 1989. *The challenge of adjustment in Africa.* Tripartite Symposiumon Structural Adjustment and Employment in Africa, Nairobi,16-19 October. WEP 2-46-02-04 (Doc. 1). Geneva.

—. 1989a. *Report of the Tripartite Symposium on Structural Adjustment and Employment in Africa,* Nairobi, 16-19 October. Committee on Employment. G.B. 244/CE/3/4. Geneva.

—. 1989b. *Women and land.* Report on the Regional African Workshop on Women's Access to Land as a Strategy for Employment Promotion, Poverty Alleviation and Household Food Security, 17-21 October. Rural Employment Policies Branch, Programme on Rural Women. Geneva.

—. 1989c. *Substantive and operational aspects of Population, Human Resources and Development Planning Programme activities.* Report of an Inter-Service Training Workshop, Geneva, October 1988.

Jackson, Cecile. 1985. *The Kano River Irrigation Project. Women's roles and gender differences in development.* West Hartford, Connecticut, Kumarian Press.

Joekes, Susan. 1988. *Gender and macro-economic policy*. Paper prepared for Association for Women in Development Colloquium on Gender and Development Cooperation, Washington, DC, April 11-12.

Joekes, Susan et al. 1988. *Women and structural adjustment*. Paper prepared for the meeting of the Women in Development Expert Group of the OECD Development Assistance Committee, Paris, April 18.

Jolly, Richard. 1988. *Women's needs and adjustment policies in developing countries*. Paper prepared for the Expert Group of Structural Adjustment and Women, Commonwealth Secretariat, London, 2-3 June.

Kershaw, G. 1975-76. "The changing roles of men and women in the Kikuyu family by socio-economic strata", in *Rural Africana* (East Lansing, Michigan State University), Vol. 29.

Khan, Mohsin S. 1986. *Macroeconomic adjustment in developing countries: A policy perspective*. Discussion Paper, Development Policy Issues Series. Washington, DC, World Bank.

Killick, Tony. 1989. *A reaction too far: Economic theory and the role of the state in developing countries*. London, Overseas Development Institute.

Kongstad, P.; Monsted, M. 1980. *Family, labor and trade in Western Kenya*. Centre for Development Research, Publication No. 3. Uppsala, Scandinavian Institute of African Studies.

Krueger, Anne O. 1983. *Trade and employment in development countries: Synthesis and conclusions*. Chicago, Illinois, University of Chicago Press.

—. 1984. "Trade strategies and employment in developing countries", in *Finance and Development* (Washington, DC, IMF), Vol. 21, No. 2.

Kumar, Shubh K. 1985. *Women's agricultural work in a subsistence-oriented economy: Its role in production, food consumption and nutrition (Zambia)*. Paper presented at the XIIIth International Congress of Nutrition. Brighton, Sussex.

Kydd, J; Hewitt, A. 1986. "The effectiveness of structural adjustment lending: Initial evidence from Malawi", in *World Development*, Vol. 14, No. 3, pp. 347-365.

Lallemand, S. 1971. *Projet d'access des femmes a l'education, mai 1968 et mars 1970*. Paris, UNESCO.

Locoh, Therese. 1988. "Evolution of the family in Africa", in International Union for the Scientific Study of Population: *The state of African demography*, Liège.

Longhurst, Richard. 1987. "Policy approaches towards small farmers", in UNICEF: *Adjustment with a human face*, Vol. I. Oxford, Clarendon Press.

McSweeney, Brenda G. 1979. *The negative impact of development on women reconsidered: A case study of the Women's Education Project in Upper Volta*. Unpublished Ph.D. thesis. Medford, Maryland, Fletcher School of Law and Diplomacy.

Monsted, M. 1977. *The changing division of labor within rural families in Kenya*. Copenhagen, Centre for Development Research.

Moock, P. 1973. *Managerial ability in small farm production: An analysis of maize yields in the Vihigia Division of Kenya*. Unpublished Ph.D. thesis. New York, Columbia University.

—. 1976. "The efficiency of women as farm managers: Kenya", in *American Journal of Agricultural Economics* (Ames, Iowa State University), Vol. 58, No. 5.

Moser, Caroline O. N. 1989. "Gender planning in the Third World: Meeting practical and strategic gender needs", in *World Development*, Vol. 17, No. 11, pp. 1799-1825.

Mueller, Eva. 1988. "The allocation of women's time and its relation to fertility", in R. Anker et al. (eds.): *Women's role and population trends in the Third World.* London, Routledge.

Mulder, Monique Borgerhoff. 1989. "Marital status and reproductive performance in Kipsigis women: Re-evaluating the polygyny-fertility hypothesis", in *Population Studies*, Vol. 43, No. 2.

Muriithi, C. N. 1980. *The role of women in small-scale farm production in Kenya.* Ford Foundation Seminar on Women in Agricultural Production in Eastern and Southern Africa. Nairobi.

Oberai, A. S. 1987. *Migration, urbanisation and development.* Training in Population, Human Resources and Development Planning Paper, No. 5. Geneva, ILO.

OECD. 1988. *The socio-economic effects of structural adjustment on Women.* Development Advisory Committee, Women in Development Expert Group Task Force. Paris.

Okale, C.; Mabey S. 1975. *Women in agriculture in southern Ghana.* Paper presented to the Conference on Manpower Planning, Development and Utilisation in West Africa. Legon.

Okpala, Amon O. 1989. "Female employment and family size among urban Nigerian women", in *Journal of Developing Areas* (Macomb, Western Illinois University), Vol. 23, No. 3.

Oppong, Christine. 1983. "Women's roles, opportunity costs and fertility", in Rodolfo A. Bulatao and Ronald D. Lee (eds.): *Determinants of fertility in developing countries,* Vol. 1. New York, Academic Press.

—. 1987. *Traditional family systems in rural settings in Africa.* International Union for the Scientific Study of Population. Seminar on Changing Family Structures. Honolulu, Hawaii, East West Population Institute.

—. 1988a. "Family structure and women's reproductive and productive roles", in Richard Anker et al. (eds.): *Women's role and population trends in the Third World.* London, Routledge.

—. 1988b. "The effects of women's position on fertility, family organisation and the labour market: Some crisis issues", in International Union for the Scientific Study of Population: *Conference on Women's Position and Demographic Change in the Course of Development; Solicited papers.* Oslo.

—; Abu, K. 1987. *Seven roles of women: Impact of education, migration and employment on Ghanaian mothers.* Women, Work and Development, No. 13. Geneva, ILO.

—; Bleek, Wolf 1982. "Economic models and having children: Some evidence from Kwahu, Ghana", in *Africa* (Manchester, International African Institute), 52 (4).

Pala-Okeyo, A. O. 1978. *Women's access to land and their role in agriculture and decision-making on the farm: Experiences of the Jaluo of Kenya.* Discussion Paper No. 263. Nairobi, IDS.

—. 1980. "The Joluo equation", in *CERES* (Rome, FAO), Vol. 13, No. 3, May-June, pp. 37-42.

Palmer, I. 1985. *The impact of male out-migration on women in farming.* West Hartford, Kumarian Press.

Patel, A. U.; Anthonio, Q. B. O. 1974-75. *Farmers lives in agricultural development: the Nigerian case.* Supplement to *International Journal of Agrarian Affairs.* Contributed papers read at the 15th International Conference of Agricultural Economics.

Pebley, Anne R.; Mbugua, Wariara. 1989. "Polygyny and fertility in sub-Saharan Africa", in Ron Lesthaeghe (ed.): *Reproduction and social organisation in sub-Saharan Africa.* Berkeley, University of California Press.

Pittin, R. 1987. "Documentation of women's work in Nigeria: Problems and solutions", in C. Oppong (ed.): *Sex roles, population and development in West Africa.* London, Heinemann Educational Books.

Phillott-Almeida, R. 1983. *Gambian rural women at work.* London, Commonwealth Secretariat.

Potter, Joseph E. 1989. "Rapid population growth, the quality of health, and the quality of health care in developing countries", in United Nations: *Consequences of rapid population growth in developing countries,* Proceedings of an Expert Group Meeting, New York, 23-26 August 1988.

Ruttan, Vernon W.; Hayami, Yujiro. 1989. "Rapid population growth and technical and institutional change", ibid.

Rwabushaija, Margaret. 1988. *The status of women and the value of children in East Africa: An example from Aukole, Uganda.* Paper presented at the International Conference on Women's Position and Demographic Change in the Course of Development. Oslo.

Sadik, Nafis. 1989. *The state of world population 1989.* New York, UNFPA.

Safilios-Rothschild, C. 1985. *The policy implications of the role of women in agriculture in Zambia.* Planning Division Special Studies, No. 20. Zambia, Ministry of Agriculture.

Sen, Amartya. 1984. "Economics and the family", Ch. 16 of *Resources, values and development.* Oxford, Basil Blackwell.

Sen, Gita. 1985. *Development, crisis, and alternative visions: Third World women's perspectives.* Norway, A.s Verbum. Also published under the same title (authors: Sen and Grown), New York, Monthly Review Press, 1987.

Simmons, George B. 1985. "Theories of fertility", in Ghazi M. Farooq and George B. Simmons (eds.): *Fertility in developing countries.* Basingstoke, Macmillan, pp. 20-66.

Simmons, E. B. 1976. *Economic research on women in rural development in Northern Nigeria.* Overseas Liaison Committee Paper, No. 10.Washington, DC, American Council of Education.

—; Farooq, Ghazi M. 1985. "Towards a policy-relevant framework", ibid., pp. 109-122.

Smock, Audrey. 1981. "Women's economic roles", in Tony Killick (ed.): *Papers on the Kenyan economy.* London, Heinemann Educational Books.

Spiro, Heather. 1985. *The Ilora farm settlement in Nigeria.* West Hartford, Kumarian Press.

Staudt, K. 1985. *Agricultural policy implementation: A case study from Western Kenya.* West Hartford, Kumarian Press.

Stewart, Frances. 1981. "Kenya strategies for development", in Tony Killick (ed.): *Papers on the Kenyan economy.* London, Heinemann Educational Books.

—. 1987. "Alternative macropolicies, meso policies, and vulnerable groups", in UNICEF: *Adjustment with a human face,* Vol. I. Oxford, Clarendon Press.

Streeten, P. 1987. "Structural adjustment: A survey of the issues and options", in *World Development,* Vol. 15, No. 12, pp. 1469-1482.

UNICEF. 1987. *Adjustment with a human face,* Vol. I. *Protecting the vulnerable and promoting growth.* Oxford, Clarendon Press.

UNIDO. 1989. *Global Report 1988/89.* Vienna.

Wills, J. 1967. *A study of time allocation by rural women and their place in decision-making: Preliminary findings from Embu district.* Rural Development Paper No. 44. Kampala, Makerere University College.

World Bank, 1979. *Small enterprises in African development: A summary.* World Bank Staff Working Paper No. 363. Washington, DC.

—. 1989. *Sub-Saharan Africa from crisis to sustainable growth. A long term perspective study.* Washington, DC.

Youssef, Nadia. 1988. "The interrelationship between the division of labour in the household, women's roles and their impact on fertility", in Richard Anker et al. (eds.): *Women's role and population trends in the Third World.* London, Routledge.